To. Dad,

Happy Fathers Day 1986,

from

Karen & Stephen
Auril & Rosemary
XXXX
XXXX

From Herring to Seine Net Fishing
on the East Coast of Scotland

From Herring
to Seine Net Fishing

on the East Coast of Scotland

by

Iain Sutherland

No part of this book may be reproduced or copied by any means whatsoever without written agreement.

Published by Camps Bookshop, Wick.
Printed by The Northern Times, Golspie.
© *Iain Sutherland*

ISBN 0 9508697 2 4

Foreword

This book is an attempt to relate how seine net fishing came to be adopted by the fishermen of the east coast of Scotland. It tries to show the circumstances which existed before, during, and after its arrival, all of which shaped its character as it is today. This is only part of the story and a book this size could easily be written about every port mentioned herein.

I have not used the bye names, or tee names, of the people concerned, although like myself they nearly all had one. My reasons for omitting them are twofold. Firstly they are not for use by strangers whose lack of knowledge of the person concerned makes them meaningless. Secondly, modern trends have devalued them and the skill and imagination with which they were created would be lost on the present day reader whose unfamiliarity with the disappearing Scots tongue is best left as it is. There are exceptions, only where I had no choice.

Iain Sutherland,
Wick.

Photograph by permission of Mr H. Carter, Wick

The 'Maid of Honour' lies in Wick harbour with a shot of 240 boxes of cod, the largest amount ever taken by a seine net boat in a single drag in the Moray Firth. The crew are, from the starboard quarter forward: Hugh Carter, jun.; Skipper Jack Carter; Don Carter; Hugh Carter, sen. at the rail; William Bremner and George Carter, later skipper of the 'Silver Cloud'. As skipper of the first 'Silver Cloud', which was 48 feet long, he landed 378 boxes of prime cod on 16th February, 1966. They were taken in two drags off the Caithness coast, and this is probably a world record catch for a single fishing in a vessel of this size. With the outstanding successes of his brother Jack and the famous 'Maid of Honour', the Carter family of Lybster have acquired a unique position in Scottish fishing achievement.

FROM HERRING TO SEINE NET FISHING
ON THE EAST COAST OF SCOTLAND

The seine net as used in Scotland is a closer cousin to the trawl net than to the net from which it takes its name. Originally the seine net was mainly used on the rivers and lakes of Europe and its method of operation was quite straightforward. It was a simple, shallow curtain of net, one end of which was held to the shore. The net was then pulled out behind a boat, in a loop, to return to the bank so that both ends could be hauled ashore with any fish that had been surrounded.

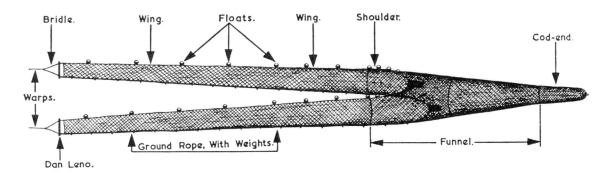

Illustration reproduced from "Sea fisheries; their investigation in the United Kingdom" under the terms of the introduction.

The Danish seine net.

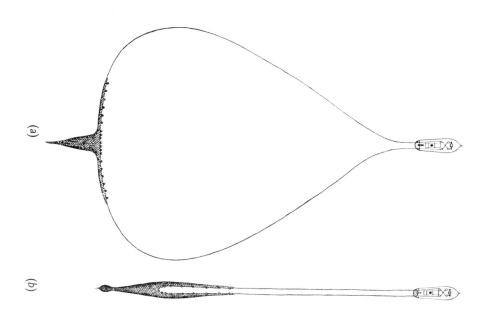

Illustration reproduced from "Sea fisheries; their investigation in the United Kingdom" under the terms of the introduction.

A seine net — (a) shot. (b) towed.

The seine net as used on the fishing grounds around the Scottish coasts, like the trawl net, consists of a cone of netting with extensions on either side, in front, called wings. These wings are in fact the original seine net which was cut in the middle to allow the bag to be sewn in. The net is then towed behind a fishing boat which moves as fast as conditions allow, and the method is not all that far removed from the original: that of surrounding the fish and bringing them to a point where they can be removed from the net. The difference is an example of how, over the centuries, man has introduced, improved and almost perfected the ways in which he has hunted one of his most valuable food sources.

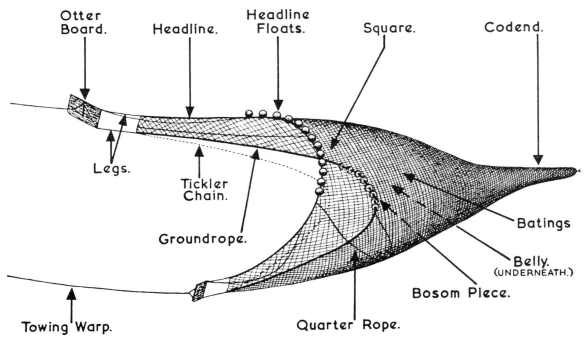

Illustration reproduced from "Sea Fisheries; their investigation in the United Kingdom" under the terms of the introduction.
The otter trawl which came into use in the 1890's. Before then the trawls were all beam trawls.

The development of fishing methods falls into three main stages: when man operated his fishing gear by his efforts alone; when he increased his efforts artificially by adding wind power; and when he mechanised his efforts as a result of the Industrial Revolution, which, with politics, has been the main influence on the situation that fish, fishermen and the fishing industry, find themselves today.

The ability of a modern fishing vessel to achieve the successes that it has, owes as much to the engineers and electronics specialists in the factories as it does to the skills and experience of the skipper. The inventions and innovations in use today would seem like magic to men who fished only two or three generations ago. Yet whether the changes are progress in the long term interest of the fishing industry is far from clear. So far the fishing industry has shown itself very susceptible to innovation, particularly in fishing apparatus, without making any compromise towards the traditional selective methods which sustained the fishing communities for so long. Houses which contained fishing families for generations have now become holiday homes or dormitories for towns like Aberdeen as the number of fishermen shrinks steadily in direct proportion to the introduction of technology.

As in many another traditional industry the introduction of scientific methods completely revolutionised it. The construction, navigation, safety and control of fishing vessels have altered almost out of recognition in the space of 60 years and the most of these changes came in the 30 years between 1945 and 1975. This was due almost entirely to the mechanical, electrical and electronic developments made as a result of the First and Second World Wars. As ever, man was at his most innovative while trying to dispose of an opponent and the effect of war-time developments on fishing has been enormous. To the effect that man now seems to be waging a war of attrition on the fish by comparison with the older methods.

On a modern fishing vessel the skipper, without moving from his personal armchair, can tell with a glance at his control panel, where he is to within three feet, the shape and depth of the bottom of the sea, how far he has come, his speed, course, where the nearest land or vessels are, and above all, where the fish are, how many there are, what kind they are, the direction they are travelling in and at what depth. This information is relayed to him from a series of detection devices which display their information on the control panel. The same control panel is also connected to a score of warning devices which monitor everything from the depth of water in the bilges to the performance of the gearbox. He can engage the automatic pilot to steer for him by satellite navigation and he can alter the net as it is fishing if he feels it is not in the best position. Modern designs have made weather conditions almost irrelevant and skippers now fish when 30 years ago their fathers would never have left the harbour.

As a result, fishing is carried out much more continuously than it ever has been, and fewer boats are catching obviously declining stocks in greater quantities than ever has been possible before the advent of modern technology. Two modern herring, or mackerel, purse seiners with about 30 men aboard can outfish 1000 boats, with 5000 men aboard, of the kind in use in the 1840's. This is in spite of the fact that where previously the fishing fleet went to sea daily during the four month season and purse seiners may only fish for a quarter of that time through the whole year. And the harvest of the purse seiners is for use as a fertiliser or animal food whereas the catch of the boats, before their advent, was for human consumption unless there was a glut.

A large purser in Fraserburgh harbour.

Yet for all the changes that have been made to date, no practical method of catching fish has been introduced which has proved to be superior to the main traditional methods, whose origins stretch away into the murky waters of time. Apart from the use of explosions and electricity to disable and disorient the fish, the 16 international classifications of fishing methods fall into three main categories. Fish may be lured to a hook or trap, entangled in a net set for that purpose, or a net may be pulled around them to enclose them. These methods grew over the years, all with their local adaptions, and developed as best they could to work on sufferance from the uncontrollable and often unpredictable sea. A sea which exacted a high price from the unready, the ill-prepared, the mis-informed, the careless and those who were simply unlucky. Yet there were those who by their studies, observation, intelligence, experience and luck found reward on the great waters and many prosperous communities grew around the shores of Europe because of the skills of their fishermen. Among these, Scotland only shared in a very minor way in the great harvest of the North Sea, or German Ocean as it was called, although it sat at the very centre of the most prolific fishing grounds. A combination of civil turmoil, wars with England, poor communications and bad legislation held the enterprise of its coastal dwellers in check until the last ten years of the 18th Century.

The growth of the many towns and villages, particularly those on the shore of the Moray Firth, comes from this time and as a direct result of money invested by companies or private individuals. Many of the settlements were of great antiquity and had conducted a foreign trade over the centuries, although it was very small and confined to a ship or two a year. In the main they had slumbered for hundreds of years till developments in the last quarter of the 18th Century sent men scrambling for any foothold that they could find on the coast. Old and new together exploded into life as if at a signal: Lossiemouth, Burghead, Portsoy, Buckie, Cullen, Whitehills, Macduff, Gardenstown, Findochty, Rosehearty, Banff, Peterhead, Avoch, Fraserburgh, Brora, Golspie, Helmsdale, Keiss and above all, Wick, responded to the conditions and, in the shadow of the Industrial Revolution, set their courses by a beacon lit by the British Fisheries Society on the Caithness shore.

The British Fisheries Society, either directly, or indirectly through the efforts of imitators, was the single most important factor in the success that the Scottish fishing industry was to achieve in the years following its creation, right up to the present day. It was by no means the only, or first, Society which attempted to promote the fishing, but succeeded on a gigantic scale, in complete contrast to the results obtained by its predecessors which at best had met with a very limited success, and more often, failure. The British Fisheries Society succeeded for two reasons. The first was that the abilities and principles of its founders, and servants, were of the highest order. The second was that the maze of legislative stupidities which had dogged earlier companies had largely been removed by the time it was incorporated. Some, not all, of the early companies had failed because of greed, but others because of incompetence and restrictive legislation.

The Society came along at the right time, at the end of a period of the the most enlightened law-making which presented the fishing industry with golden opportunities if only they would realise them. And the Society did just that. The legislation was almost exclusively concerned with the expansion of the herring fishing, with white fishing confined to the small print and the afterthoughts, but nevertheless this same legislation was the forerunner of present day regulations. It was also the successor to centuries of trial and error by politicians before they succeeded in creating the conditions which were almost to guarantee the success of the British Fisheries Society. It is a story that has its beginnings some centuries before the Act of July 1786 which incorporated the Society as a joint stock company, and thence quite unwittingly, changed the history of the North and North East of Scotland.

Although the Scots had never been able to pursue fishing on the scale of England, France, Holland and Denmark, they were by no means ignorant of the presence of herring and other fish in their waters. Up to 1707 Scotland had its own parliament and over the centuries this had made many efforts to promote fishing as both a source of employment and wealth. By wealth it usually meant taxation and revenue, but it did also try to operate on capitalist principles in as much as efforts were made to ensure that those who invested money got a return on it. The earliest record of the Government taking a positive step to raise revenue from the fishing is to be found in the Burgh Tallys of 1240 when a Value Added Tax was imposed in the following words: "Burghe tallys of a last of hering 1111D, dry hering at ye further passing 1D, of a thousande hering an thai be lade on a hors. 1D for ilk birding for ye stalling of the mercat. 1d½D. Item for a last of freshe hering 1111D, and gif thai be lade throu ye byar yat byis thame, bot gif ye be lade to ye havyne with ye fishcar, he sall gif naithing for ye hering bot for his set."

This imposed a tax of four pennies on a last, or 10,000 herring and a further 1d per 1000 when they have been cured and loaded for sale. Another penny was charged for being allowed to sell them in the market. Dry herring presumably means dry salted or smoked herring. It is doubtful if the Scots were salting herring in barrels of brine at this time, otherwise the legislation would not have referred only to dry and fresh herring. There was also a tax of four pennies on fresh herring, and one and a half pennies on resale, but only when the fish have been removed from the harbour. The fact that a tax had been imposed on fish indicating that it must have been carried on to quite a large extent, and could provide a substantial source of revenue to the perpetually impoverished Scottish kings, who were always on the look-out for their next bawbee.

Because of the troubled times of the next 150 years very little seems to have been legislated in connection with the fishing until the turn of the 15th Century.

Fishings seem to have been picking up again after the numerous English harryings of the previous hundred years and attempts were being made to impose a fishing limit on foreign vessels. In an effort to enforce this the Scots had made several attacks on Dutch vessels off the coast and a treaty was made in 1416 to try to keep the peace.

Further evidence that prosperity of a kind was being enjoyed by the fishermen comes from the first parliament of James I when it passed the following on 26th May, 1424:

"Alsua for thay that mony thingis passes out of the realme withoutten custome, it is ordained and decreeted that there be paid to the King for custome of ilke thousand of fresche fish sauld, of the sellar, one penny, and of the last of herrings barralled foure shillings; and of ilke thousand red herringe made in the realme, foure pennies."

This was a tax on exports and the mention of fresh herring can only mean that they were sold fresh to foreign curers for processing, either ashore or on board their ships. They would be processed at once as a light salting would not keep them fresh until they reached a foreign port and ice was not in use for some centuries later. The benefits of having foreign merchants buy and pay tax on their herring seems to have escaped governments in the 20th Century, as can be seen from the factory ships which are in the proximity of the purse net fleet.

The red herring referred to were smoked, salted herring, but by no means the familiar kipper. Red herring were smoked whole, not split as in the case of a kipper, which was another process that did not develop till the 19th Century.

However, the herring referred to in this Act seem to be cured in brine and attracted the fairly steep tax of four shillings per 10,000. The imposition of this taxation does not seem to have restricted the industry in any way and by 1471, in the reign of James III, there appears to be a shortage of supply and an Act was passed to try to boost the amount of boats that was being built.

"Lordes, Barrones, and Burrowes gar mak schippis, busches and great pink boats with nettes. The Lordis thinkis expedient for the common guide of the Realme, and the great encris of riches to be brochte within the realme of other countries."

This means that the Scottish Parliament, which was called the Three Estates because it was made up of three parties, the Lords spiritual, the barons and the representatives of the burghs, caused ships of various kinds to be built. At that time fishing was conducted from vessels which were much larger than those used in the first half of the 19th Century, and usually were called busses, the "busches" referred to above. The reference to "pink boats" does not describe the colour, but another kind of vessel in use on the continent at the time.

The Act was the first attempt by a Scottish Parliament to encourage fishing by statute, but it was not ready, nor would it be for many years, to actually put any financial encouragement in the direction of the fishermen or companies. Some shipbuilding obviously took place as a result for within a few years there seems to have been difficulty in finding crews. In 1491, 20 years later, the Act was

Photograph by permission of Mr J. D. Storer, Keeper, Royal Scottish Museum, Edinburgh.

A model of an English herring buss of the kind in use during the 18th Century. The Scottish busses must have been very similar and most of those in use in Scotland were bought either from Holland or England.

amended at the direction of James IV to include what seemed to be a Job Creation Scheme but in actual fact was little more than a charter to enslave the unemployed.

"In ilke Burgh of the Royaltie, that officares of the burgh make all starke, idle men within their boundes to pass with the said schippes for their wages, and gif the said idle men refuses to passe, that they banish them the burghe."

And if the officers of the burgh omitted to banish reluctant fishermen, then they in their turn could be fined 20 pounds, a very large sum then, for neglect of their duties. It was no coincidence that those who passed this pernicious piece of lawmaking were also the only people who could afford to build ships. And they quickly realised the advantages of being legally provided with forced labour. The Act effectively turned most fishermen into bonded slaves and men could be forced to sea in old and dangerous vessels, with the inevitable high casualty rate. As late as 1683 shipowners were still applying to the courts for the return of men who had left their employment to work elsewhere. And by that time the scope of the original legislation had been extended to include the activities of other property owners who had seen the benefits derived by their fellows with fishing interests.

This monument, which I presume to have been a well originally, is built into the wall of the church at Newhaven. It bears the legend "Erected 1775, re-erected 1901. Society of Free Fishermen." This is an obvious reference to the day when the grip of landowners was finally broken. Newhaven has lost all the character which one would associate with fishing ports of such fame and antiquity. Its redevelopment has been catastrophic as far as its heritage is concerned.

In 1606 the idle in the countryside, among whom no doubt were men who had fled from the coastal towns, could be made to work in the mines or saltpans, both very unpleasant occupations. So, for over 200 years there was very little to encourage the ordinary man to go to sea, and this unquestionably limited its expansion until the legislation finally came good.

By the standards of the day, when witches were being executed in Europe by the thousand and the Spanish Inquisition was running out of new ideas for torture in the name of religion, these pieces of legislation were not all that extraordinary and they seem even to have met with a limited success.

SARCLET HARBOUR

SHEWING RECENT IMPROVEMENTS

Jos.ᵗ Mitchell, F. R. S. E. Engineer.

1843.

J. Smith. Lithog. 30 Hanover St. Edin.

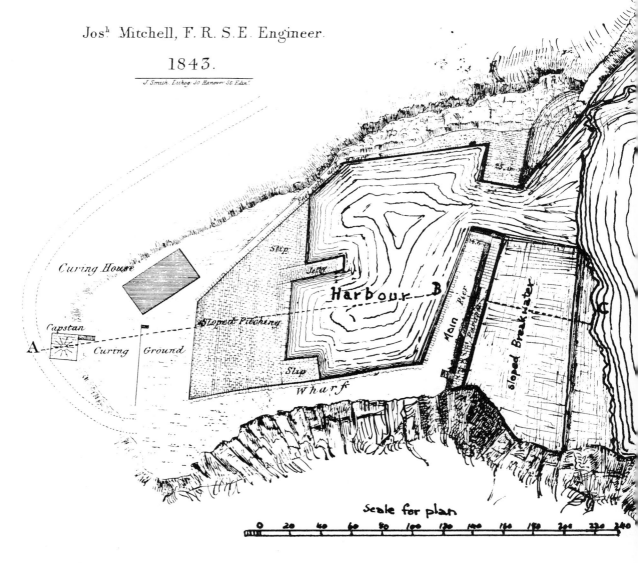

Curing House

Slip

Jetty

Harbour

Capstan

Sloped Pitching

Main Pier

Sloped Breakwater

Curing Ground

Slip

Wharf

Scale for plan

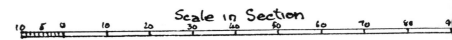

Scale in Section

The harbour at Sarclet in Caithness which was built by the British Fisheries Society. It was destroyed by a succession of storms in the 1860's

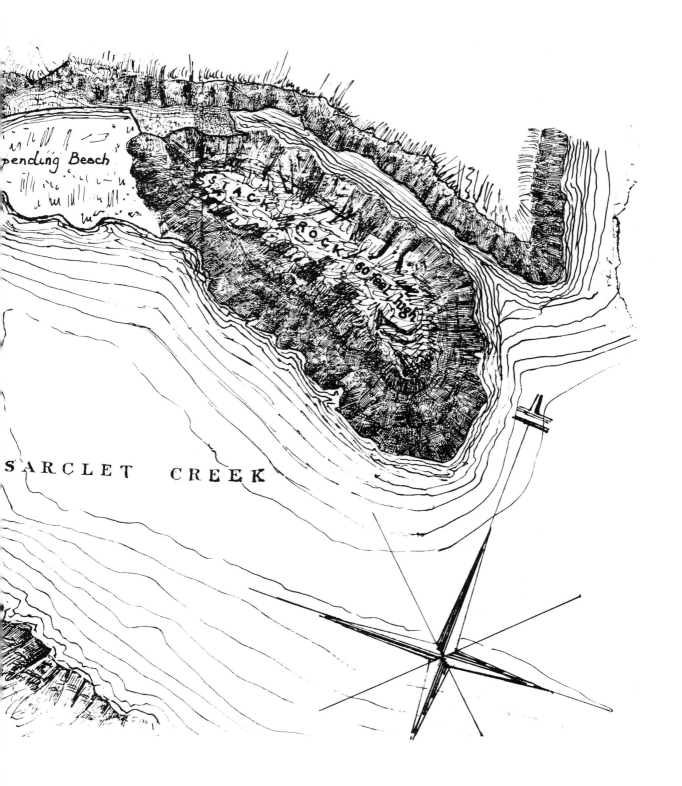

pending Beach

STACK
ROCK 60 feet high

SARCLET CREEK

On 14th March, 1540, during the reign of James V an Act was passed to try to ensure that the home market was provided for, obviously as a result of successful exporting and perhaps because of food shortages:

"It is statute and ordainit that no maner of person to burgh nor to lande, bye ony maner of fische in mercat nor other places, to pack or peile, quhil elleven houres of day, and fra elleven houres to twa houres afternoon, it sall be leasum to bye fische, and pack or peile the samin, as they maist think expedient. And not the lesse that all our Soveraine Lordes lieges, cadgers and others within that time of day, be served for their money, of fische to the furnishing of the countrie; And sic lik fra twa houres after noone to sex houres even, it sale not be leasum to bye, pack, or peile the saidis fish, bot that all our Soveraine Lordis lieges at the saidis times of day may be served al maner of fische, and bye the samin for their silver, for sustenation of their house, and serving the countrie about: And that na maner of persone in this realme, merchand or uthers, send, or have ony maner of quhite fische furth of the samin, bot it sall be leasum to strangers to cum within the realme to bye the samin fra merchands and free men of the burrows with reddie gold or silver, or be bartouring of sufficient merchandice with the saidis merchands, or with the owners thereof, for their sustenation, necessares of their houses allanerly; And quhair ony persons hes ony fish packed or peiled, that they be ready at all times to sell the samin to all our Soveraine Lordis lieges for furnishing and sustenation of their houses, and the countrie, under pain of confiscation of the samin."

Apart from evidence that the public had access to clocks then, there was obviously a brisk foreign trade because the Act prohibits the sale of fish till 11 o'clock presumably to allow merchants from the country areas to get to the markets before selling began. Between 11 and two fish could be bought for curing and resale at home or abroad. After two, until six, the fish could only be bought for the home market while foreigners were restricted to their own personal needs. This is an odd clause and seems to be a deliberately left loophole because it is hardly likely that a foreign buyer would wait till the afternoon to cater for his household needs. It is more likely to allow a foreign buyer to acquire fish left after the home market was satisfied.

Any curer who had fish which he refused to sell for the home market was liable to forfeit it, but this also looks like window dressing because the Act goes on to say that the price of fish will be fixed every day by the town magistrates. They were to make enquiries if anyone was offering a higher price than they had set. Human nature being as it never changes, there almost certainly was a black market, if demand caused prices to rise or fall from the levels set by the Baillies. They were required to take and punish the "said persones, coropares, forestallers and regratours against the common weill."

Corruptors, forestallers and regraders still flourish today, but this was an attempt at ensuring supplies for the home market at a regulated price. It was very similar in concept, if not in form, to the legislation passed to control the price of fish in the Second World War, almost exactly 400 years later. The Act also refers to white fish, and while very often fresh herring were referred to as white fish, it seems in this instance to actually mean white fish in the sense that is used today.

The fishings were obviously becoming successful and as the prospect of an easy way to prosperity has never been far from the consciousness of politicians, the most influential sections of the Three Estates soon found a way. On 30th April 1573, by which time control of the town councils was in the hands of the merchants, which meant that they would be representing the burghs at the Three Estates, they succeeded in having passed one of the most restrictive pieces of legislation ever enacted about fishing in Scotland. And it was purely for the benefit of the merchants who represented the Royal Burghs, most of which were fishing ports.

The merchants had already benefited from the expansion of the fishing, but not enough for their liking and this Act placed complete control of the fishing in their hands. It restricted the landing of all fish to the free, or Royal, burghs. Very few ports had a harbour, or even a quay at that time and the absence of a landing stage of some kind did not matter all that much as the then minute catches could easily be manhandled ashore from shallow draught vessels lying close by. Some, mainly Royal Burghs, did have harbours. They were very small by modern standards and a good example of what they looked like may be seen at Crail in Fife.

While these harbours were shelter in bad weather, fishing was by no means confined to these ports, or towns, and neither were exports. It was unfortunate for the towns which were not Royal Burghs, that, unless they had a baron or land owner for a feu superior, they were not represented in Parliament and had no say in opposition to this legislation. Once it was passed the fishermen were left with the choice of either moving to a Royal Burgh or bringing their catches there, a journey which could take two or three days depending on the weather. And while they were doing that they were not fishing, with the resultant loss of earnings. The effect was immediate, disastrous to many communities, and long lasting. Having now cornered the market and encouraged by the effect that this had on their personal fortunes, the merchants, in their capacities as representatives of the Royal Burghs, managed to keep this iniquitous piece of legislation on the statute book for another 131 years, till 1704.

Obviously there was some resistance to the Act but without representation not much was achieved. In fact it was reviewed and toughened in 1579 and again in 1584. This time the greed of the Burgesses ran away with them and they enacted that all fish caught in the Firth of Forth had to be landed at only Crail or Leith; all fish from Fifeness to the Dee had to be landed at Dundee or Perth; fish caught north of Dumbarton had to be landed there, and south of the town, at Ayr. There is no mention of the ports north of these towns and, although a lot of fishing was done in both the Moray Firth and the Minch, very little seems to have been landed there. Either that or communications were so poor that the bureaucrats in Edinburgh were not interested in anything north of Perth, something that has a familiar ring to it in the 20th Century. However, for whatever reason, the legislation clamped down firmly to ensure the landing of fish in the south of Scotland only.

If this was not enough the Act proceeded to limit the export of fish, which by now it was clearly meaning white fish as well as herring. It also took a faltering step towards improving the reputation of the exports by attempting to introduce a standard size of barrel, in which all fish were transported. At that time each town had its own size of barrel, and no two were the same, with the resultant complaints from foreign buyers over the different quantities of fish that they were being sent for the same money. The Act also required that all barrels be branded with the iron of the town of origin and, contrary to the legislation that it had just passed about fish being landed only at specific ports in the south, nominated Elgin as one of the towns required to appoint "ane discrete man to be visitaire, wracker, and gager and burner." As Elgin is four miles inland this "visitaire" must have been required to examine exports in the district between Lossiemouth and Buckie. It is a contradictory piece of legislation, in the context of the other clauses, and the "visitaire" may have been inspecting commodities other than fish, such as tallow, beef or mutton, which were packed in the same size of barrels as herring. However, the stupidity of confining the landings to six ports soon became apparent and on 10th December, 1585 this restriction was withdrawn, but the other clauses remained.

James VI seemed to have a great interest in fishing, more as a good source of revenue rather than from any desire to foster the industry for its own sake. In furtherance of this he imposed a tax of one third of the catch on vessels fishing in the north and west, obviously to encourage them to fish elsewhere. Yet he also was the first to attempt to promote fishing by governmental direction, and hinted at the way which was to be so successful 200 years later. In 1601, with a distinct lack of regard for local feelings, he sent a force of 600 men to take possession of a large tract of the Isle of Lewis and to establish a fishing colony there. The inevitable resistance to the colony, led by Murdoch MacLeod, prevented a start being made beyond the construction of some stone houses and some of the adventurers were captured and killed. That was the end of the expedition and MacLeod with 12 of his men were rounded up and executed at St Andrews for rebellion. Unpromising though this episode may appear it was another faltering step towards the successes of the 19th and 20th Centuries.

In 1603 James departed for England to become King of the new United Kingdom, but Scotland was to retain a more or less independent Parliament for another 104 years. Towards the end of this period the Three Estates put on the statute books, and not just in respect of fishing, a concentration of enlightened legislation that has rarely been equalled by any Parliament in such a short time.

After the King's removal to London it took the Parliament some time to adjust to the fact that he had gone and that they were now dealing with a Secretary of State. The fishings were left to struggle on as best they could under the burdens that had been placed upon them. An enquiry was set up in

1630 to see how the scale of fishings could be increased. This was part of a general movement which was begun in England but did not come to much. A charter was granted to a company in 1633 to establish a fishing colony in the Hebrides again, but this too fizzled out even though it was conducted in a much more diplomatic manner than the previous attempt. Part of the reason for the failure was that the backers, for the first time, were English aristocracy who had only a shallow interest in making the company successful.

Photograph from the Johnston Collection by permission of the Wick Society.

Basket making in Wick, July 1907. Quarter-cran baskets are stacked to the rear and every boat carried about a dozen. They were inspected by Fishery Officers before use as they were the official, standard measure of herring. They only came into use in the last 20 years of the 19th Century. Before then the cran measure was a bottomless barrel which was filled with herring on the back of a cart and then lifted clear, leaving the herring.

1661 is a year in which the fishing industry may be described as turning the first real corner on the road to success as far as parliamentary influence was concerned. The legislation which the Scottish Parliament passed that year was by no means original as it followed lines that had already been laid down, but there was one very significant and far reaching innovation. For the first time a cash incentive, in the form of tax exemption, was allowed to fishing companies. Taxation due on the various materials required to pursue the fishing was considerable and "our Sovereign lord being willing to cherish and encourage the foresaid Societies and Companies in the said trade, hath, out of his innate beneficience and royal bounty, ordained, and by the tenour here-of discerns and ordains that salt, cordage, hemp, cork, pitch, tar, clapboard, knaple, skewhoops, and Holland nets, imported for the trade of fishing aforesaid, by the foresaid companies respective, are and shall be free of custom or other imposition, whatever. And that the herring and white fish taken, made, or prepared therewith, are and shall be free of any manner of taxation or burden in the exportation of the same.'' It is noteworthy that as a result of the Union of the Crowns in 1603, Scots Laws were now written in more or less standard English, as opposed to the Scots in use before then.

Ropemakers in Wick about 1900. Most towns were self-sufficient in the needs of their fishing fleet until the 20th Century.

The Act went on to give a few more concessions but the exemption of duty was a major step forward. The prosecution of fishing was still confined to companies and most of the restrictions still applied, but faltering as these steps were, they were still in the right direction. And before long yet another company was being formed. In 1663 the Royal Fishery Company, although it did not get under way for some time, was established. The delay in getting started seems to be largely due to the fact that the shareholders did not appreciate the complexity of the restrictions surrounding fishing in Scotland. They never succeeded in promoting fishing as they intended but they apparently did understand the benefits of the tax exemption because they soon gave up their own half-hearted attempts to promote fishing themselves and sub-let their fishing stations to others. And part of the terms on which they sub-let their rights was that they continued to exact a fee of £6, Scots, on every last of herring exported. Clearly, this could not go on as they were in breach of the legislation which had allowed them to set up in the first place. They were putting nothing into fishing by way of investment in boats, nets or any of the materials required. It took some time but eventually complaints caused the Three Estates to abolish the company in 1690, by which time William and Mary were on the throne.

"Our Sovereign Lord and Lady, with the consent of the estates convened in Parliament, con-

Mr John Gunn, the last cooper to work at the trade in the traditional manner. He is seen here raising a barrel in the Bloomfields cooperage in Wick about 1977. If a trade has to cease, it could not finish with a more powerful personality than Mr Gunn whose life, times and doings would easily fill a book this size by themselves.

sidering that the late Royal Company erected for fishing, is now dissolved by retiring their stocks and quitting the prosecution of that trade in company, as was designed in its institution, and yet they continue to exact six pounds Scots per last of all herring exported forth of the Kingdom, to the hurt and prejudice of their Majesties lieges: Therefore their Majesties, with the advice and consent of the estates of parliament, do rescind, reduce and annul, the aforesaid gift of erection of the company, called the Royal Company of Fishing, with the whole priviledges and immunities belonging thereto, together with all acts, confirmations and ratifications thereof, and declares the aforesaid company to be dissolved; discharging hereby, and strictly prohibiting, the exacting of the six pounds Scots for the last of herrings etc.''

The Act went on to confirm that others could form companies if they had the money and edged away from the hithertofore monopoly which had existed in all legislation setting up a fishing company. There had obviously been disputes about how much salt had been used in curing and the measurement of this was tightened up by allowing a refund of £10.4s tax on a last of salted herring rather than on the salt itself, as this was obviously easier to assess. The buyer of the herring paid the refund to the fishing company, paying at one and the same time his export tax and the tax concession to the producer without any further paperwork.

Of course the privilege of exporting still rested with the merchants of the Royal Burghs and the Act confirmed that this would continue but it also proceeded to open a crack in a hitherto firmly closed door. "And their Majesties with the consent aforesaid, do recommend to the Lords of their Majesties Privy Council to receive such overtures from royal burrowes, *Or Others* (my italics) and to interpose their authority to such of those overtures that they find the most convenient, and to conduce most for the better curing of the fishes, and for the profit and honour of the trade.''

This clause is of great importance because it does two things. The first is that it permits towns which were not Royal Burghs to apply for permission to set up an export trade, and the second is that the application or representation was to be made to the Privy Council. The Privy Council in Scotland, which was abolished in 1708, was the crowns adviser on most matters. The fact that representations were to be made to them and not Parliament itself, meant that plaintiffs would receive a fairer hearing, as the Three Estates contained a large section of merchants from the Royal Burghs, who were not likely to consider any attempt to break their monopoly on fish exports with impartial detachment. It is a matter of wonder that the implications of the legislation slipped them when they agreed it in the first place.

If the history of the fishing were to be imagined as a vessel setting out on a voyage after being becalmed almost since she was built, then these two words "and others" were the first stirrings in the sail. Before this voyage was completed she would be comparable to a big Fifie in a half gale, charging across the sea with every sail set and not a reef down. It would be some time yet before the sail would belly away from the mast, but in 1704 the breath of air was becoming quite noticeable.

On 6th July of that year a quite momentous piece of legislation was passed, obviously as a result of the representations made to the Privy Council by the towns who could not foster a fishing of their own because they were not Royal Burghs. That, and possibly the will of a Parliament that was moving to its death-bed and subconsciously was trying to leave the best inheritance that it could to its dependants. This was the case with legislation on other subjects and the Act of 1704 was about as wide ranging in the removal of the restrictions that had built up over the centuries as it was possible to be. It stopped just short of the ideal but the main parts are as follows. The Sovereign Lady is Queen Anne.

"... Her Majesty, with the advice and consent of the estates of parliament, authorises and empowers her good subjects to take, buy and cure herring and white fish in all and sundry seas, channels, bays and firths, lochs and rivers etc, of this her Majesty's ancient kingdom, and to the islands thereto belonging, wheresoever herring or white fish are or may be taken, and ...'' There was nothing new about that but the next sentence was stupendous "... for their greater conveniency, to have the free use of all ports, harbours, shores, foreland, and others, for bringing in, packing, drying, unloading, and the loading of the same, upon payment of ordinary dues, where harbours are built, that is, such as are paid for ships, boats and other goods ....''

They could now land where they found it most convenient and cure on any suitable spot in return for fair rent or harbour dues. And there was more: ". . . and discharges all other exactions, as a nights fishings in the week, commonly called Saturdays fishing, top money, stallage and the like."

It had long been the practice of fishing companies to take the best nights fishing of a week as a right so that the pittance paid to their employees was taken as a share of the remainder, or poorer catches. The companies still deducted all expenses from the balance and the fishermen were actually paid about 1/16th of a share, and there may have been eight shares, depending on how the boat was owned. The skipper received 1/16th more than the crew, but again there was no exact share-out and it varied from vessel to vessel. In any event the wages were those of almost slavery and the Act of 1704 abolished the practice of taking this "Saturdays fishing" as it was most usually known.

Fishery officers had been appointed in 1693 and their duties were clearly defined: ". . . and the collectors and other officers of the custom are hereby commanded to take and seize all salmon, herring or white fish, that shall be shipped in their several precincts of exportation, unless made and marked as aforesaid." Barrels were required to be to a certain standard of manufacture and had to be clearly marked according to their contents. When these had been inspected the crown brand was burned on them as a guarantee of quality. It was forbidden to forge these brands or to attempt to export without them. "And it is hereby declared, that it shall be lawful to the sheriffs, bailies of regalities, and magistrates of the burghs, or any having commission from them, not only to visit, on all occassions, the curing and packing of herring or white fish in their respective bounds, and also to pitch upon any barrel after it is made up and marked up, and cause to break open the same, and raise the herrings, if they think fit, from the very bottom." Defaulters would have their herring confiscated and fined into the bargain. This time, for almost the last time, the Three Estates meant business. The previous tax refund, drawback or bounty as it was coming to be called, was confirmed on exports, either at the time of export or by way of deduction of import tax if the merchant was also an importer, as most of them were. Various materials were also exempted from tax and salmon fishing was banned between midnight on Saturday and midnight on Sunday. Then there was the problem of salt, which was used in very large quantities. Salt was exempted from duty in Scotland, when used for fishing purposes, but not in England, and there was obviously many flourishing cross-border rackets because a ferocious list of penalties was laid down for anyone caught importing English or Irish salt. In the Treaty of Union of 1707, when the Three Estates gave up its sovereignty to join the English Parliament, there was inserted a special clause to guarantee exemption from English duty for seven years after the Union became fact. And although the imposition of this salt tax did have a restricting influence on the expansion of the fishing for a time, it was beginning to gather momentum in a way that nothing would restrain for long.

After the trial, and usually, error of centuries most of the obstructions had been lifted, but there remained one which it had not yet occurred to the lawmakers to remove. That was that a company still had to be formed, and officially recognised, before fishing on any scale other than for domestic needs, could be undertaken. But pressures were building up and in the next 20 years, two or three attempts were made to take advantage of the new conditions. They came to nothing because the old story repeated itself where those with money did not have the experience and the fishermen had no money. In 1726 a group of 21 commissioners was set up and their purpose was a widely spread one. They were required to report on several industries such as banking, linen, hemp and fishing and to see what could be done to foster these. Most of their attention was confined to the land based industries, particularly linen, and flax growing and spinning began to spread over the country. However, the men with the brains, experience and money to do something about the fishing industry were just a little way around the next corner and most of that corner was removed in 1750, as a direct result of the fright that the Government and Crown got during the Jacobite Rising of 1745.

Mainly to create employment among the thousands of Highlanders who were not to emigrate in numbers till a century later, the Society of Free British Fisheries was set up for a period of 21 years with a subscribed capital of £500,000, a truly gigantic sum for these days. The Government offered them an annual payment of 3% on this and, in addition, a bounty of 30 shillings per ton on all decked vessels built or fitted out, which were between 20 and 80 tons, — comparable in size to modern seine net boats. The Act also permitted other companies to be formed, provided they had a subscribed capital of £10,000. The amount of money required to get started was coming down but control was still in the hands of the moneyed classes, the aristocracy usually.

The most important point was that the Government was actually offering a cash subsidy which was not simply a return of your own taxation. It took some time for the implications to be grasped by investors, but this was a very generous injection of money, for which it was possible to qualify without paying a penny. It worked this way. The subscribed capital did not have to be paid right away but only over a period of time as the expenditure required it. The fact that the money had been subscribed, or promised, was supposed to guarantee its eventual payment if necessary. On the strength of this promise the Government paid out the 3% which amounted to £15,000. Together with the bounty on the ships, which were probably bought with the £15,000, not a penny of the subscribed capital was used up. With careful planning the company could have set itself up nicely, with very little expenditure of its own money, and indeed it set out with great enthusiasm. It even went to the lengths of importing Dutch fishermen and curers to advise and train its employees. At the same time some other smaller companies, with less subscribed capital, also set up in business but things proved to be a flash in the pan as the subscribers to the Society of Free British Fisheries were unwilling to pay up when the subsidies could not keep abreast of the expenditure by themselves. It was a time when India, America and Australia were attracting attention and possibly they offered better prospects to investors. For whatever reason the Society's momentum faltered and in 1755 another Act, which really was an amendment to the earlier one of 1750, allowed them to hire out their busses to others. This amendment was of great importance as it meant that people of little capital, who were willing to take a chance, could hire a vessel although they still had to form a company. All that was needed now was for the obvious to be stated and stated it was in July 1786. As a result of pressures, mainly from expatriate Scots in London, an Act incorporating ''The Society to extend the Fisheries, and improve the Sea Coasts of the Kingdom'' by ''building of free towns, villages, harbours, quays, piers, and fishing stations in the Highlands and Islands of North Britain.''

There was nothing new at all in the enabling legislation, in fact some of it was over two hundred years of age. But all the errors had been removed just before the Society was set up.

The conditions were right, but what was of supreme importance was the will and the attitudes, of the men who subscribed, and this time meant it, the capital of £150,000 to the British Fisheries Society, as it would go down in history.

Their motives, as indeed were their principles of business, were of the highest, and they had a genuine desire to help the Highlands of Scotland which were living in a condition of absolute poverty and degradation as a result of, among other things, the reprisals which followed the Rising of 1745. Whether their attitudes came from guilty consciences, as many of them were from the rebellious Highlands, is a matter of conjecture, but the humanity and generosity of their actions is not. From the very beginning they set about their business in a most workman-like fashion to the extent that, within a very few years the evidence of their determination was to be seen in the north and west. Briefly what they did was this; they personally visited many likely spots for development, which in itself was a considerable achievement in a country which had neither roads nor a charted coast. They then sent surveyors and engineers to examine and report in detail on the most likely areas which were closest to the fishing grounds. And the men in their employ, Thomas Telford, Joseph Mitchell, John Rennie and James Bremner among others, sound like the roll of honour of civil engineering. In less than 25 years of their arrival the Society had transformed the Highlands which had remained unchanged almost since men had arrived there. Ullapool, Tobermory, Lochbay, where incidentally one of the earliest experiments with concrete was carried out, and above all Wick, awoke between 1790 and 1803. The development at Wick was to be named Pultneytown in honour of their chairman. It had a population of six families and no name when John Rennie visited it in 1793. By 1850, 4000 people lived there and another 12,000 came every summer to the largest herring port in Europe at that time. And the Society which concentrated almost exclusively on the promotion of herring fishing achieved this and other blinding successes by fulfilling to the letter the undertakings which it had given at its incorporation.

Photograph from the Johnston Collection by permission of the Wick Society.

Wick at its zenith in 1864. Two pursers, with about 36 crew can easily outfish the boats in this picture.

It built the houses, schools, churches and streets, many of which were named after members of the Society's board. Meeting halls, mills and even breweries were constructed and then let at a very moderate rental to whoever was prepared to migrate to work in the new settlements. Money was loaned to fishermen, and other trades, at a reasonable rate of interest, to acquire the equipment that they needed. People could also buy their rented property and finance was also available for that. The Society was limited by law to taking no more than 10% profit on any of its transactions, and at no time did it hire any smart mouthed lawyers, a practice that is painfully prevalent today, to find a way of milking more out of the fishing.

The awesome 'Chris Andra', 'Vigilant', 'Quantus', 'Chrystal Sea', 'Lunar Bow', 'Krossfjord', and 'Andra Tait' waiting menacingly in Fraserburgh harbour. They can outfish the whole Scottish herring fleet of the 1860's when it was at its peak of employment, with 1100 boats in Wick alone.

There was one outstanding difference, above all, between the Society and all the companies that had gone before it. This was that it did not pursue the fishing itself, because it was debarred from doing so in the Act that incorporated it. It must be remembered that at that time Acts of Parliament passed about trade or industry, were greatly influenced by the people who wished to have them passed and they had a lot to do with the wording. This disbarment from fishing themselves was more than likely inserted at the Society's request, as they realised that they could improve the fishings by creating the right atmosphere rather than encouraging men to fish without any real shore based organisation. It was in the drafting of this wording that the Society showed its real worth, because it resisted the almost irresistable temptation of taking the government subsidies on boats and materials and then withdrawing without involving any of its own money. Their revenue was derived from the shareholders, harbour dues, rents, grants from the revenues of estates which had been confiscated from Jacobites, interest on loans and latterly government grants and loans when the expenditure on Wick harbour, once the jewel in its crown, turned to a nightmare.

Photograph from the Johnston Collection by permission of the Wick Society.

The ill-fated breakwater, under construction in Wick Bay, which was to be instrumental in the demise of the British Fisheries Society.

The Society provided a much wider service to its immigrants than merely the provision of harbours, stores and homes. It undertook the recruitment of teachers, ministers and even provided horticultural advice for those with gardens. Settlers were guaranteed access to a peat bank for fuel and often their title deeds allowed other privileges such as quarrying, mining and storing equipment on Society property, if this was for their own needs. The attitude of the Society, and the relaxation of the laws which allowed men with little or no capital to prosecute the fishing, came together as if pre-ordained and by the beginning of the 19th Century the foundations for the prosperity of the future had been firmly laid.

Although the Society stood as a colossus over the rest of the industry it was by no means alone. Apart from private landlords who were fostering fishings in imitation of the Society, there was a fair amount of fishing going on in ports around the Firths of Forth and Clyde. While this too was mainly in connection with the herring fishing there also was a large element of white fishing as it had been for centuries. The presence of these towns was due of course to the good fishing grounds but also to the proximity of the most heavily populated part of Scotland. So, while life was being breathed into the north and west coasts, ports such as St Monans, Anstruther, Crail, Tayport, Dunbar, North Berwick and Eyemouth were carrying on more or less as ever.

The Industrial Revolution was just getting under way at the same time as the fishing began to flex its muscles. In the middle of the 18th Century the population of Scotland was much more evenly spread than it is today and amounted to about a million and a quarter. Of these about 50,000 lived in the Edinburgh district, which at that time was made up of the many villages that are its suburbs today. By 1800 the population of Scotland had risen to 1,600,000 and both Edinburgh and Glasgow had 80,000 each. Within a few years, where previously there had been only the crudest of footpaths, communications were revolutionised by the construction of canals, then roads and railways. While much of the production of the fishing industry went for export, at the same time the easy access to an expanding home market provided a steady, if small, flow of ready money.

But the years between the Act of the 1750's and the construction of the main canals in 1822 were not without their difficulties. In spite of increasingly favourable legislation, ports outside the influence of the British Fisheries Society were subject to a series of fits and starts, but from them came two changes which were to have an enormous effect in the coming century. One of these was primarily concerned with the fishing industry, and the other part of a much wider field.

The first change was that the size of the boat used in commercial fishing was dramatically reduced and it seems to have come about for the wrong reasons. The change was probably coming anyway but it received a push from the fact that in the late 1760's and early 1770's the payment of bounties was very badly administered and often there were delays of several years before some payments were made. It appears that the lessons of these delays were not lost on those who set up the British Fisheries Society in 1786. The effects of the delays could be serious because many of the smaller companies used up their capital far more quickly than they had expected because busses were not cheap and there was a heavy tax on many of the materials. The larger companies survived better but the amount of busses fishing declined, because of the delays, and of course the fishings with them. This happened at a time when on paper companies should have been receiving £300 bounty per year as the minimum, from the Government, plus about £15 for each buss and 3/- per barrel of fish exported; enough to add a new buss to the fleet each year.

The original bounty had been in Scots money and this was recalculated at the union to allow for the fact that English money was worth 12 times as much. The bounty had been paid on a last, 10,000 herring, but by the late 18th Century this had been rounded to between three and four shillings per barrel, another factor that gave a boost to the industry because of the smaller quantity of herring necessary to qualify. A crew in 1800 would consider a catch of 1000 herring, roughly a barrel-full to be a good nights fishing. And it was the difficulties with the bounties that, together with the barrel bounty gave rise to the use of smaller boats.

The use of the smaller boats meant the end of the fishing companies or Societies in Scotland, although not in England, until the advent of trawling in Aberdeen in 1880 and thence until the 1960's

Photograph by permission of Mr J. P. Campbell, Halkirk.

The spectacular Whaligoe steps in Caithness. Built privately by the Sinclairs of Ulbster about 1770 it remained in use as a harbour till the 1950's. Fishermen's wives carried the catch up the steps in heather creels and thence as far as Wick, seven miles away for sale. On the third corner from the bottom can be seen the spot where the last of the Caithness crofter fishermen, "Canadian" Jock Sutherland, and the author quarried the stone they used to repair the steps when they had been damaged by vandals. It is extremely dangerous to attempt to get this view.

A closer view of the steps, showing "Canadian" Jock's quarry at the bottom. This is the fourth traverse above the "Bink" as the level part was called.

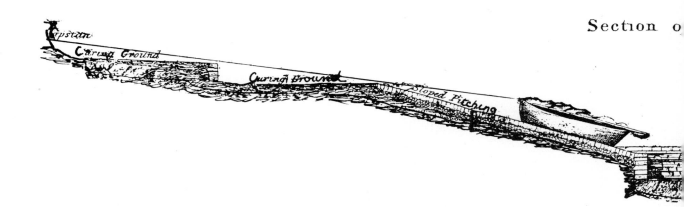

Section o

CAPSTAN erected at S⌁

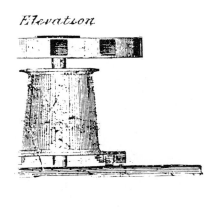

Elevation

Pull Rack

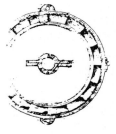

Section through

Timber

Masonry

5'4"

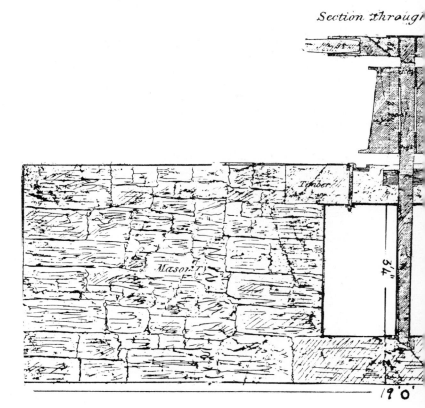

19'0'

Scale for Cap

1   2   3   4   5

B, C.

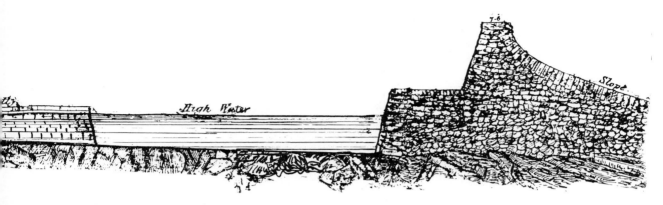

ET HARBOUR

an

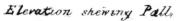

Elevation shewing Pall.

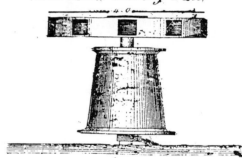

Masonry

Socket

Top of Capstan

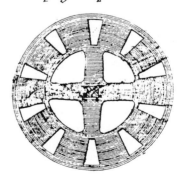

7   8   9   10 feet

The capstan at Sarclet today, 140 years later.

when investment companies such as the Wood Group began shareholding in boats. It was about 1780 that the move towards smaller boats began and the companies which were previously handling the fish from catch to export began to specialise in one branch. Either as curers, exporters, chandlers or in some other capacity while, at last, the fishermen began more and more to fish for themselves from their own boats. These boats did not attract a bounty from the Government in the way that a buss had, but that was offset by the barrel bounty. Originally a buss had to be a minimum of 20 tons burthen and had to carry a specific size of crew, with a regulated amount of nets, salt, barrels into the bargain. They were not cheap and caused a large outlay even when bought second-hand from England or Holland. The equivalent of £100,000 in modern terms could be required to get it to sea, and the irony was that there never was a need for busses in Scotland anyway. It really was a heavy duty, distant water drifter, designed by the Dutch to go anywhere in the North Sea when their own herring stocks became inadequate for their needs.

As far as the Dutch were concerned it had been an outstanding success and had made Holland a wealthy country. The Scots, who took about 300 years to realise that they could catch herring from their shores almost, saw no reason to change this design until circumstances overtook them. In the beginning these circumstances produced the famous "Scaffie" in the north and "Fifie" in the south, both between 15 and 20 feet long, completely undecked and costing around £10 ready for the sea. By modern standards about £4000 with all gear and nets and there was an excellent chance of recovering their costs in the first season. So about 20 of these boats, with 80 men aboard, could be sent to sea for the cost of one buss with 20 crew. Or, as was becoming the practice, the fishermen were buying their own boats to be crewed usually by their families. By the turn of the century bounties were being paid regularly, the export markets were being established and through the British Fisheries Society an ordinary man could easily borrow money, without security, on the strength of the barrel bounties that would be paid on the fish he was to catch. As a result the industry leapt forward, first in the north and west, in spite of yet another, but lesser irritation. It took a little time to sort this problem, which was that there was not a lot of money in circulation with which to pay the increasing number of people being attracted to fishing.

It will be recalled that the subsistence level of existence being eked out on the Scottish coasts up to about 1760 was such that most people rarely saw money, far less use it. However, as the Industrial Revolution got under way events inland and on the coast was to change that state of affairs. Up to then, employment in the modern sense of a hired employee who was paid regularly existed only in a very limited way. It had always been a master and man relationship where the master was a landowner, merchant or tradesman and there usually was a set of laws governing the use of labour. On the land where ordinary people either provided labour in lieu of rent, or worked in their own cottage industries, little or no money was in circulation. In the towns nearly all the businesses were family affairs, controlled by trades guilds, who employed outsiders when there were no relations available. The result was that very little money moved out of the control of those who had it for long and there was comparatively little in circulation.

The rapid build up of the fishings between 1770 and 1800, particularly in the newly established ports of Staxigoe, Broadhaven and later Tobermory, Ullapool and Wick required a ready supply of cash to meet the needs of people who had migrated there. They needed ready finance for the many transactions which were taking place and although there were three banks in existence, none had penetrated to the north in 1800. The village of Staxigoe, two miles north of Wick, made one of the first attempts to get around the difficulty of a lack of ready money.

Photograph by permission of Mrs M. Sutherland, Wick.

Staxigoe near Wick, birthplace of the Caithness herring industry, of which only the rock in the middle remains recognisable. This photograph was taken about 1880.

Staxigoe may very well be regarded as the pioneer of the Scottish herring industry, in its modern form, and fishings on the bounty began there 19 years before the creation of the British Fisheries Society and by the time they started building Wick, Staxigoe was flourishing.

In 1767, Alexander Miller, estate factor and businessman with interests in meal milling and smuggling, formed a company and sent a boat on the bounty system to the herring fishing. Like many others they were not paid until a year or so later, but could carry on and by 1770 had created a fishing centre at Staxigoe. As people were attracted to the village pressure began to build up on the money supply and for some years Miller and his partners were hindered by having to carry out complicated paper transactions with his suppliers. They were another example of a company which had given up fishing by this time, and were now exporting, curing and providing various services to the fishermen. They had a shop and stores and Miller hit on a convenient solution. That was to give credit tokens to his employees, or fishermen for herring, in lieu of cash which he did not have. This was not an original idea as the British Linen Bank had been using a similar system since 1746 for the purchase of linen, and these credit notes had acquired such a reputation for trust that they eventually became bank notes.

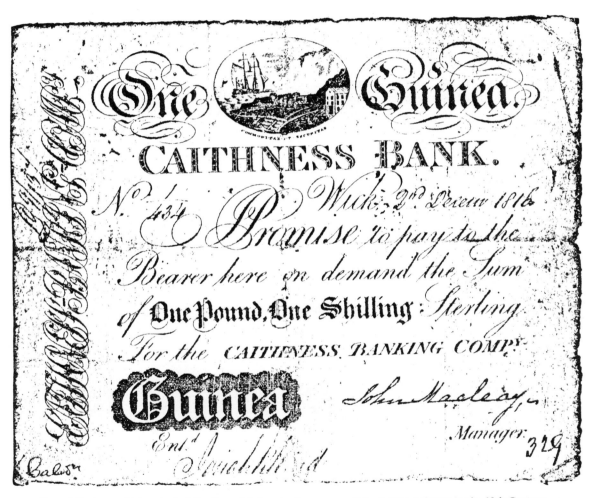

One of the keys which unlocked the financial door to the success of the fishing industry in the 19th Century.

Miller's tokens, or counters as he called them, were made of tin and lead, and varied in size according to value. These could be exchanged for goods at the shop in Staxigoe and in spite of the obvious temptation to cheat, they do not seem to have exploited their customers. The counters were in use for about seven years until a blacksmith called Cormack perfected forgeries and put an end to their use. By that time, 1800, there was more money in circulation because of the growth of trade and the effect of the withdrawal of these counters was hardly noticed. In 1812 the Caithness Banking Company was set up in Wick and this provided the readily available finance that was so badly required.

They issued their own bank notes but the bank was not a success and was taken over by the National Commercial Bank in 1825. But a banking service had now been established in a town which was beginning to expand at a phenomenal rate. Progress on the other side of the Moray Firth, and further south, was not as dramatic and it was a slow, cautious growth as befitted the character of the people there.

The herring fishing was a seasonal affair, which in the Moray Firth ran from about the middle of June to the middle of September at that time. It was on this comparatively short period of the year that the fishing communities relied for their main source of income once commercial fishing began in earnest. Outside these months, in the south, line fishing occupied the men for the other nine months or so and in the north time was divided between crofting and line fishing. There were few full-time fishermen in the modern sense until 1820 or even later in many places.

From about 1785 fishermen from Nairn, Moray and Banff coasts, and even as far as Eyemouth,

Photograph by permission of Mrs M. Sutherland, Wick.

The nursery of the great herring fishery in the north of Scotland. Ramsigoe harbour in Caithness with Broadhaven in the background. This photograph was taken about 1890 and both have almost completely disappeared. Visible in the middle of the picture with its roof fallen in is Willie Oman's Mill. In 1909 David Petrie wrote the following:-

A lang the road
As aft I've trod
To see the Pilot Row, man
A place I saw
An it they ca
The mill o Willie Oman

Ablow a bridge
At the sea's edge
An biggit aside aknowe man
A store o heicht
Half shades the sicht
O the mill o Willie Oman

In it nae mair
Is heard the roar
Nor whistle o the plooman
Nor horses go
Nor corn put to
The mill o Willie Oman

But fading fast
In storm and blast
The place wi weeds doth grow, man
That did adore
Broadhaven's shore
The mill o Willie Oman

For it wid nae
Ootlive its day
Sae baith hae fa'en noo, man
Time wrocht the ill
On Willie's mill
An time killed Willie Oman

began to come to the Caithness coast to fish from Staxigoe and its neighbouring inlets of Elzy, Ottergoe, Greenigoe, Broadhaven, Ramsigoe, with the overspill going into the shelterless Wick bay itself. Their presence helped to influence the British Fisheries Society to its decision to build at Wick, and their descendants assured its success for the next 150 years as Wick was a regular feature of their lives until the very end of the herring fishing. Ironically their attendance in such numbers at the Caithness fishings at the turn of the 19th Century seems to have slowed developments on their own coasts by about 20 years. Their absence in the north meant that the herring they were now catching were being processed in the north. Most of the ports on the south side of the Moray Firth, many of great antiquity and with a history of exporting going back hundreds of years, such as Burghead, Cullen and Macduff, did not begin herring curing operations on any scale till between the years of 1815 and 1830.

There were herring shoals off these coasts which were just as accessible as those off the Caithness coast but in the early days the organisation to service the fishing industry properly existed only in the north and around the Firth of Forth, mostly on the south side from Grangemouth to Eyemouth. Caithness was not only close, it was also visible and less than a day's sail away. The export markets had been created mostly in Ireland and the slave plantations of the West Indies, but pioneering representatives were beginning to examine the possibilities of Russia and Germany as there were no herring stocks of any consequence left in the Baltic Sea. The original trading was done on the barter system, exchanging herring for timber as the Scottish forests were cut down in ever increasing numbers.

To a small extent Miller's tokens served a purpose in Caithness but only in Wick and Staxigoe, although it was possible that they were used as collateral elsewhere. It was the establishment of the banking system which finally provided the credit facility which did not exist on the other side of the Moray firth for another 15 years. It seems quite likely that it was the money earned in Caithness that made the creation of a curing and marketing organisation possible on the Moray coast, together with the creation of branch yards there by established curers.

It will be recalled that under the Act of 1750 a company was allowed to hire out its vessels to others and over the years there grew from this the practice of fishermen contracting to supply the curers with an agreed amount of herring at a fixed price; even if, by 1800 the vast majority of the fishermen were quite independent of the curers and using their own boats. Once the quantity of the original contract had been supplied, it could be extended, or not, as things suited the parties involved. The price remained for the duration of the contract, regardless of how the market behaved, and there were advantages and disadvantages accordingly. One of the conditions which were to fisherman's advantage, and was a very important factor in the huge increase in the number of boats in the first 30 years of the 19th Century, was that he could be given credit, or even advanced cash, to the value of the herring which he had contracted to sell. This way he could finance a boat, and with ordinary luck in these extraordinary times, could even come out of the season owning his boat with cash in his pockets, where a few months previously he might not even have had a net. The secret of the course was that the investment was low, the herring plentiful, the demand was high and the market expanding.

So for the first 30 years of the century matters proceeded at an ever quickening pace as far as herring fishings were concerned and with them glimmerings of the white fishing that was to come began to appear. In the Moray Firth particularly, fishermen found themselves with boats which, apart from the four months herring fishing, were doing nothing for the rest of the year. While most of them were hauled for the winter a few began to take a more serious interest in the small line fishings, particularly in the spring time. The story was quite different for the ports south of Aberdeen as they always followed the line fishing from time immemorial and it was the herring fishing that was to be a novelty for them. It was only really from Fifeness and beyond that there had previously been a herring fishing on any scale. But it was from the ports which turned to the line fishing in the early 1800's that the seine net fishing was to come 100 years later.

Some localities developed line fishing more vigorously than others and one of the most progressive on the coast was Buckie. By 1865 there were about 40 boats long and small lining there and it was the largest white fishing fleet in Scotland at the time. Buckie, like Wick and Helmsdale, had begun to rival the traditional suppliers of the main markets and Dunbar, Newhaven, Eyemouth, St Monans, and Anstruther faced serious competition. Before the arrival of the coastal steamship in the 1830's and the railways in the 1850's, not till 1875 in the north, supplies to the home market were as difficult as those for the export market. The only fresh fish came either from these ports or in welled smacks, of which modern chilled sea water tanks are merely a development, which kept the fish alive till it reached the market, usually London. Apart from these vessels fish were sent in salted or smoked condition, and it was for smoked fish from the north-east that the improving communications created a huge demand. And this demand could no longer be met by the traditional methods. Finnan Haddies had originally been cured in the peat reek of a fisherman's home by his wife, usually a couple of dozen at a time. This was on much too small a scale and mass production kilns which could smoke hundreds at a time, when not in use for herring, had to be used.

A similar story in fact had taken place about 50 years earlier when the original corf-houses, rather like beehives for smoking salt herring, which were not yet split open to make kippers, were enlarged in response to market demands. This expansion of the kilns for herring was the first sign of the introduction of mass production methods, although it was a manual as opposed to mechanical innovation. It was in 1826 that the first mechanical appliance was invented and this was the net loom developed by William Paterson of Musselburgh. This loom wove the yarn into meshes, a job which previously, and for some time till its reputation spread, was done by the fishermen and their families. The spinning machine took a great deal of painstaking labour out of the weaving of nets although the netting still had to be laid to the cork and sole ropes manually for a hundred years after.

The nets themselves were originally made of hemp or flax and at the time of Paterson's invention were only about one third the size of the nets used in the 20th Century. This increase in the size of nets came about in the 1860's with the introduction of cotton yarn which was one third the bulk of hemp but twice as durable. But that was 40 years into the future and much change was to be introduced in the meantime.

The first of these changes, even though it was the end of an era, passed almost unnoticed. On 5th April 1830, bounties on herring were repealed and no longer was a government subsidy paid on the barrel of herring. By that time the fishing was in full flight under its own momentum and the withdrawal of the bounty made no difference. But their passing is worth more than a casual mention because their long and mostly honourable career of 150 years had been of paramount importance in the growth and success of the fishing by directing the flow of money to where it did most good. First to the herring fishing and thence indirectly to the white fishing. And yet bounties have never really passed away because modern grants are basically the same. They also direct government money into the industry. It is only the way that it is done that is different. But no form of subsidy, because of changing circumstances, ever achieved the same dramatic success. The original bounties, through the response of the fishermen, and the teeming seas, brought towns to life around the coasts like stars awakening in a winter sky. Recent subsidies are more in the form of a prop to an industry which would have declined more rapidly without them, because the Golden Age has passed. The Golden Age lasted from about 1830 to 1914 during which the industry neither needed, asked for nor got, direct government financial assistance. The Government did not lose its interest in the fishing industry during these years, far from it. It was much too important a source of food and employment for that and a fairly close watch was kept on what was going on. Many attempts were made to bring order to the basis on which it proceeded and one of the first of these came about on 22nd August, 1843. This was a major piece of legislation.

A convention had been held between the governments of France and Britain in 1839 to see what could be done about fighting between English and French fishermen in the English Channel. It also investigated the possibilities of taking steps to curb smuggling which was reaching epidemic proportions all around the coasts. The contraband was mainly spirits and tobacco and if it seems strange that it was profitable to smuggle spirits into Scotland it must be remembered that the distilling industry was still in its infancy having only been organised in 1823. The fact that a convention had been held to sort out the differences between rival fishermen was in itself a novelty because until recently the practice had been to send the navy to sink nuisances. The French had sunk about 400 Dutch vessels off Bressay in 1801, only 40 years before.

The novelty of the conference spawned a couple of new ideas in itself. The first was that fishing vessels had to be registered and numbered in the following manner:—

ARTICLE VI.

All British and French fishing boats shall be numbered.

There shall be a series of numbers for the fishing boats belonging to each Collectorship of Customs in the United Kingdom, and a series of numbers for the fishing boats belonging to each district of Maritime Registry in France; and to these numbers shall be prefixed the initial letters of the names of the respective collectorships or districts.

ARTICLE VII.

Whereas there are in the United Kingdom several Collectorships of Customs, and in France several districts of Maritime Registry, the names of which begin with the same letter, in which case the initial letter alone would not suffice; the distinguishing letter or letters for the boats of each collectorship or district shall be designated by the Board of Customs in the United Kingdom, and by Ministry of Marine in France.

ARTICLE VIII.

The letters and numbers shall be placed on each bow of the boat, three or four inches (eight or ten centimètres French) below the gunnel, and they shall be painted in white oil colour, on a black ground.

For boats of fifteen tons burthen and upwards, the dimensions of these letters and numbers shall be eighteen inches (forty-five centimètres French) in height, and two and a half inches (six centimètres French) in breadth.

For boats of less than fifteen tons burthen, the dimensions shall be ten inches (twenty-five centimètres French) in height, and one and three-quarter inch (four centimètres French) in breadth.

The same letters and numbers shall also be painted on each side of the mainsail of the boat in black oil colour on white sails, and in white oil colour on tanned or black sails.

These letters and numbers on the sails shall be one-third larger in every way than those placed on the bows of the boat.

ARTICLE IX.

In order that the fishing boats of Jersey, Guernsey, and other islands of the same cluster may be distinguished from the fishing boats of the other British Islands, their numbers shall precede the initial letter of the name of the island to which such boats may belong.

Each of these islands shall have a separate series of numbers.

ARTICLE X.

All the buoys, barrels, and principal floats of each net, and all other implements of fishery, shall be marked with the same letters and numbers as those of the boats to which they belong.

These letters and numbers shall be large enough to be easily distinguished. The owners of nets or other fishing implements may further distinguish them by any private marks they judge proper.

ARTICLE XI.

The letters and numbers of British fishing boats shall be inserted on the licences of those boats, after having been entered in the Registry book kept at the Collectorship of Customs.

The letters and numbers of French fishing boats shall be inserted on the muster rolls of those boats, after being entered in the Registry book kept at the Maritime Registry Office.

ARTICLE XII.

The licences of British fishing boats and the muster rolls of French fishing boats shall contain the description and tonnage of each boat, as well as the names of its owner and of its master.

ARTICLE XIII.

The fishermen of both countries shall, when required, exhibit their licences or muster rolls to the commanders of the fishing cruisers, and to all other persons of either country, appointed to superintend the Fisheries.

ARTICLE XIV.

The name of each fishing boat, and that of the port to which she belongs, shall be painted in white oil colour on a black ground on the stern of the said boat, in letters which shall be at least three inches (eight centimètres French) in height, and half an inch (twelve millimètres French) in breadth.

ARTICLE XV.

It is forbidden to efface, cover, or conceal, in any manner whatsoever, the letters, numbers, and names placed on the boats and on their sails.

It later became the practice of Scottish skipper/owners to paint their names on the stern as well as the port of registration.

Regulations were laid down in respect of trawl nets and this is the first sign that trawling, the parent of seine netting as we know it, was by now being conducted on a scale large enough to attract governmental attention. Herring net sizes are also described but there is no reference to steam powered fishing vessels. The only kind of boats mentioned are decked and undecked, to which the decked boats had to give priority in all respects, particularly sea room.

There are 89 Articles, or paragraphs, including the historic Article 2, which fixes a fishing limit of three miles, and closes all bays less than ten miles wide, for foreign vessels. There was nothing new about the idea of a fishing limits as most maritime countries had been trying for centuries to apply them.

The Scots had one of 17 miles or so in 1497, known as the "landkenning," or the distance at which the land was visible from the top of the mast. The weakness of this was twofold. Firstly the Scots could never enforce it around their enormous coastline and secondly it was very imprecise, as the land in Scotland is sometimes visible for 30 miles, it depends on which part is being observed.

Limits had always, as indeed these were, only applied to foreign vessels. Their application to native boats was to come later. By this time the herring fishing had almost reached its zenith in terms of boats fishing and numbers of people employed. In Scotland in 1856 there were 90,000 people working in the fishing industry, nearly all of them concerned with herring. There were 11,250 boats fishing with approximately 40,000 men aboard them. Wick still dominated the scene, handling a third of the Scottish catch itself, but Peterhead was by now challenging its position with Fraserburgh, Banff and Lerwick also showing signs of toppling it as they would within the next 30 years. In fact the 1850's ushered in the era which was to last to the beginning of the First World War, when the fishing industry went through its most prosperous times and also its most innovative period.

It was as if a giant hand was drawing together all the threads which were being spun in the various districts and was twisting them into a cable of immense strength. Such was the scale, and across so many subjects, that it is only in retrospect that events can be seen in perspective. The industry went in a mere 60 years from open boats of 50 feet which fished only in summer to decked steam and motor powered boats which could fish all year round.

The first move to modernisation began gradually enough in Fife where between them the carpenters and fishermen developed the hull style which was to become renowned as the "Fifie" or "Fyfie." Elsewhere in Scotland the "Scaffie" dominated the fishing and until the 1840's both types were completely undecked. The "Fifie" was a more heavily wooded hull and by 1850 many of them were half decked with some fully decked. This of course made it a much stronger vessel than the Scaffie which was very light by comparison and could be easily hauled ashore in the event of bad weather in the exposed areas. Although many harbours had been built around the coasts as a result of the boom in fishing, at the same time there were many fishing villages and hamlets with no shelter at all and these depended on the small Scaffies for a living. These small Scaffies, up to about 25 feet in length kept such places going for long after the size of the general fishing boat had greatly increased elsewhere. By the 1850's the average size of the larger herring drifters was in the region of 40 to 45 feet and, apart from Fife, were completely undecked. However, as a result of an enquiry set up to

Photograph from the Johnston Collection by permission of the Wick Society.

Boats hauled on the now deserted island of Stroma about the beginning of the Century. The vessel in the foreground carries the sprit sail rig of which the fishermen all around the Pentland Firth were the supreme masters. Stroma was deserted during the 1940's and 1950's when the inhabitants lost the will to seek a living there. It has the distinction of being the most rapidly abandoned district in Scotland, where there were no pressures such as Clearances or disease. The yawls were all line boats called Firthies but were very similar in general appearance to the Scaffie workhorse of the herring fishing until the latter half of the 19th Century.

look into the causes of the disaster of 19th September, 1848 when there was a heavy loss of life, especially at Wick where 37 men were drowned in one night, there was a general move towards the construction of first half, and then, fully decked boats. It took some time for the new design to become widely accepted and it was not till about 1865 that half decked vessels were used in any quantity. And these boats, coming as they did during the Italian wars of Independence under the leadership of Garibaldi, attracted the name of Baldies, often spelled Bauldies. The advent of the Baldies coincided with three other events which were to have a profound effect on the fishing. The first of these was the introduction of the cotton herring net which was one third the weight of the hemp nets that had been used till then, but twice as strong. What it meant was that boats could carry at least twice as many nets, and its introduction began a steady increase in the size of boats as the smaller vessels had difficulty in carrying what they could catch. The rate at which the new net was adapted was slowed by the American Civil War which interrupted the supply of cotton from the Southern States but that was only a temporary set back. The effect of the cotton net on the hemp net was almost the same as the polypropelene net was to have on the cotton seine net; it made it obsolete over-night. In 1800 a boat carried ten nets or so, each of about 12 fathoms long. Nets were in fact measured by the score of meshes, each mesh one inch square, so a 12 fathom net would be called a 45 score net. By 1840 boats were carrying 20 to 25 nets, and by 1880 the average was about 50 nets.

Photograph by permission of Mr P. McCabe, Peterhead.

The 'Spindrift', built as a motorised Zulu, and the Fifie 'Ivy' lying in Wick harbour.

But these 50 nets were by now 50 yards long or 25 fathoms. This represented about a four-fold increase in catching power since 1840 and thus the material which was to create the first seine nets of 60 years later arrived.

The other, and again not exactly obvious at the time, but as dramatic in its way, took place in the south of England in the town of Dartmouth in Devon. There at the yard of Mr George Bidder, the 49 feet long 'Thistle' specially constructed as a steam trawler was launched. In a letter to the Marine Engineer of the 1st Act, 1883, Mr W. E. Redway of Milford Haven assured the survival of the details of the introduction of steam trawling, when he wrote to the editor on the following terms.

"STEAM TRAWLERS."

To the Editor of THE MARINE ENGINEER.

SIR.—In your columns of the 1st instant I notice an article headed " Steam Trawlers." I beg to correct the statement that steam trawling originated on the Tyne. The origin of steam trawling was in South Devon in 1867, when the late Mr. George Bidder, the celebrated calculating engineer, applied to Mr. S. Lake, of Dartmouth, who then owned a lot of sailing vessels, to induce him to go into steam.

A small steam trawler was built called the *Thistle*, followed by the *Florence*, constructed by Mr. Bidder, and launched in 1868. She was after a trial condemned, as being too small. Following her another vessel was laid down in 1869, and launched in 1870, George Bidder providing the hull, and George Robert Stevenson the engines. This vessel, the *Bertha*, was built at Dartmouth, went round the coast under sail, and had her engines fitted by George Robert Stevenson in the Tyne. She was fitted with simple jet-condensing engines, a pair of 15-in. cylinders, multitubular boiler, and attained the speed of eleven knots. She had wire hawser, patent winding drum worked by the main engines, and disconnecting propeller. Her dimensions were 66 ft. keel, 15ft. 6in. beam, and 10 ft. 6in. depth of hold. She was a great success as a fishing machine, but one great drawback was very apparent. The towing warp was constantly being cut by the propeller. This vessel was, however, found too small, as there was not accommodation sufficient in her for the fish and the crew, and her sailing power was of little benefit to her. She is still in existence as a sailing trawler, her engines having been taken out, and placed in a larger vessel, No. 3, called the *Edith*, built at Dartmouth, in 1872. The dimensions of this vessel are 85 ft. keel, 20 ft beam, and depth of hold 11 ft. 6in. She was fitted with a lifting propeller, and had the first steam capstan placed in her, which formed the model for all future capstans in the North Sea (although trawlers are now being fitted with a similar winch to that which was used in No. 2, the *Bertha*, and which was considered of such importance that it was patented).

The *Edith* had full sailing power, and was a perfect trawler in every respect, and with good accommodation. She worked on the west coast of England for some time. Afterwards she was sent to the North Sea, and worked as a carrier with the Lowestoft fleet.

So strong, however, was the "ring," that although she carried to London what was equal to six sailing cutters, they would only allow her two shares out of ten, and consequently she had to be taken off the station. The sailing trawlers would not join her under any conditions on anything like fair terms. It was found impossible to work the vessel in strong tideways owing to the net fouling the propeller, and the warp being cut, and also the disadvantage of having to go to market daily with her own fish. The application of the encased propeller has made it possible and practicable to work the trawl in all weathers. This encasement, which is termed " Griffith's Patent," and was discovered by Mr. Griffiths and Mr. Lake at the same time, has rendered steam trawling a possibility, but in no case can it be considered advisable or found profitable to work only one or two boats alone.

A number of vessels fitted with these encased propellers are under construction at Milford Haven for the deep Irish fisheries.

The design you have put upon paper appears to take us back thirteen years.

Appended is a drawing of the vessels now being constructed for the Irish fisheries, and outline sketches of those above described, which are entitled to be called the pioneers of steam trawling.—I am, sir, yours obediently,

W. E. REDWAY.

Milford Haven, South Wales, *September 3rd,* 1883.

The "ring" referred to was the Billingsgate Monopoly.

Within 40 years there were to be about 1500 steam trawlers fishing from these islands, a rate of expansion both in numbers and catching power which was without precedent in the history of fishing. Of that number, about 200 trawlers were fishing from Scottish ports but not, legally, in Scottish waters because by that time the legislation exluding them had been enacted.

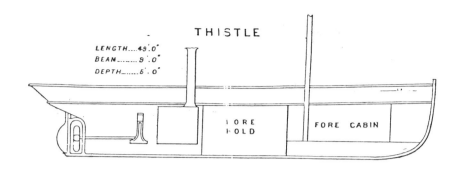

THISTLE

LENGTH....49'.0"
BEAM........9'.0"
DEPTH......5'.0"

FORE HOLD   FORE CABIN

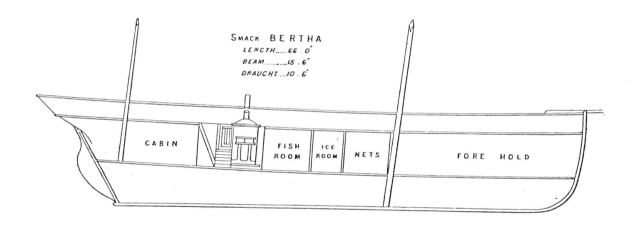

Smack BERTHA
LENGTH....66'.0"
BEAM.......15'.6"
DRAUGHT...10'.6"

CABIN   FISH ROOM   ICE ROOM   NETS   FORE HOLD

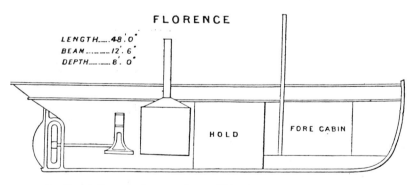

FLORENCE

LENGTH....48'.0"
BEAM.......12'.6"
DEPTH......8'.0"

HOLD   FORE CABIN

For Description, see Correspondence, "STEAM TRAWLERS" (*page* 187).

Illustration by permission of the National Maritime Museum, London.

An illustration of the earliest steam trawlers built in England. The earlier steam fishing boat with a screw propeller in Scotland seems to have been the 50 ft long 'George Loch' which was launched with a six hp engine on 18th March, 1869 at Wick. She was built by Robert Steven for J. Mackenzie, fishcurer and was modelled on the hull of the RNLI safety boat. I came into possession of this information through the invaluable assistance of Mr Joe Reid of Edinburgh but too late for me to follow through her career for the purposes of this book.

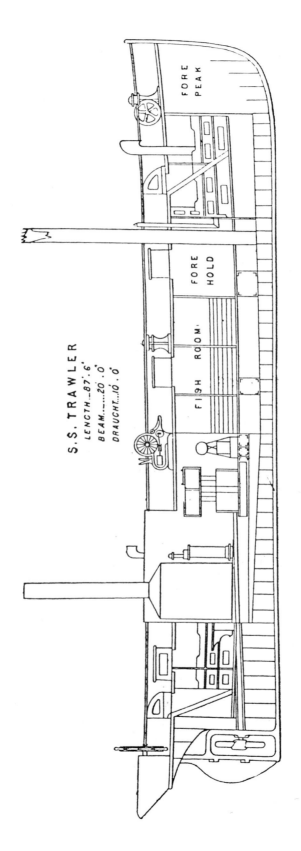

S.S. TRAWLER
LENGTH..87'.6'
BEAM......20'.0"
DRAUGHT..10'.0"

FORE PEAK

FORE HOLD

FISH ROOM.

Illustration by permission of the National Maritime Museum.

Drawings of the trawler referred to in the correspondence to the Marine Engineer.

The process of law which eventually excluded trawling from inshore waters began in 1868. This was really an updated version of earlier Acts, particularly that of 1843. This Act, although it does not exactly say so in so many words, hints at the existence of steam driven vessels being used in support of fishing, but not actually fishing. It also mentions, at paragraph 68 that: "No person between the 25th July and 25th November in any year, shall, within half a mile of any sea fishing boat stationed for seine netting, anchor any seafishing or other boat not engaged in seine netting."

This clause applied to the coast of Cornwall only and obviously refers to seine netting of the traditional kind where the seine net was hauled to the shore. Trawling is still not mentioned in any important sense, but nevertheless it was beginning to expand at an accelerating rate on the east coast of England. In England trawlers were to be largely sail powered until the 1890's and some English skippers and owners persisted with sailing trawlers till just before the Second World War. This may be explained by the fact that they were superbly built, probably the finest sea-boats ever launched in England, or anywhere else for that matter, and because the English, in spite of their progressive outlook, cling tenaciously to their traditions.

Trawling of course had been going on in England for centuries while the Scots seem to have ignored it completely until the creation of the Aberdeen industry in 1882. As in Scotland, but to a far greater degree, the Industrial Revolution had a profound effect on the English fishing industry. As in Scotland it was the improvement in communications ashore to the fishing ports which unleashed the great expansion. The effect was most noticeable in East Anglia and on the Lincoln and Yorkshire coasts where the previously isolated villages of Grimsby, and Kingston-upon-Hull grew at incredible rates, after the arrival of the railway in the 1850's. It was this, combined with the proximity of the then apparently unexhaustable Dogger Bank, that was to shape the character of fishings in Europe, and beyond, over the next century. The date when steam trawling began in earnest, and seine netting took an irrevocable step closer, has to be reckoned from the launch of the 'Zodiac' of Grimsby in 1881.

It was no coincidence that as the first English steam trawlers were fitting out, the Scots, who had up till now almost completely ignored the potential of trawling, began to develop the industry in Aberdeen. Aberdeen was not the first port to pursue trawling and the first Scottish trawl owner was probably David Walker of Johnshaven who began beam trawling under sail in 1872 and gave evidence to this effect before the Royal Commission on Trawling in 1883.

He had adapted the English method and there is the strange paradox that the English trawling industry was mainly fostered by a Scotsman. He was Scrymgeour Hewett who developed the Short Blue Fleet in Barking in 1764. The trawling industry in Aberdeen was mainly organised by Englishmen, the most notable among whom was Peter Johnstone of Birmingham who came to Aberdeen about 1872 to buy fish for his father. But Aberdeen was the first port in Scotland where trawled fish was landed regularly and it was to have a great influence on the future of the fishing generally because, as the fleet grew, many of the crews in Aberdeen came from the Buchan and Moray coasts, The result was that a basic knowledge, if not practical experience, of how this method of fishing worked soon became fairly widespread along the coasts. What the vast majority of fishermen learned about trawling, they did not like in the least, but in the fullness of time they were to put this knowledge to use in seining. Over the next 40 years trawling was to be prosecuted from Fraserburgh, Peterhead and Buckie although much of it was attempted with underpowered steam drifters in the desperate years of the early 1920's. But the advent of the steam trawlers in Aberdeen was to have a much more immediate effect on things around the coasts than that.

By the 19th Century the rural population of Scotland was among the most literate in the world. This was due to the Education Acts, especially that of 1696, stretching back into history. The result was that the fishing communities were very well informed through their local newspapers, many of which like the *Aberdeen Free Press and Daily Journal,* to become the *Press & Journal* in Aberdeen, the *John O'Groat Journal* in Wick, *The Courant* in Elgin, the *Banffshire Journal, Fraserburgh Herald, Northern Scot, Fife Herald* and the *Buchan Observer* were well established by the middle of the century. These papers, before the advent of national dailies in the early 1900's, carried a great deal of news from outwith their local areas, most of which they acquired from the pages of the *Scotsman, Glasgow Herald* and even English papers.

The contents of the papers would range from local news to the goings on at the court of the Tzar, cannibalism in Africa, punishment of runaway servants in South America and there was usually a large sprinkling of gruesome murders, reported in great detail, but very importantly as far as public opinion was concerned, there were large sections devoted to reporting the fishing at various ports. Not only that but governmental activities in respect of the fishings such as Laws, Enquiries and debates were very fully reported for the enlightenment of the readership. And as far as governmental activity was concerned, the 1880's were the most important ten years that the fishing industry were ever to see as they laid the foundations on which all the future was to be built.

From the 1860's onwards works were published which came about as a result of the study of fishing carried out by scientists in conjunction with the practical experience and observations of the fishermen. Reports and observations had been produced in pamphlet or leaflet form for 60 years before then but they were usually the work of some observant fishery officer who produced them on his own initiative. These pamphlets had a limited circulation and often they were more like a memorandum to the board of the British Fishery Society, or the governors of the Fishery Board. The result was that a great deal of valuable information and far-seeing observations was confined to a comparative handful of people who, while often recognising the worth of what was being said, had other more pressing matters to think about and nothing much was done as a result.

That was changed in 1864 when Mr John M Mitchell published his masterpiece, "The Herring, its Natural History and National Importance." In this outstanding work, which will never be surpassed for its quality, Mitchell wrote not only a history of the fishing up to his time, but an analysis of the life cycle of the herring, how it was caught and processed in various countries, and some opinions on the future of the industry. Mitchell was already an established international authority whose words carried considerable weight and among his observations was that trawling posed a serious threat to the herring industry because of the destruction of the herring spawn. He argued that between man and its natural enemies, the herring would not be able to survive the additional burden of a trawl being dragged through its spawning grounds. This point he illustrated in the following manner: "Let us suppose that there are 200,000 Solan geese in the colony of St Kilda, feeding there, or thereabouts, for seven months of the year. Let us suppose that each devours, by itself or its young, only five herring a day, this amounts to one million; seven months (March to September) contain 214 days; by which if we multiply the above, the product is 214 million fish for the summer sustenance of a single species near the island of St Kilda."

At that time the Scottish curing and fishing activities were accounting for another 750 million or so, and Mitchell made no attempt at estimating how many adult herring were consumed by other predators in Scottish waters alone, such as cod, haddock, ling, whiting, seals, whales and sea birds too numerous to mention. The scale of the depredation may be gauged from the report in 1878 that a cod was landed in Wick with 32 small herring in its stomach. Dr R. G. Hislop of the Torry Research Laboratory in Aberdeen saw similar numbers of young mackerel or cod caught off the west coast in the 1970's.

Mitchell confined himself to the observation that, in 1856, there were 39,000 fishermen in Scotland and that if this number were increased by 6000, they would then catch the same amount of herring as the cod were estimated to do; in other words about 800 million a year. What Mitchell did not say, possibly because research had not established the fact by that time, is that herring in their turn lived on the spawn of their predators. The cycle was therefore to the greater or lesser degree self perpetuating but for one key fact that no-one observed. Man alone was the only predator who injected nothing into the cycle but only took from it. Dead whales, seals or seabirds are consumed by one organism or another and thence recycled to the sea for the benefit of its inhabitants. The early writers such as Mitchell, while they did not say so in so many words, implied as much and were at some pains to make it clear.

Another writer of great influence was James G. Bertram, author of the "Harvest of the Sea." He was much more forthright than Mitchell and he wrote the following at a time when Wick by itself was exporting nearly a third of all the herring leaving Scotland.

I have always been slow to believe in the inexhaustibility of the shoals, and can easily imagine the overfishing, which some people pooh-pooh so glibly, to be quite possible, especially when supplemented by the cod and other cannibals so constantly at work, and so well described by the Lochfyne Commission; not that I believe it possible to pick up or kill every fish of a shoal; but, as I have already hinted, so many are taken, and the economy of the shoal so disturbed, that in all probability it may change its ground or amalgamate with some other herring colony. I shall be met here by the old argument, that "the fecundity of fish is so enormous as to prevent their extinction," etc. etc. But the certainty of a fish yielding twenty thousand eggs is no surety for these being hatched, or if hatched, of their escaping the dangers of infancy, and reaching the market as table food. I watch the great shoals at Wick with much interest, and could wish to have been longer acquainted with them. How long time have the Wick shoals taken to grow to their present size?—what size were the shoals when the fish had leave to grow without molestation?—how large were the shoals when first discovered?—and how long have they been fished? are questions which I should like to have answered. As it is, I fear the great Wick fishery must come some day to an end. When the Wick fishery first began the fisherman could carry in a creel on his back the nets he required; now he requires a cart and a good strong horse!

Bertram was to be proven all too accurate in his prophecy and if Wick's demise was not entirely for the reasons he gave, but he was not all that far off the mark as far as the fishing generally was concerned.

The concerns of Mitchell and Bertram were mainly directed against overfishing by the traditional methods and, although neither of them liked trawling, their criticism of it was put in mild, almost apologetic terms. Their comments were of course made when trawling was still being carried out by sailing beam trawlers off the east coast of England and the level of activity was still a long way from the heights it would reach in the 1880's and provoke the violent reactions of 1884 and 1885. It must also be remembered that Bertram and Mitchell lived at a time when men of their social background could only point to shortcomings in the system in a very respectful manner if they wished any attention to be paid to what they were saying. Fishermen, for whom trawlers became increasingly annoying, did not have such restraints placed upon them.

Trawling had been unpopular with those not engaged in it, just as purse netting is today, from the very beginning. It seems to have begun in the 15th Century in England or Holland and local magistrates always seemed to be harassing trawler men to the greater or lesser degree. There was not much active discrimination against them about till 1880 by which time the North Sea was becoming extremely crowded with tens of thousands of fishing boats on its surface. And inevitably, all local and national jealousies apart, when somebody is dragging a net around an area where others are lying to lines or drift nets, trouble soon develops. With the built-in resentment of this newfangled trawling, and the fact that the growing use of steam gave the advantage of manoeuvrability, and speed from the scene if gear was fouled, aggrieved fishermen had very little patience with the newcomers. On top of claims for losses, real or imagined, there could be added the accusation likely to be most damaging of all, that trawlers were destroying the spawning grounds.

In the decade up to 1880 matters deteriorated in proportion to the increase in trawling, mainly off the coast of East Anglia as trawling was still in its annoying infancy in Scotland. Fuelled by the notorious Dutch and German grog ships, which led to the establishment of the Royal National Mission to Deep Sea Fishermen in 1881 because of the loss of life and injury through drunkenness, there was a constant and increasing friction between the fishermen of the various methods and countries. Fights, rammings, boardings, shootings and even sinkings became frequent until it was evident that something had to be done by governments to sort out both their national and international problems.

Ashore matters had progressed from the mild criticisms of Mitchell and Bertram. Organisations to combat trawling had been created, such as the Sunderland Sea Fisheries Protection Society, the Honorary Secretary of which, Mr Joseph John Hill, frequently wrote all local newspapers encouraging fishermen to get up and at trawlermen. He implied that localities which did not resist were suffering from a docility just short of cowardice. Mr C. A. Vansittart Conybeare travelled all over the country, addressing large and excited gatherings of fishermen and succeeded in sparking off a few riots.

These matters all contributed to the pressures which were building up and they came to various heads in the 1880's. In 1883 an international convention, for the purpose of regulating the Police of Fisheries in the North Sea outside Territorial Waters took place in the Hague. This convention, and by no means for the last time in fishing history, turned out to be a talking shop, that did no more than draw up a series of rules which had been approved already, and long ago at that. The cast of characters who attended the conference is quite interesting if only for the fact that they must have spent the opening session trying to upstage one another with their medals and decorations, viz:—

HER Majesty the Queen of the United Kindom of Great Britain and Ireland; His Majesty the Emperor of Germany, King of Prussia; His Majesty the King of the Belgians; His Majesty the King of Denmark; the President of the French Republic; and His Majesty the King of the Netherlands, having recognised the necessity of regulating the police of the fisheries in the North Sea, outside territorial waters, have resolved to conclude for this purpose a Convention, and have named their Plenipotentiaries as follows:—

Her Majesty the Queen of the United Kingdom of Great Britain and Ireland, the Honourable William Stuart, Companion of the Most Honourable Order of the Bath, &c., her Envoy Extraordinary and Minister Plenipotentiary at the Hague; Charles Malcolm Kennedy, Esq., Companion of the Most Honourable Order of the Bath, &c., Head of the Commercial Department of the Foreign Office; and Charles Cecil Trevor, Esq., Barrister at Law, Assistant Secretary to the Board of Trade, &c.;

His Majesty the Emperor of Germany, King of Prussia, Veit Richard von Schmidthals, Knight of the Order of the Red Eagle of the Third Class, and of the Order of St. John, &c., Councillor of Legation, his Chargé d'Affaires at the Hague; and Peter Christian Kinch Donner, Knight of the Order of the Red Eagle of the fourth class with the Sword, and of the Crown of the fourth class, &c., his Councillor of State, Captain in the Navy, on the Reserve;

His Majesty the King of the Belgians, the Baron d'Anethan, Commander of the Order of Leopold, &c., his Envoy Extraordinary and Minister Plentipotentiary at the Hague; and M. Léopold Orban, Commander of the Order of Leopold, &c., his Envoy Extraordinary and Minister Plenipotentiary, Director-General of the Political Department in the Ministery of Foreign Affairs;

His Majesty the King of Denmark, Carl Adolph Bruun, Knight of the Order of the Danebrog, &c., Captain in the Navy;

The President of the French Republic, the Count Lefèbvre de Béhaine, Commander of the National Order of the Legion of Honour, &c., Envoy Extraordinary and Minister Plenipotentiary of the French Republic at the Hague; and M. Gustave Emile Mancel, Officer of the National Order of the Legion of Honour, &c., Commissary of Marine;

His Majesty the King of the Netherlands, the Jonkheer Willem Frederik Rochussen, Commander of the Order of the Lion of the Netherlands, &c., his Minister of Foreign Affairs; and Eduard Nicolaas Rahusen, Knight of the Order of the Lion of the Netherlands, &c., President of the Committee for Sea Fisheries;

The conference was the first truly multinational discussion about fishing and is noteworthy for that if nothing else. It did not make much physical difference to what was going on at sea in the short term, but at least it defined the three mile limit all around Europe from the 61st parallel of latitude north of Unst, all the way around Europe and back to the 61st parallel off Lindesnaes lighthouse in Norway. Apart from that it really was a re-statement of earlier agreements but nevertheless it is an indicator of how things were going, particularly that the tempo of fishing expansion was speeding up.

Photograph by permission of Mr R. Smart, Keeper of Muniments, University of St Andrews.

Professor William Carmichael McIntosh, MD, FRS, photographed about 1863. He regarded Professor G. O. Sars of the University of Christiana, later to become Oslo, as the pioneer of modern marine biology. Professor Sars first discovered cod spawn floating off the Lofoten Islands in fantastic quantities in 1864.

Alongside these events other matters to be of great future import, were proceeding. One was that Marine Research Laboratories were set up in Dunbar and St Andrews. The laboratory in St Andrews is worth mentioning as it came about as the result of the right man being in the right place at the right time. That man was Professor William McIntosh who had a keen interest in marine biology although

Photograph by permission of Mr R. Smart, Keeper of Muniments, University of St Andrews.

Professor McIntosh's original laboratory. The men in the foreground are probably students and fishermen assistants. The vessel is either the 'Goldseeker' or the 'Garland', a yacht bought by the Trawling Commission for research for which she was totally unsuited. A close and highly regarded associate of the professor was Mr Alexander Wallace Brown, a line fisherman who became known as "Professor" to the students.

he had in fact trained as a doctor of medicine. He had been appointed professor of Civil and Natural History at St Andrews in 1882, just as the trawling controversy was reaching full swing and steam trawlers were making their appearance along the coast. In 1883 he was given a grant, which eventually over the years reached a total of £335, to set up a marine research laboratory to identify fish fry and spawn, their food chains and a general enquiry into fish caught as food for this country. He set up his laboratory in an old wooden building which had been built near St Andrews harbour as an isolation hospital and for 12 years pioneered in marine biology research. His research was not by any means confined to the laboratory and the way and standard to which he conducted it earned him an international reputation. Almost at the same time as McIntosh received his grant, and perhaps this may have

Photograph by permission of Mr R. Smart, Keeper of Muniments, University of St Andrews.

The inside of Professor McIntosh's laboratory showing the tanks where he kept his live specimens.

been one of the conditions of the grant, he was invited on 1st January 1884, to act as one of the scientific advisers to the Commission of Enquiry set up on 30th August, 1883, to "inquire and report upon complaints that have been made by line and drift net fishermen of injuries sustained by them in their calling owing to the use of the trawl net and beam trawl."

This Commission obviously resulted from the increasing national and international dissatisfaction over the disarray at sea, but there may very well have been one factor above all which drew fishermen and their livelihood to the attention of the Government, in a way which immediately won their sympathy and probably did more than anything to ensure the Commission of Enquiry.

That occurred on 14th October, 1881 when a storm of unprecedented ferocity hit the fishing fleets of Eyemouth, Newhaven, Burnmouth, St Abbs and Cockburnspath. 189 men and boys were drowned on that dreadful day and these are the souls who perished along with their vessels:—

EYEMOUTH—129 MEN.

"HARMONY," 6—Lost in east entrance to Eyemouth.

	Years		Years
William Angus ⎫ (Brothers)	35	James Ward . . .	29
Peter Angus ⎬	32	George Cribbes . .	55
Henry Angus (Uncle) . .	53	Alexander Craig . .	37

"RADIANT," 7—Lost in east entrance to Eyemouth.

	Years		Years
John Windram . . .	57	David Fairbairn ⎫	37
James Crombie . . .	37	John Fairbairn ⎬ (Brothers)	35
William Gray . . .	36	Alex. Fairbairn ⎭	28
		John Burgon, 30 years.	

"PRESS HOME," 6—Lost in east entrance to Eyemouth.

	Years		Years
Andrew Collin . . .	36	Robert Stott ⎫	26
Leonard Dougal . . .	18	John Stott ⎬ (Brothers)	22
George Windram . . .	25	James Stott ⎭	20

"JANET," 6—Lost at Burnmouth.

	Years		Years
John Maltman, Father .	45	George Maltman . .	17
Alex. Maltman ⎫ (Sons)	22	Henry Young . . .	47
Robert Maltman ⎬	20	Thomas Swanston . .	19

"LILY OF THE VALLEY," 6—Lost at Burnmouth.

	Years		Years
Thomas Miller . . .	37	David Ritchie . . .	34
James Lough . . .	40	James Dougal . . .	23
Robert Lough . . .	38	Alexander Swanston .	19

"FORGET-ME-NOT," 7—Lost near Berwick.

	Years		Years
William Nisbet . . .	35	Andrew Dougal . .	33
Alexander Nisbet . .	37	Alexander Cribbes .	31
Robert Collin . . .	41	William Scott . .	28
		James Simpson, 17 years.	

"WAVE," 6—Lost near Berwick.

	Years		Years
Peter Paterson . . .	49	Robert Johnson . .	40
John Paterson (Son) .	17	David Johnson (Son) .	19
Peter Burgon . . .	42	John Hastie . . .	34

"BLOSSOM," 5—Lost in Goswick Bay.

	Years		Years
George Dougal . . .	40	William Crombie . .	26
William Young . . .	51	Robert Young . . .	20
John Burgon . . .	44	(One Saved)	

"BEAUTIFUL STAR," 7—Lost at Sea.

	Years		Years
George Scott (Father)	54	Robert Collin . .	28
John Scott ⎫	26	James Broomfield . .	28
George Scott ⎬ Sons	23	Edward Fisher . . .	24
William Scott ⎭	21		

"INDUSTRY," 7—Lost at Sea.

	Years		Years
Andrew Cowe . . .	52	Andrew Craig . . .	52
James Paterson . . .	47	James Dougal . . .	43
William Paterson (Son) .	17	Thomas Spouse . .	40
		Thomas Scott, 21 years.	

"FIERY CROSS," 7—Lost at Sea.

	Years		Years
Robert Collin . . .	45	Joseph Collin . . .	41
William Collin (Brother) .	43	Hugh Grant . . .	38
John Cowe . . .	41	Robert Wilson . . .	34
		James Young, 24 years.	

"MYRTLE," 7—Lost at Sea.

	Years		Years
William Hood . . .	43	George Bone . . .	41
John Hood (Son) . .	19	George Bone (Son) .	17
James Purves . . .	51	Thomas Collin . . .	24
		James Collin (Brother), 21 years.	

"GUIDING STAR," 7—Lost at Sea.

	Years		Years
Henry Dougal ⎫ Brothers	38	George Dougal . . .	25
John Dougal ⎬	28	Thomas Fisher . . .	30
William Maltman . .	35	James Dougal . . .	24
		George Whillis, 39 years.	

"FLORIDA," 7—Lost at Sea.

	Years		Years
John Paterson . . .	44	Thomas Dougal . .	33
William Crombie . . .	41	Paul Paterson . . .	37
John Paterson . . .	35	John Craig . . .	18
		Thomas Fairbairn, 19 years.	

"LASS O' GOWRIE," 7—Lost at Sea.

	Years		Years
George Windram (Father) .	60	James Windram . .	33
David Windram ⎫ (Sons)	37	Robert Kearney . .	30
William Windram ⎬	25	Charles Burgon . .	25
		Peter Collin, 21 years.	

"SIX BROTHERS," 6—Lost at Sea.

	Years		Years
Robert Collin (Father) .	44	James Collin (Son) . .	18
James Collin (Son) . .	21	James Windram ⎫ (Brothers)	40
George Collin (Father) .	41	John Windram ⎬	28

"SUNSHINE," 6—Lost at Sea.

	Years		Years
George Grant . . .	28	Richard Windram . .	28
Robert Scott . . .	28	Alexander Collin . .	17
John Broomfield . . .	22	Robert Longh . . .	19

"MARGARET AND MARY," 5—Lost at Sea.

	Years		Years
John Maltman . . .	28	Robert Gillie . . .	23
James Maltman (Cousin) .	22	John Gillie (Cousin) .	22
		William Collin, 30 years.	

"MARGARET AND CATHERINE," 6—Lost at Sea.

	Years		Years
John Lough ⎫ Brothers	23	Alexander Storey . .	25
Peter Lough ⎬	21	Henry Paterson . .	24
Peter Craig . . .	32	Johnston Borthwick .	17

"GOOD INTENT," 2—Lost at Spittal.

	Years		Years
John Lough . . .	32	James Cribbes . . .	25

"ECONOMY."

Alexander Maltman, 48 years.

"ENTERPRISE."

James Windram, 28 years.

"INVINCIBLE."

John Dougal, 50 years.

"ONWARD."

Alexander Dougal, 21 years.

"JAMES AND ROBERT."

Andrew J. H. Dougal, 24 years.

"FISHER LASSES."

William Young, 58 years.

"VELOX."

Andrew Henderson, 23 years.

"PEARL."

John Fairbairn, 32 years.

NEWHAVEN—15 MEN.

"PERSEVERANCE," 7—Lost near May Island.

	Years		Years
John Carnie	32	Boreas Hall	31
William Inglis	30	Peter Inglis	18
Johnston Wilson	21	William Liston (Rutherford)	37
	David Lyle, 25 years.		

Yawl "STORMY PETREL," 3.

	Years		Years
David Stevenson (Father)	58	Philip Stevenson (Son)	30
Hugh Stevenson (Son)	32		

Pilot-boat "CONCORD," 3—Swamped off Dunbar.

John Johnston	37 years	}
James Johnston	30 years	} Brothers
William Johnston	23 years	}

Yawl "ROBINAS," 2.

	Years		Years
William Liston	20	Alexander Noble	42

FISHERROW—7 MEN.

"ALICE," 7.

	Years		Years
Alexander Hamilton	23	John Cunningham	22
William Walker	39	Thos. Langlands	} (Brothers) 19
Robert Halley	21	Geo. Langlands	} 21
	William Caird, 27 years.		

COLDINGHAM SHORE (ST. ABB'S)—3 MEN.

"TWO SISTERS"—Lost at Sea.

	Years		Years
Charles Purves	55	James Thorburn	42
	William Thorburn (Brother), 38 years.		

BURNMOUTH—24 MEN.

"TRANSCENDENT." 7—Lost at Sea.

	Years		Years
Thomas Kerr	32	John Anderson Wood	25
George Martin	48	George Wilson	32
James Anderson	24	James Lindores	25
	James Lindores, 27 years.		

"GUIDING STAR," 7—Lost at Holy Island.

	Years		Years
Mark Anderson	51	William Johnston	30
James Johnston	28	George Anderson	30
Robert Anderson	53	Alexander Anderson	30
	Thomas Aitchison, 30 years.		

"EXCELLENT"—Ashore at Goswick.

	Years		Years
Alexander Affleck	22	Thomas Martin	24
	Both washed overboard when nearing the shore.		

Two Small Cobles Lost at Sea—"CHRISTINA" and "ALICE," 4 of each Crew.

	Years		Years
Robert Lindores (Father)	51	James Lindores (Son)	24
John Martin	18	William Lindores	21
William Martin	20	Thomas Mackay	18
John Aitchison	17	William Struthers	18

COVE (COCKBURNSPATH)—11 MEN.

"RENOWN"—Lost at Sea.

	Years		Years
Richard Gordon	33	John Fairbairn	31
	Thomas Fairbairn, 19 years.		

"SNOWDON"—Lost at Sea.

	Years		Years
David Fairbairn	34	David Fairbairn	17
John Fairbairn	24	Robert Grieve	24
Thomas Fairbairn	24	James Gordon	18

Reproduced from "Eyemouth an Old Time Fishing Town".

Mr William Nisbet who was lost in the Eyemouth Disaster and whose remains were so tenderly prepared for burial.

They left 86 widows and 314 children. The story is very movingly told by the Rev Daniel McIver in his book: ''An Old-Time Fishing Town'' from which the above information is reproduced. The appalling scale of the calamity is almost beyond comprehension but, even in this disturbing catalogue of suffering there shines an incident of almost devine character. That was when the body of Mr William Nisbet, obviously a man held in the highest esteem, was recovered. Women of the village, who by that time must surely have been in the furthest stages of emotional exhaustion, cleaned and dressed his remains with a care and delicacy that must have been similar to the anointment of a Saint.

Public response to the bereaved was immediate and magnificent. £54,000, an enormous sum in these days, was raised in a very short time, with donations from all over Scotland, England and Wales. Donations ranged from £100 from Queen Victoria to six pence from ''May and Katie'' and a trust fund was set up to administer it so as to provide an income for widows as long as they lived. The disaster gripped the public attention even more than the equally terrible English trawling fleet disaster of March 1883 when 255 men and boys were drowned and almost certainly was one of the factors influencing the establishment of the Commission.

The Commission itself is worthy of more than a passing mention if only for the way in which it went about its business. If modern information-gathering agencies of governments did their work half as well as this illustrious body, the fishing industry would not be in the state of uncertainty and confusion that it finds itself in the 1980's. Its terms of reference were short and to the point.

COMMISSION.

𝔙𝔦𝔠𝔱𝔬𝔯𝔦𝔞, by the Grace of God of the United Kingdom of Great Britain and Ireland Queen, Defender of the Faith.

𝔗𝔬 our right trusty and right well-beloved Cousin John William, Earl of Dalhousie, Knight of Our Most Ancient and Most Noble Order of the Thistle ; Our trusty and well-beloved Edward Marjoribanks, Esquire (commonly called the Honourable Edward Marjoribanks) ; Our trusty and well-beloved Thomas Henry Huxley, Esquire, Doctor of Laws, President of the Royal Society, Inspector of Fisheries ; Our trusty and well-beloved William Sproston Caine, Esquire ; and Our trusty and well-beloved Thomas Francis Brady, Esquire, Inspector of Irish Fisheries, greeting.

𝔚𝔥𝔢𝔯𝔢𝔞𝔰 We have deemed it expedient that a Commission should forthwith issue to inquire into the Complaints which have been made by Line and Drift-net Fishermen of injuries sustained by them in their calling, owing to the use of the Trawl-net and Beam Trawl in the Territorial waters of the United Kingdom ; and to ascertain how far these Complaints are well founded, and whether any, and what, legislative remedy can be adopted without interfering with the cheap and plentiful supply of fish :

𝔑𝔬𝔴 𝔨𝔫𝔬𝔴 𝔶𝔢, that we, reposing great trust and confidence in your ability and discretion, have nominated, constituted, and appointed, and do by these Presents nominate, constitute, and appoint you, the said John William, Earl of Dalhousie, Edward Marjoribanks, Thomas Henry Huxley, William Sproston Caine, and Thomas Francis Brady, to be Our Commissioners for the purposes of the said Inquiry :

𝔄𝔫𝔡 for the purpose of enabling you, Our Commissioners, to make the said inquiries, We do hereby authorise you, and empower you, or any three or more of you, to invite such Persons as you may judge most competent by reason of their situation, knowledge, or experience to afford you correct information on the subject of this Inquiry, to attend before you and bring with them all such Books, Documents, Papers, Accounts, &c., as may appear to you, or any three or more of you, calculated to assist you in the execution of Trust hereby reposed in you :

𝕬𝖓𝖉 We do further by these Presents authorise and empower you, or any three or more of you, to visit and personally inspect such places in Our United Kingdom as you may judge expedient for the more effectual carrying out of the purposes aforesaid :

𝕬𝖓𝖉 We further ordain that you, or any three or more of you, may have liberty to report to Us your proceedings under this Our Commission from time to time, if you shall judge it expedient so to do :

𝕬𝖓𝖉 Our further will and pleasure is that you do, with as little delay as possible, report to Us, under your hands and seals, or under the hands and seals of three or more of you, your opinion upon the several matters herein submitted for your consideration.

𝕬𝖓𝖉 We will and command that this, Our Commission. shall continue in full force and virtue, and that you, the said Commissioners, or any three or more of you, may, from time to time, proceed in the execution thereof, and of every matter or thing therein contained, although the same be not continued from time to time by adjournment.

𝕬𝖓𝖉 for your assistance in the execution of these Presents, We do hereby authorise and empower you to appoint a Secretary to this Our Commission to attend you, whose services and assistance We require you to use from time to time as occasion may require.

> Given at Our Court at Saint James, the thirtieth day of August one thousand eight hundred and eighty-three, in the Forty-seventh Year of Our Reign.
>
> By Her Majesty's Command.
>
> (Signed)   W. V. HARCOURT.

The Commission reported back in March 1885 in the following manner:

MAY IT PLEASE YOUR MAJESTY :
    Your Majesty having been graciously pleased to issue a Commission under the Great Seal authorising and empowering the Commissioners therein named to inquire and report upon the complaints which have been made by line and drift net fishermen of injuries sustained by them in their calling, owing to the use of the trawl net and beam trawl, in the territorial waters of the United Kingdom, and to ascertain how

far these complaints are well founded, and whether any and what legislative remedy can be adopted without interfering with the cheap and plentiful supply of fish ; and signifying Your Majesty's will and pleasure that three or more of the said Commissioners should under their hands and seals report to Your Majesty their opinion upon the several matters submitted for their consideration in the said Commission ; We Your Majesty's Commissioners whose hands and seals are hereunto set, having inquired into all the subjects committed to us for consideration, do humbly certify to Your Majesty the proceedings under the said Commission in furtherance and execution of Your Majesty's commands.

1. We have held sittings in London, Aberdeen, St. Andrews, Edinburgh, Dunbar, Berwick, Sunderland, Scarborough, Hull, and Brixham, and have examined witnesses from the following places :—-

Golspie.	Cellardyke.	North Shields.
Peterhead.	Anstruther.	South Shields.
Port Erroll.	Pittenween.	Whitburn.
Whinnyfold.	St. Monance.	Sunderland.
Newburgh.	Buckhaven.	Hartlepool.
Footdee.	Leith.	Staithes.
Aberdeen.	Edinburgh.	Whitby.
Torry.	Newhaven.	Scarborough.
Burnbanks.	Granton.	Filey.
Cove.	Prestonpans.	Hull.
Findon.	Cockenzie.	Great Grimsby.
Portlethen.	North Berwick.	Yarmouth.
Downies.	Dunbar.	Lowestoft.
Stonehaven.	Coldingham.	London.
Johnshaven.	Eyemouth.	Brixham.
Broughty Ferry.	Burnmouth.	
St. Andrews.	Berwick-on-Tweed.	

We have received from witnesses and other persons books, documents, papers, and accounts bearing upon the subject of our inquiry.   Such of these as we think material are printed in the Appendix.

Shortly after the commencement of our inquiry we obtained from the Lords Commissioners of Your Majesty's Treasury, a sum of 200*l*., to be expended in scientific observations upon the results of the use of the beam trawl-net, and the distribution of the food-fishes taken by trawling on the various grounds frequented at different seasons of the year.

On the 1st January 1884, we appointed Professor McIntosh of St. Andrews to conduct the observations.   Arrangements were made with the Granton Steam Trawling Company, Limited, and with Mr. W. Meff, smackowner of Aberdeen, to accommodate Professor McIntosh on board their steam-trawlers, when trawling for the market in the usual way.   Printed forms were supplied by us for the registering of the contents of the net at each haul.   Professor McIntosh began to work on the 2nd January 1884, and continued until the end of the following August.   The observations were chiefly carried on off the Scotch coasts, between Buchanness and St. Abb's Head, with the exception of one expedition to Smith's Bank, off the coast of Caithness.   The trawl was shot and hauled in the usual manner in the ordinary course of business. on the ordinary grounds ; and every facility was afforded to Professor McIntosh for inspecting and registering its contents.   Three days were also spent in trawling off Scarborough and two days off St. Andrews, in small steam trawlers.

Ninety-three hauls were made under the supervision of Professor McIntosh, and the contents of the trawl carefully registered in every case.

The chairman and certain members of the Commission were present on several occasions, for the purpose of seeing the mode in which the experiments were carried out.

Professor McIntosh made his report on the 1st November 1884 ; a copy of which, together with our instructions to him, and registers of the hauls, will be found in the Appendix.

The members of the Commission asked a total of 12,929 questions of those invited to attend to give their evidence. Each session was reported verbatim and the clarity of purpose is exemplary. The first session was held in the Sheriff Court House, Aberdeen on Tuesday, 25th September, 1883 and the minutes were reported in the following manner.

MINUTES OF EVIDENCE

TAKEN BEFORE

ROYAL COMMISSION ON TRAWLING.

SHERIFF COURT HOUSE, ABERDEEN.

Tuesday, 25th September 1883.

PRESENT :

The Right Hon. THE EARL OF DALHOUSIE in the Chair.

Mr. W. S. CAINE, M.P.	PROFESSOR HUXLEY,
Mr. MARJORIBANKS, M.P.	Mr. T. F. BRADY.

Mr. C. A. PIDCOCK, Acting Secretary.

[CHAIRMAN.] Before we begin I think I ought to state the object for which the Commission has been appointed. The Commission is appointed for a very strict and definite purpose.   Complaints have been made by line and drift net fishermen of injuries which have been sustained by them in their calling, owing to the use of the trawl net and beam trawl in the territorial waters.   The Commission has been appointed to ascertain how far these complaints are well founded, and whether any and what legislative remedy can be adopted without interfering with the cheap and plentiful supply of fish.   But our inquiry is limited to the territorial waters.   Any grievances that drift and line fishermen may have against trawlers outside the territorial waters the Commission are not empowered to inquire into ; but within the territorial waters the Commissioners are anxious to hear all complaints that the drift net and line fishermen may have to make against trawlers.   They will of course hear what the trawlers have to say in their defence.   The Commissioners will also inquire what may be the effect of any legislative measures, or any remedies that may be proposed by any of the witnesses upon the supply of fish, because you will readily understand the Commission would hesitate very much before they would recommend to the Government any legislation that might have the effect of diminishing the supply of fish in the markets. It is our intention to examine first of all the line and drift net fishermen from the various places, to hear what they have to say, and having heard them to hear what the trawlers have to say.   After that we will hear the fish salesmen.   So we are now to begin with a line fisherman who has come from Golspie.

HECTOR MACDONALD.

1. [CHAIRMAN.] Where are you from?—Golspie.

2. What calling do you follow at Golspie?—That of a fisherman.

3. What sort of a fisherman?—Haddocks, flounders, cod, &c.

4. Do you fish with drift net and line?—Yes, we fish with herring nets.

5. Would you tell me what complaint you have to prefer, on behalf of the line and drift net fishermen against the trawlers?—I hope you will excuse me, gentlemen, because I may go wrong in the English language. I was not brought up in the English language. I only learned it since I came to manhood.

[CHAIRMAN.] You speak it very well; we shall understand you; go on.

(*Witness, continuing.*) When the trawlers first began to come to our bay it was smacks that used to come. Well, we felt the loss then, but this year, when we went away to the west coast fishing, there were some steam trawlers in our bay. We do not try the long line fishing till we come back from the herring fishing. We call it the home fishing.

6. You have been fishing round the west coast?—Yes. The time we were at the west coast fishing these trawlers were working in our bay all the time.

7. While you were away at the west coast fishing these trawlers were working in your bay?—Yes. On coming from the west coast some went to Peterhead, some went to Fraserburgh, others went to Wick and Helmsdale, and all these places. When we came back we tried the small line, and, where we used to get a lot of fish, haddocks and flat fish, we could hardly get any, because these trawlers had been trawling where we used to get as much flat fish as pay our bait, and haddocks besides. This year we cannot get any flat fish or haddocks.

8. Is this the first year you cannot get any flat fish or haddocks there?—Yes, this is the first year that we are not able to get flat fish among the haddocks, as we used to.

9. Your complaint is that while you were away fishing on the west coast, trawlers were trawling in your bay, and when you came back you did not find the same supply of fish you used to find?—Nothing like it.

10. Is there any other complaint you wish to make?—There is the complaint that the trawlers spoil the spawn, and tear up the feeding beds as well, the beds that the fish feed upon.

11. Then your complaint is a double complaint against the trawlers, that, while you were away, they fished your bay and took away all the fish?—Yes.

12. And that by trawling they have destroyed your supply of bait?—Not the bait, but the beds that the fish used to feed upon.

13. These are your two points. I understand you are anxious to tell the Commission your experience while

. . . and so the report went for, including the index, 157 pages of the most fascinating reading that anyone interested in the history of fishing will ever come across. Witnesses were line fishermen, drift net fishermen, fishery officers, fish salesmen, smack owners, sail and steam trawl skippers, pilots, solicitors, fishmongers, harbour masters, fishing fleet owners and a striking part of the evidence lay in the confidence and clarity with which the fishermen expressed their opinions and the total impartiality of the inquisitors.

Evidence was also being collected at sea by Professor McIntosh whose report ran for 81 pages. Everything was meticulously recorded and the following extracts illustrate the manner in which he recorded the details of the contents of the trawl:—

are nearly equal, many of the former being small, while all the latter were large. With all the wealth of young coalfishes swarming round our shores, it is surprising so few adults are captured. Fifteen herring occurred in the trawl, and some of these were alive. It might reasonably be supposed that the majority were captured either during the descent or ascent of the trawl, but the men avowed that they occasionally frequented the bottom. Only 15 brill appear in the list, yet in St. Andrews Bay it sometimes happens that a single fishing boat will in 12 hours capture a dozen small examples in its trawl. The sandy and sharp-nosed rays are few (seven and eight), the former chiefly occurring in Aberdeen, the latter on the island of May. All the examples of the sharp-nosed ray were large, and for the most part males. Four specimens of the common bream, and two halibut complete the list; the paucity of the latter is noteworthy, one young specimen occurring near Smith Bank off the Caithness coast and the large example south-east of Aberdeen. The halibut seems to be scarce within the 10-mile limit.

The small number of edible crabs (*Cancer pagurus*) obtained is noteworthy. With the exception of the inshore trawling north of Aberdeen, only one or two were occasionally picked up. The condition of these appeared to be good, and several were eaten. In the first week of April 18 edible crabs were procured at Aberdeen, and 19 in the same locality the first week in May. No spawn was observed in either case. All were of good size.

The cuttle-fishes (chiefly *Loligo vulgaris*, Lam.,) occurred in varying numbers, both on the sandy ground at Aberdeen and St. Andrews, and the deeper waters near the Forth and Smith Bank. They were most abundant off Aberdeen.

---

3. *The proportion of Living and Dead, and the condition of the Fishes when brought on deck.*

The proportion of living fishes varies according to the nature of the ground, the length of time the trawl has been down, the condition of the weather and the sea.

After inshore trawling on clean ground (sandy or hard) it has happened that every fish has been alive, while on a muddy bottom, on the other hand, almost every one has been dead. When the bag of the net is emptied the fishes, as a rule, form a seething and lively mass on deck, the large—such as cod, green cod, ling, catfish, plaice, and turbot, making violent efforts and flapping over the deck. It will be convenient to take the various kinds of fishes in succession and indicate their condition.

Grey Skate.—In almost every instance in which this species occurred it was alive, and in the majority of hauls very vigorous, and this is not surprising since the heart has been found in active condition 35 hours after the removal of the fish from the sea. Even when subjected to considerable pressure, and after the surface has been "diced" by the net, this species survives. Occasionally a little ecchymosis (bruising) has been observed on the outer surface, but to a trifling extent. The activity of a large example in the water is remarkable, and its dexterity in escaping from the mouth of the trawl under favourable opportunities is considerable. One had a hook in the pectoral fin.

Thornback.—Scarcely a dead specimen was observed. Almost all came on board alive. Occasionally a few bruises are visible on the white side.

Starry Ray.—A few dead examples only appeared on deck, these probably having been compressed in an exceptional manner, or injured in hoisting. All were in excellent condition as food-fishes, though its small size renders this species less acceptable in the market. No noteworthy injury occurred.

Sandy Ray.—The few examples of this species were alive and uninjured.

Sharp-nosed Ray. — The specimens were in perfect condition, and all alive.

Herring.—A few (15) examples of this surface fish occurred, and in several cases they were landed on deck alive and in excellent condition. It is probable that some of these were captured as the net went down or came up, but on the other hand one or two might have come from the bottom.

Cod.—It rarely happens that a dead cod is brought on board, and their condition as a rule is faultless. Their large frames and tenacity of life enable them to withstand the accidents incident to such a mode of capture; their skins are fresh and clean, and in many cases the fish-lice (*Caligus rapax*) actively glide over their surfaces. This common crustacean parasite not only occurs on the external surfaces of cod, haddock, ling, coalfish, plaice, and other forms, but is found in the mouth of both cod and coalfish. So far as injury to the tissues is concerned, these are not worse than those caught on the lines, for they escape the laceration of the hook and gaff. The only injury noted in some instances is slight fraying of the fins and tail from their efforts in the trawl. Some of the large old cod procured in winter showed many cicatrices of former wounds, it may be from the bites of dog-fishes or predatory cetaceans.

Codling.—The condition of the young cod is almost as satisfactory as the adults as regards food-qualities, though a large number, especially among the smaller examples, succumb to the effects of the pressure in hoisting the trawl, and of some the stomach is thrust out of the mouth. Many live a considerable time on deck. Slight bruising of the snout occurred in a few.

Haddock.—The large haddocks show greater vitality than the smaller, about a third at least being generally alive, and sometimes a larger number. The smaller haddocks suffer more from the pressure as well as from friction against the meshes of the net. Then their snouts, as a rule, and at times their tails, show distinct reddish patches (from ecchymosis), and their fins are occasionally frayed. This reddening of the snout is one of the most distinctive features between a line-caught and a trawled fish. On cutting into the tissues beneath such marks effused blood is found, and some show a similar escape over the brain. It occasionally happens that this effusion of blood from injury takes place in the abdominal organs (such as the liver), or into the peritoneal cavity. Such effusions, however, are not extensive, and do not materially affect the value of the fishes. Thus fishes that have gone to port and returned again to sea have been found to be in a fair

condition, and the edible qualities of even unfavourable examples have been tested. Some of the haddocks with reddened (ecchymosed) heads and tails are lively, so that it is possible this reddening is merely due to the efforts of the animal to escape from the trawl. In other cases fracture of the premaxillaries shows that they have been pressed against the side of the vessel in hauling the net on deck. In critically examining the trawled haddocks, and comparing them with those caught by hook and line, it is found that the fine cupreous lustre so characteristic of the hooked fish as it is pulled on board is not always present in the larger examples, and generally absent in the smaller, and many of the scales are abraded. It has to be stated, however, that in favourable hauls of the trawl many of the large haddocks are in fine condition, both as regards the cupreous sheen and otherwise, and even many of the smaller are as satisfactory. Moreover, though the snouts of the smaller are generally ecchymosed, and and occasionally an eye protrudes, they do not have the lacerations from the hook. These lacerations occasionally involve the tearing out of portions of the gill-apparatus (branchial arches), and of the gullet or the stomach. One or two small haddocks have indeed been found in the trawl with the hook adhering to the gullet. They all become rigid like line-caught fishes. One of the most trying periods for such fishes is when the trawl has dropped into mud, either from the sudden stoppage of the ship or otherwise. Then very careful washing is necessary by the hose or by towing the net behind the steamer after drawing up the beam, but even this does not remove all the particles of mud that lodge about the gills. This, however, is a comparatively rare occurrence, for the trawlers carefully avoid soft muddy ground or steam more rapidly over it. On the whole the condition of the trawled haddocks, both when landed on deck and on the pier, is often very good, and in no instance has anything been observed that would interfere with their value as food.

Very fine haddocks are occasionally got on various grounds. Thus on June 5th, some weighing 7 lbs. and 7½ lbs. were procured at Aberdeen. Those having gill-parasites (*Lernea branchialis*, L.) are generally much out of condition.

Whiting.—This is a more delicate fish than the haddock, and the mortality is much greater. In favourable hauls the majority have been found alive, but generally most succumb. In some cases every whiting is found dead. Their pointed snouts show the bruises formerly alluded to very distinctly, and it has happened in a few instances that from their projecting outwards through the meshes of the net the premaxillary and other bones have been broken by rubbing against the ship during the elevation of the net by the derrick.

Whiting Pout.—These were invariably dead, and the conjunctival membranes often project as aqueous bullæ. Their condition otherwise is good.

Coalfish—The fins of the coalfishes are usually frayed, and the fishes are generally dead. The men are of opinion that they are very active and rush about in the net till they are exhausted.

Hake.—The fins of the hake, both large and small, are as a rule rather extensively frayed, as if their struggles in the net had been desperate. Slight ecchymosis of the snout is also present in some. Few hake are bought on board alive. Only in one or two in Aberdeen Bay have a few muscular twitches been noticed. Their condition as food is good. A large example measured 40 inches at Aberdeen (June).

Ling.—Most of the ling are alive, and the great muscularity of the larger renders it difficult to lift and place them in the hold. Those brought on board in a dying or dead condition have a pouting reddish mass of the alimentary canal projecting from their mouths. This occurs likewise in line-fishing, just as the wrasses and other fishes from great depths off the

Channel Islands have their intestines thrust out of the vent on being drawn on board. No injuries were observed in the ling. A large ling (6 feet) was caught by the "Buccleuch" off St. Abbs. It was greenish all over, and the muscles, liver, and viscera had the same colour, while in its stomach was a greenish mass. The men thought it had eaten green paint. Unfortunately it was not kept for investigation.

Halibut.—Only two halibut came under observation. The smaller (about 14 inches) was dead, the larger (4 feet) was lively. No fish could be in a more satisfactory condition.

Sail-Fluke (Arnoglossus megastoma).—Some of these were alive on being let out of the bag, but they speedily died. The species is by no means hardy. The state as regards food was good.

Craig-Fluke.—This fish is considerably more tenacious of life than the foregoing, and withstands pressure better. It, however, is liable to ecchymosis, the dull whitish or greyish under surface thus showing pinkish patches. Their condition, however, is not materially affected.

Long Rough Dab.—Comparatively few large examples of this species occurred, but the majority of those usually encountered were alive on issuing from the trawl. As the larger fishes struggle to the top of the heap on deck this and other smaller forms generally succumb before the packing is completed in an ordinary haul. Moreover, the trampling of the men in securing the other fishes is occasionally injurious to this and other small specimens.

Turbot.—As a rule, these are active when freed from the trawl, and the only injury observed was an ecchymosis here and there on the white surface, in the region of the gills. No exception could be taken to their condition. One in St. Andrews Bay had its eye destroyed—probably by the pincers of an edible crab. A turbot 23 inches from tip of snout to tail weighed 10 lbs. in Aberdeen Bay in June. After spawning many are extremely thin. Several large examples in this exhausted condition were caught at St. Andrews in September. Both small and large turbot are frequently brought on shore (by the fishing-boat trawlers) alive.

Brill.—All the brill were alive and in fine condition. Many small examples are brought alive by the local trawlers to the harbour at St. Andrews.

Plaice.—No flat fish is so hardy as the plaice, many surviving in the fish-boxes after a lengthened journey. They suffer little in the trawl, the flapping of the larger examples on deck being both powerful and long continued. Rarely a deposit of mud has proved fatal to many. Ecchymosis is not conspicuous. Very many come to shore alive in the fish-boxes of the local trawling-boats at St. Andrews.

Common Dab (Pleuronectes limanda).—This and the large rough dab are the forms which suffer most from the action of the trawl, large numbers occasionally being brought on deck, and since their size is inconsiderable pressure is more readily felt. Very many, however, are lively on issuing from the bag, but before the collection of the other fishes is concluded most are dead. As they are of no interest to the trawlers, since they are not sold, little attention as a rule is paid to them, and they are thrown overboard. There is nothing, however, in their condition to prevent their being utilized as food in almost every instance, for their size is not so inconsiderable, few being under 6½ inches, and the majority larger. Many of these and the long rough dabs stick in the meshes of the net in their efforts to get out, and therefore are liable to have their heads bruised and lacerated. It is to be remembered, however, that the men do not always remove them in their haste to unship the trawl, and thus the same form is seen several times. A comparatively small dab sticks in the meshes of the cod-end. Many reach the harbour at St. Andrews alive.

Lemon-Dab.—A hardy fish, which shows no noteworthy injury by this mode of capture. The majority are alive and active.

Sole.—One of the most tenacious amongst flat fishes. All were alive and in fine condition.

Common Flounder.—An inshore form, and tolerably hardy. The state of these was without exception good. Many of those caught by the local trawlers are brought to shore alive in the fish-boxes.

Grey Gurnard.—A few specimens exhibited slight fraying of the fins, and a trace of ecchymosis, but otherwise their condition was excellent. The majority, however, were dead; indeed, it was comparatively rare in deep-sea trawling to bring them alive to the surface, though in shallow water and short hauls such did occur. They are more delicate in this respect than the whiting. No sound was emitted by these fishes. Lately most were thrown overboard both at Aberdeen and off the Forth.

Bream.—Of four examples two were alive. As might be expected from their firm nature they were uninjured.

Catfish.—Every catfish came on board alive, their dense bony skulls and lithe tough bodies giving them great advantages in the seething mass in the trawl-net as it is brought on board. Besides, the Blenny-group includes others of great tenacity, such as the shanny. No injury of note occurred to any of these fishes, but on the other hand they occasionally inflicted severe, though in the main purposeless, wounds on others in their neighbourhood. They fix their teeth so tenaciously in pine that they may be drawn along the deck, and the wood is penetrated about one-fifth of an inch. Their jaws do not always seem to be able to crush large horse-mussels. They are seized by the sockets of the eyes with the thumb and forefinger of one hand, caught under the gill-cover with the other hand, and thrown over the bulwarks.*

In regard to the condition of the food-fishes in the trawl, the proportion of the living is, as already mentioned, greatest when the haul is short and the ground clean. Thus, for instance, No. XI. in St. Andrews Bay, in a few fathoms water and after two hours and 50 minutes, contained only living fishes, 189 in number, and the succeeding one presented similar results, only a gurnard having succumbed. In the same way the fishes captured at Scarborough were almost all alive. The plaice landed on the quay at St. Andrews from the boats of the local trawlers are often alive. On the other hand, the mud in XVI. proved very fatal, though the duration of the haul was less. It is also of moment that there was an essential difference in taking the net on board, this being rapidly accomplished in the shallow water and with the low gunwale of the fishing-boat, while the hoisting of the bag of mud and fishes in IX. and XVI. by the derrick places the living forms at great disadvantages. If the fishes could be taken out of the net by any apparatus before leaving the water, a very great change would at once occur in regard to their condition. It can easily be imagined that the individuals in a mass of fishes suspended from the derrick and compressed by their own weight (it may be over a ton) and the strain of the net, suffer very materially, and they fare no better in a square-meshed net if the derrick is used in boarding. Moreover, when the derrick be at work during the latter operation the heavy mass in the net rolls along the side of the ship, and the snouts of such small fishes as project from the meshes are so severely rubbed that laceration and bleeding occur. It may happen, also, that a heavy lurch of the ship brings the weighty net with force on the bridge or the gunwale, and seriously stuns the fishes.

When much mud has been scooped by the trawl active measures are taken. The distal extremity of the net is allowed to float behind the ship, while the vessel steams in circles. The tenacious greyish mud east of the Island of May, however, is seldom wholly disposed of in this manner, and it is necessary to use the donkey engine and hose on the mass of fishes, and again in each basket. This entails a considerable amount of extra labour, which alone would cause the skippers to avoid such ground. The appearance of the fishes after such handling is not quite so good, and a little mud is apt to lodge in the gills. In many hauls, also, those fishes last gathered from the deck are less presentable from the débris and mud. In June, at Aberdeen, the fishes were landed on deck in the midst of masses of jellyfishes (chiefly *Cyanea*), so that the whole formed a quivering mass that swayed to and fro, and slid across the deck with every lurch of the ship. "Sluthers" is the not inappropriate vernacular name given to the jellyfishes.

Heavy seas, as in L. to LIII., also seem to be unfavourable to the vitality of the fishes, especially if horse-mussels and their accompanying muddy débris are present.

In passing the dandy, bridles, and ropes aft, and again in unshipping the trawl, it also happens that some damage is done to the fishes by the feet of the men, and still more injury to the invertebrates such as Norway lobsters, sea- and heart-urchins.

It is to be borne in mind that while the trawled fishes are thus in the way of certain injuries, they escape the occasional decimation by dogfishes on the lines, the ravages of cod, the insidious attacks of the glutinous hag (" eel " of the fishermen), the decapitation so common in herring-fishing, the blows on the snout in the case of the cod and salmon, and the bites of the cuttle-fishes when hooked. Moreover, they do not hang for a day or two on a hook as in the lines left in the sea, or in the gill-net of the cod-fishermen of the Norwegian coasts.

To summarise, therefore, it is evident that the general condition of trawled fishes, as shown in these investigations, is excellent, many of the haddocks in favourable hauls having the cupreous lustre so characteristic of healthy fishes drawn singly from the sea. A large proportion are living, and no saleable fish was observed to be landed from the trawl in a condition that would render its acceptability doubtful, even though the bruising in some instances might make its preservation less satisfactory.

The *cuttlefishes* are either sickly or dead, the soft skin being much frayed from overcrowding and pressure in the trawl-net. The fishermen remove them as quickly as possible from their fishes, as the ejection of the inky fluid renders the latter unsightly.

Norway lobsters, notwithstanding their apparent delicacy, are generally vigorous on reaching the deck. They can easily be transported alive a long distance.

The condition of the edible crabs in every case was good. There is no foundation for the statement that the ground-rope crushes them. Soft northern stone crabs even come up uninjured.

The only disagreeable contents of the trawl were a number of dead herrings brought to the surface on August 15. They had probably been thrown from a fishing boat on becoming tainted. One or two dead and putrid frogfish also occurred off St. Abbs, and once a dead starry ray. The frogfishes had been on board another ship (a slit having been made on the ventral surface), and this was evidence that the ground had been carefully gone over. Indeed, it has happened that articles which have fallen overboard have again been recovered in the trawl-net.

---

4. *Proportional quantity of Immature Fishes taken at various seasons* * *Growth of Fishes.*

The uncertainty that exists on this head is alluded to in the report of the Sea-Fisheries Commission of 1866. [†]
The total number of immature fishes procured in these investigations amounted to 11,609 or thereabout, and therefore they formed a considerable proportion (numerically) of the whole. They occurred not only in the shallow, but likewise in the deep water. The great majority of these, however, were formed of two kinds, viz., long rough and common dabs, two fishes which are small and variable in value. Thus they are unsaleable for the most part at Granton and Aberdeen, but readily find a market in St. Andrews. At Macduff they are sometimes sold for 1s. per box, so that comparatively little attention is paid to them by the trawlers. Both occurred in large numbers off St. Abbs Head in July and August. It is rare that one of either species is seen 13 inches in length, the majority being much smaller. As a rule in the steam trawlers the long rough dabs are seldom observed under $5\frac{1}{4}$ inches in length, only one here and there being so small as $3\frac{1}{4}$ inches by $1\frac{1}{8}$ inch. The common dab similarly is generally larger than 5 inches in total length, very rarely so small as $3\frac{3}{8}$ inches. By using a smaller mesh in St. Andrew's Bay, as in the yacht " Medusa," small specimens $2\frac{1}{4}$ inches in length were obtained. Diminutive forms like the latter, so far as observed, never occurred in the steam trawlers. Those caught by the lines in St. Andrew's Bay range from 6 to 10 inches.

Though very young flat fishes abound at low watermark along the sandy beach at St. Andrews none occurred in the net in trawling close inshore. No young plaice, again, were found in the deep water off St. Abbs Head and the Island of May.

In regard to the total bulk of immature fishes in a single haul it is found that even in such as No. XCIII. (where the total number was 700) the whole did not exceed a basketful and a half. In one instance 15 boxes of craig-flukes had been brought to Aberdeen from the Moray Firth, and beside them lay two heaps (of about a bucketful and a half each) of young, 8 or 9 inches in length.

The number of immature round fishes unfit for the market was insignificant. The majority of the young haddocks and young whiting having been obtained from the mouths of the cod and large fishes as they came on deck. It will be observed from the returns that a considerable number of young cod (codling) were present in most of the good hauls, but all were saleable fishes, indeed, only a single example 6 inches long, trawled off St. Abbs Head in April, came under observation, and it does not fall under the present returns, as it was sent from another ship. Quite as many immature cod (codling) are caught by the liners in the same waters, and off the Bell Rock, perhaps, the proportion is even greater. In former days the codling-fishing formed a feature in the year's proceedings at St. Andrews and elsewhere, but such is not now followed to any extent, though on the west coast and in Shetland they are more abundant. Smaller cod than that from the St. Abbs' trawler are occasionally caught by line-fishermen. The small cod caught between December and September were apparently last year's fishes, and they range over the entire area examined.

The number of young haddocks and whiting, moreover, caught by the liners in summer and autumn is considerable, the men being annoyed in certain places by such immature fishes taking their bait. They return many of them to the sea, or eat them at home, if unfit for sale.

A hiatus yet remains in the history of the young cod between the date of the absorption of the yolk-sac, when it is a pelagic creature carried about near the surface of the water, and the period when it is found

. . .

Further in this monumental work he broke down the catch into saleable and unsaleable fish, mature and immature fish, and commented in detail on what their condition was when taken aboard. The saleable fish he tabulated as follows.

S.

Column locations and months (left to right):

- **January** — I. St. Andrews Bay; II. Off Haddington Coast; III.–VII. Off St. Abbs Head; VIII. St. Andrews Bay
- **February** — IX.–XIII. Off Haddington Coast; XIV. Aberdeen Bay (*Blank.—Trawl torn by wreck.*)
- **Mar.** — XV. Off Isle of May
- **April** — XVI. Aberdeen; XVII.–XVIII. Off Caithness; XIX.–XXIV. S.E. of Isle of May
- **May** — XXV. St. Andrews Bay; XXVI. Aberdeen Bay; XXVII.–XXVIII. Off St. Abbs Head; XXIX.–XXXI. Off Isle of May
- **June** — XXXII.–XXXVI. Off Isle of May; XXXVII.–XXXVIII. Aberdeen Bay

	I	II	III	IV	V	VI	VII	VIII	IX	X	XI	XII	XIII	XIV	XV	XVI	XVII	XVIII	XIX	XX	XXI	XXII	XXIII	XXIV	XXV	XXVI	XXVII	XXVIII	XXIX	XXX	XXXI	XXXII	XXXIII	XXXIV	XXXV	XXXVI	XXXVII	XXXVIII
Grey Skate	1	3	6	3	6	—	5	5	2	1	2	2	—		8	2	9	1	—	—	2	2	7	7	2	—	10	—	1	—	—	—	1	—	1	—	1	2
Thornback	2	5	3	3	2	1	4	1	1	1	1	3	4		2	—	1	—	—	1	1	—	1	5	1	—	—	1	1	—	—	—	—	1	—	—	—	—
Starry Ray	—	—	—	—	—	—	—	—	—	—	—	—	—		—	—	6	1	—	—	—	—	—	—	—	—	1	—	13	5	5	3	15	9	13	2	—	—
Sandy Ray	—	—	—	—	—	—	—	—	—	—	—	—	—		—	—	—	—	—	—	—	—	—	—	—	—	—	—	—	—	—	—	—	—	—	—	—	—
Sharp-nosed Ray	—	—	—	1	2	—	1	—	—	—	—	—	—		—	—	—	—	—	—	—	—	—	—	—	—	—	—	—	—	—	—	—	—	—	—	—	—
Herring	1	1	—	1	2	—	—	1	—	3	5	—	—		—	—	—	—	—	—	—	—	—	—	—	—	—	—	—	—	—	—	—	—	—	—	—	—
Cod (large)	6	4	5	6	8	12	14	3	3	6	1	2	4		13	—	10	2	21	15	25	22	37	27	—	—	—	2	—	2	8	12	10	13	15	4	3	
Codling	9	15	7	2	14	9	11	4	—	4	4	4	1		20	—	18	12	31	21	2	3	8	2	—	12	3	31	2	11	12	3	6	9	13	5	—	—
Haddock (large)	402	959	363	363	301	268	317	98	187	179	364	185	177		323	48	33	354	961	497	146	76	135	148	14	3	96	10	281	—	79	49	700	352	145	223	145	176
Do. (small)	—	902	499	951	1039	900	895	639	200	486	841	526	430		344	115	—	—	—	213	70	114	144		—	—	60	935	91	271	54	740	343	411	348	77	40	
Whiting	24	774	582	578	281	531	366	122	720	337	926	893	1522		163	113	—	5	7	9	71	149	73	70	—	—	3	77	16	36	8	172	142	151	357	11	65	
Whiting-Pout (Bib)	—	1	—	—	2	—	—	—	—	—	—	—	1		—	—	—	—	—	—	1	1	—	—	—	—	—	—	1	8		—	—	1	2	—	—	—
Coalfish	—	—	—	1	—	—	—	—	—	—	—	—	—		—	—	1	—	—	—	—	—	—	—	—	—	—	—	—	—	—	2	—	1	2	—	—	—
Hake	—	—	—	1	—	—	1	—	—	—	2	—	—		—	—	—	—	—	—	—	—	—	—	—	—	—	—	—	—	—	—	—	—	—	—	—	1
Ling	—	3	—	—	1	—	3	—	—	—	—	—	—		1	—	—	4	—	2	1	1	—	—	—	1	—	3	—	—	—	2	2	—	—	—	—	—
Halibut	—	—	—	—	—	—	—	—	—	—	—	—	—		—	—	—	1	—	—	—	—	—	—	—	—	—	—	—	—	—	—	—	—	—	—	—	—
Sail-Fluke	—	—	—	—	—	—	—	—	—	—	—	—	—		—	—	—	—	—	—	—	—	—	—	—	—	—	—	—	—	—	—	—	—	—	—	—	—
Craig-Fluke (witch)	—	6	15	44	46	20	76	—	14	7	5	14	9		—	5	2	3	—	—	7	4	9	1	—	—	—	6	—	—	—	1	1	9	3	4	—	—
Long rough Dab	—	—	—	—	—	—	—	—	—	—	—	—	6		—	—	—	—	—	—	—	—	—	—	—	—	—	—	—	—	—	—	—	—	—	—	37	—
Long rough Dab, small saleable.	—	—	—	11	—	5	7	5	—	—	—	—	—		—	—	—	—	—	—	—	—	6	3	—	8	2	2	—	—	—	3	—	6	2			
Turbot	3	1	—	1	—	1	—	3	—	—	—	—	—		—	1	—	1	—	—	4	3	6	—	1	1	1	1	—	—	—	—	4	—	—	—	—	3
Brill	—	—	—	—	—	1	—	2	—	—	1	1	—		—	—	—	1	1	—	—	—	—	2	—	—	2	—	—	—	—	—	—	—	—	—	—	—
Plaice	34	17	8	4	2	8	3	77	12	2	6	15	10		5	1	9	15	100	78	9	4	6	3	158	211	134	9	41	28	51	65	42	16	20	3	60	66
Common Dab	18	50	—	—	—	—	—	—	—	2	—	—	—		—	—	7	21	14	—	5	1	2	—	—	25	—	150	5	8	—	5	—	17	1	—	82	34
Lemon-Dab	—	—	—	1	3	—	—	—	1	4	2	—	—		5	—	29	97	26	8	1	7	2	—	1	—	8	19	17	41	35	37	17	15	2	—	—	—
Sole	—	—	—	—	—	—	—	—	—	—	—	1	—		—	—	—	—	—	—	4	—	—	—	1	—	—	—	4	3	3	—	—	—	—	—	14	12
Common Flounder	—	—	—	—	—	—	—	—	—	—	—	—	—		—	—	—	—	—	4	—	—	3	—	9	2	26	44	17	—	—	—	—	—	—	—	—	—
Grey Gurnard	—	3	3	—	1	—	—	—	—	—	—	—	—		—	6	—	37	160	152	109	9	12	35	316	224	35	20	12	41	37	4	—	16	6	2	18	20
Bream	—	—	—	—	—	—	—	—	—	—	—	—	—		—	—	—	—	—	—	—	—	—	—	—	—	—	—	—	—	—	—	6	—	—	—	1	—
Catfish	—	—	—	1	—	—	—	—	—	—	—	—	1		—	—	11	12	4	—	—	—	—	—	—	—	5	—	3	2	1	2	—	—	—	—	—	—
	503	2744	1489	1971	1712	1775	1763	960	1140	1033	2167	1645	2159		895	281	92	481	1412	818	598	350	420	444	528	494	339	113	1591	211	555	251	1739	925	813	1009	424	790

I.

...ISHES.

Column station groupings (left to right): ...borough (XLV.–XLIX.); **E. by S. of Isle of May.** (L.–LI.); **St. Andrews Bay.** (LII.–LX.); **Aberdeen Bay.** (LXI.–LXIII.) — *July* — ; **Off St. Abbs Head.** (LXIV.–LXIX.); **Aberdeen Bay.** (LXX.–LXXI.); **Off St. Abbs Head.** (LXXII.–LXXIII.); **S.E. of Isle of May.** (LXXIV.–LXXVI.); **St. Andrews Bay.** (LXXVII.–LXXXV.); **Aberdeen Bay.** (LXXXVI.–LXXXVII.); **S.S.E. of Isle of May.** (LXXXVIII.); **Off Haddington Coast.** (LXXXIX.–XCIII.) — *August*.

XLV.	XLVI.	XLVII.	XLVIII.	XLIX.	L.	LI.	LII.	LIII.	LIV.	LV.	LVI.	LVII.	LVIII.	LIX.	LX.	LXI.	LXII.	LXIII.	LXIV.	LXV.	LXVI.	LXVII.	LXVIII.	LXIX.	LXX.	LXXI.	LXXII.	LXXIII.	LXXIV.	LXXV.	LXXVI.	LXXVII.	LXXVIII.	LXXIX.	LXXX.	LXXXI.	LXXXII.	LXXXIII.	LXXXIV.	LXXXV.	LXXXVI.	LXXXVII.	LXXXVIII.	LXXXIX.	XC.	XCI.	XCII.	XCIII.	Total
-	-	-	-	-	-	-	2	2	-	-	-	-	-	-	-	-	-	-	4	2	8	8	4	-	-	-	-	-	2	3	-	-	-	-	-	-	-	-	-	-	12	1	6	5	5	-	1	1	161
-	1	-	-	-	-	-	-	-	-	5	1	6	-	-	-	-	-	3	-	-	-	-	-	1	-	-	-	1	4	-	1	2	-	-	-	-	2	3	-	-	-	-	-	-	-	-	-	-	158
-	-	-	-	-	8	12	6	5	-	-	-	-	-	-	-	-	-	-	11	12	35	16	18	1	-	1	-	-	-	1	4	-	1	2	-	-	-	-	-	-	-	14	15	43	39	13	27	31	388
-	-	-	-	-	-	-	-	-	-	-	-	-	-	-	-	-	-	-	-	-	-	-	-	1	2	-	-	-	-	-	-	-	-	-	-	-	-	-	-	-	-	1	-	1	-	-	-	-	7
-	-	-	-	-	-	-	-	-	-	-	-	-	-	-	-	-	-	-	1	-	-	1	-	-	-	-	-	-	-	-	-	-	-	-	-	-	-	-	-	-	-	1	-	1	-	-	-	-	8
-	-	-	-	-	-	-	-	-	-	-	-	-	-	-	-	-	-	-	1	-	-	-	-	-	-	-	-	-	-	-	-	-	-	-	-	-	-	-	-	-	-	-	-	-	-	-	-	-	15
-	-	-	-	-	1	-	9	3	-	-	-	-	-	-	-	-	-	-	-	1	4	-	-	-	5	3	-	-	-	2	-	-	-	-	-	-	-	-	-	-	12	3	-	2	5	-	-	-	365
-	-	-	-	-	11	5	3	5	-	-	-	-	-	-	-	1	1	-	4	2	3	-	3	28	127	9	1	7	40	-	-	-	-	-	-	-	-	-	-	-	42	13	5	7	29	6	5	14	681
-	-	-	143	128	83	34	-	-	-	-	-	-	-	62	387	1	103	51	279	76	77	212	322	49	110	41	525	235	-	2	-	-	-	-	27	416	256	86	228	595	226	181	275							14,373
-	-	206	205	96	10	-	-	-	-	-	-	-	-	-	610	-	677	437	1578	705	870	455	480	270	581	31	826	817	-	-	-	-	-	81	625	340	296	561	348	301	424	587							25,459
-	-	15	45	57	24	-	-	-	-	-	-	-	-	5	283	-	1042	73	580	360	585	314	221	374	205	35	72	85	-	-	-	-	-	49	41	58	635	551	524	805	948	596							17,949
-	-	-	-	-	-	-	-	-	-	-	-	-	-	-	-	-	-	1	-	-	-	14	10	-	8	4	-	-	-	-	-	-	-	-	2	-	1	3	1	-	-	-	-	-	-	51
-	-	-	-	-	1	1	1	-	-	-	-	-	-	-	-	-	-	-	-	-	-	-	-	-	-	-	-	16	-	-	-	-	-	-	-	-	-	-	-	-	-	1	-	-	-	-	-	36
-	-	-	1	-	-	-	-	-	-	-	-	-	-	-	-	-	-	1	-	-	-	12	-	-	-	-	-	-	-	-	4	8	7	-	-	-	-	1	-	-	39
-	-	-	-	-	2	-	-	-	-	-	-	-	-	-	-	1	1	2	-	-	-	2	2	-	1	1	1	-	-	1	1	-	-	-	-	-	-	-	-	42
-	-	-	-	-	-	-	-	-	-	-	-	-	-	1	1	-	-	-	-	-	-	-	-	-	-	-	-	-	-	-	-	-	-	-	-	-	-	-	-	2
-	-	-	-	-	-	-	-	-	-	-	-	-	-	6	-	-	-	-	-	-	2	14	22	-	1	2	-	-	-	-	-	47
-	-	-	-	-	-	-	-	-	-	-	-	-	26	11	41	19	21	4	1	-	5	-	9	-	-	-	-	-	-	9	16	18	-	31	13	15	36	668
-	-	-	-	-	-	-	-	-	-	-	-	-	1	-	-	-	-	-	1	-	-	-	-	-	-	-	-	49
-	-	-	-	-	-	-	-	-	-	-	-	-	-	-	-	-	-	-	-	-	-	-	-	-	-	-	-	-	144	109	-	-	-	-	-	316
-	3	-	-	-	-	-	2	2	-	-	-	-	-	-	-	-	-	1	-	-	-	-	1	-	-	-	-	-	1	-	-	62
-	-	-	-	-	-	-	-	-	-	-	-	-	-	-	1	-	-	-	-	-	-	-	1	1	1	-	15
1	2	10	-	8	134	29	36	63	1	54	1	41	140	8	8	36	69	2	5	2	3	44	17	19	42	17	6	-	65	100	2	4	2	29	-	24	5	-	-	9	14	10	15	11	17	15	19	21	2736
2	3	6	8	18	-	-	1	-	5	-	15	20	27	8	-	-	-	-	-	-	-	-	-	-	-	-	2	1	15	26	-	7	1	4	5	-	8	10	-	-	-	-	-	704
-	-	-	82	29	22	37	1	-	-	-	-	-	-	-	2	10	7	19	16	21	36	73	6	49	1	65	60	-	-	-	3	-	-	-	9	128	74	8	9	11	-	2	4	1157
-	2	12	26	11	-	-	-	-	-	-	-	-	-	-	-	-	3	-	-	-	1	-	-	-	-	1	-	78
-	-	-	-	-	-	-	-	-	9	2	2	5	-	-	-	-	-	-	-	4	6	-	2	3	-	-	172
-	3	-	-	51	16	9	16	-	-	-	-	1	-	-	55	23	82	209	135	90	105	97	14	4	383	456	1	1	1	-	-	-	-	1	7	218	126	93	230	162	40	4076
-	-	-	-	-	-	-	-	-	-	-	-	-	-	-	-	-	-	-	-	-	1	-	-	-	-	-	-	4
-	-	-	-	-	2	1	-	4	-	-	-	-	-	-	1	-	-	-	-	-	-	-	1	-	-	-	-	3	1	-	-	2	-	62
3	7	34	34	37	654	474	327	203	1	76	4	64	165	36	16	104	1357	3	1941	624	2637	1435	1752	1233	1397	814	963	116	1967	1839	19	15	7	45	3	31	13	182	1482	946	1482	1622	1617	1612	1785	1605			69,880

Notes (vertical annotations within the table): "Trawl upset on being put overboard." (Off St. Abbs Head column); "No saleable fishes." (S.E. of Isle of May column).

Some of his comments on the fish as they came up in the net were presented thus:—

No. of Place in Chart where Trawl let down; and Time.	Course Run during Trawling, and Distance from Land.	Depth in Fathoms.	Temperature of Air.		Temperature of Surface.	Temperature of Bottom.	Nature of Bottom.	Surface-Fauna.	Length of Time Trawl down.	Time when Trawl taken up.
			Dry Bulb.	Wet Bulb.						

XXI. *Thursday, the 17th day*

2.50 p.m.	In loops S.E. of Island of May. Distance from Island of May 4 to 8 miles S.E. Distance from coast 10 to 12 miles.	24 to 30	42°·5	40°	44°·5	Cold 43°·5 Heat 42°	Muddy -	Vast numbers of floating ova of cod, haddock, and several others. Copepods, Nauplii, Zoeæ, and other crustaceans, Sagittæ, and young of fishes.	4 hours 10 minutes.	7 p.m.

XXII. *Thursday and Friday, the 17th and 18th days of*

7.25 p.m. (Thursday).	In loops S.E. of May, 10 miles from land.	32	42°·5	40°	43°	Cold 43°·5 Heat 45°	Muddy -	Vast numbers of floating ova of cod, haddock, and several others. Copepods, Nauplii, Zoeæ, and other crustaceans, Sagittæ, and young of fishes.	5 hours 50 minutes.	1.15 a.m. (Friday).

XXIII. *Friday, the 18th day of*

1.40 a.m.	S.E. from and and in loops (N.E.) back towards Island of May, 9 to 10 miles from coast.	27 to 32	44°·5	41°	43°	Cold 43° Heat 42°	Muddy -	Vast numbers of floating ova of cod, haddock. and several others.	5 hours 45 minutes.	5 a.m.

	CONTENTS OF TRAWL.				
	Saleable Fish.	Unsaleable.	Description and Quantity of Young Fishes.	Spawn or anything resembling such.	Wind, Weather, and other Observations.
Total Number.	Description and Number of each.	Description and Number of each.			

of April, 1884.

598	*Grey Skate - - 2 *Thornback - - 1 *Cod (large) - - 25 Codling - - - 2 §Haddock (large) - 146 § ,, (small) - 213 Whiting - - - 71 *Ling - - - 2 Craig Fluke - - 7 †Plaice - - - 9 Lemon Dab - - 8 Grey Gurnard - - 109 Common Flounder - 3 [Large number (hundreds) of Norway lobsters.] 1 edible Crab.	Frog fish - 5 (2 alive, none large). 1 dead green Cod with muscles re-moved, leaving only skin and bone. Probably work of glutinous hag-fish.	Long rough Dab 19 Common Dab - 8 Grey Gurnard - 10	No spawn of fishes. Some pieces of spawn of Bucci-num un-datum (Whelk).	Wind N.E., but light, sky clear. Slight swell in Forth and outside. Mud in trawl; required washing behind ship.

April, 1884.

350	Grey Skate (1 alive) - 2 *Thornback - - 1 *Cod (large) - - 22 *Codling - - - 3 §Haddock (large) - 76 § ,, (small) - 70 §Whiting - - - 149 Whiting Pout - - 1 *Ling - - - 1 Craig Fluke (2 alive) - 4 Long rough Dab - 2 Plaice (2 alive) - 4 Common Dab - - 5 Lemon Dab - - 1 Grey Gurnard - - 9 [A good many Norway lobsters]	Frog Fish - 1 (small).	§Long rough Dab 37 Common Dab - 3 Grey Skate - 1 Sandy Ray - 1 Ling - - 1	A few pieces of spawn of Whelk.	Wind N.E.; slight breeze; slight swell. Mud in trawl; required washing as before.

April, 1884.

420	*Grey Skate - - 7 *Cod (large) - - 37 Codling (2 dead) - - 8 ‡Haddock (large) - 135 § ,, (small) - 114 §Whiting - - - 73 Whiting Pout - - 1 *Ling - - - 1	Frog fish - 7 (none large).	Long rough Dab 24 Ling - - 2	None except ova of Whelk.	Wind N.E. Swell on sea less; weather good. Ova of cod removed from fish in ripe condition. Ling and grey gurnard also fairly ripe. Mud in trawl.

SYNOPTICAL TABLE OF EVIDENCE AS TO DECREASE OF FISH—*continued.*

PLACE.	Pro. State of Fishery Inshore.	Offshore.	Species affected Inshore.	Offshore.	Name and Position of Witness.	Contra. State of Fishery Inshore.	Offshore.	Species affected Inshore.	Offshore.	Name and Position of Witness.	General.
—	Decrease	-	Haddock	-	J. Gourley, line and net fisherman.						
Broughty Ferry	Decrease	Decrease	Plaice, flounders, and cod.	Haddock	Peter Sims, line and net fisherman.						
Broughty Ferry	Decrease for last 8 years, worse last 2 or 3.	Decrease in 1883	Plaice	Herring	John Lorimer, line and net fisherman, R. Webster, J. Knight.						
Anstruther	Decreased by one-third.	-	Haddock	-	-	-	No change	-	Haddock	W. Mair, fishery officer.	
Cellardyke	Decrease since 35 years ago.	Decrease	Haddock	Herring	J. Smith, line fisherman.						
—	Decrease	-	Crabs	-	H. Jack, line fisherman, David Boyton.						
St. Andrews	Disappearance	-	Haddock ?	-	J. A. Welsh, magistrate.						
Pittenweem	Decrease, specially last 2 years.	-	Haddock ?	-	G. Heugh, line, fisherman.						
Pittenweem	Great decrease	-	Haddock	-	W. Gay, line and net fisherman.						
St. Monance	Large decrease	-	All kinds, specially turbot	-	T. Murray, fish curer.						
Firth of Forth	Decrease for about 2 years.	-	Haddock	-	W. Carnie, line and net fisherman.	More abundant in 1882-3 than for many years.		Haddock			L. Lamb, Inspector-General of Fisheries.

APPENDIX.   **497**

Authority	Fish	Nature of decrease	Remarks
J. W. Driver, line fisherman.	Codlings, flounders, and lemon sole.	Great decrease	Due to circle trawl.
J. Young, line fisherman.	Haddock, whitings, codlings, and cod.	—	
W. Main, line fisherman, T. Wilson, J. Young.	Herring	Gradual falling off last 6 or 7 years, until last year.	
J. Wilson, line fisherman.	Haddock	General disappearance	
T. Wilson, line fisherman.	Haddock	Decrease	
J. Young, line fisherman.	Haddock	Decrease	
C. Baillie, line fisherman.	General	Decrease in last 6 years.	
John Howden, line fisherman, George Ross, line fisherman.	—	Fallen off about a half.	
P. Thompson, line fisherman.	Bait	Great decrease	
J. Anderson, fishmonger.	General (?)	Gradual decrease for last 50 years.	
J. Johnstone, crab fisherman.	Crab and lobster.	Almost total disappearance.	
W. Hannam, line fisherman.	Haddock	Bait beds injured	Decrease in size and quality.
John Dickson, line fisherman.	Haddock	Decrease since commencement of trawling.	
J. Thomsor, fish merchant.	General	Decrease of about half since 1880	

It will be observed from the table devoted to the decrease of fish that the fishery officers, who maintained the record of catches, were the only people to report little or no change in fishing stocks. There were also the claims of the anti-trawling agitators, none of whom were invited to give evidence because none of them were directly involved with the fishing, to be examined, in particular to their claims about the destruction of spawn. They made much of their contention that all spawn, regardless of the fish species, lay on the bottom of the sea and that trawl warps were destroying enormous quantities, McIntosh easily disproved this claim and made a serious attempt at public relations with the fishermen by allowing them to drop fertilised cod eggs into buckets of seawater. There, to their almost total incredulity, the eggs floated on the surface like cream on milk. But herring spawn, unlike that even of its first cousin the sprat, sticks to any bottom surface, whether it be sand, gravel, rocks or mud, like glue and unquestionably any ropes dragged across spawning areas destroys huge quantities. It was not uncommon in the last century for trawl warps to be so heavily coated with herring spawn that the ropes would slip on the capstan barrels. It was this that the anti-trawling lobby used as their main argument, not knowing that it was only herring spawn that was affected. McIntosh, in spite of his efforts and scrupulous methods was unable to counter their claims and was burnt in effigy by fishermen outside his front door. In a sense, inasmuch as herring, in spawn, fry and adult form, is a principle food source for many species, then trawling did affect all of the coastal fish stocks, one way or another. The anti-trawling movement was right for the wrong reasons. By the time seining came along all organised resistance to this method of fishing had abated.

The 1880's found the fishing industry in the grip of change and controversy as it had never been. Trawling, and the anti-trawling movement, were daily reaching new heights as the steam trawler began to make its presence felt. Aberdeen began expanding, Wick was visibly slipping from its position as premier herring port, and Peterhead, Fraserburgh, Buckie, Whitehills, Lerwick and Stornoway all grew rapidly with the arrival of the big Zulus and Fifies. There was neat legislation ashore and disorder afloat. A lot of the disorder stemmed from the fact that while fishing limits had been imposed on foreign vessels, and they were supposed to be no less than three miles from the coast, home vessels could fish where they liked with the exception of a few mussel and oyster beds.

There was a clause in the Act of 1883 which made allowances for compensation to be paid for gear damaged by trawlers but this was almost totally ineffective as the evidence was usually on the bottom of the sea. To a large extent, and encouraged by the anti-trawling movement, local communities frequently took matters into their own hands and often attacked steam trawlers if they came into harbour, particularly where herring fishing predominated. There were many instances of the rough handling of trawler crews and, as usual, these stemmed mainly from hooliganism than anything else. Trawlers were attacked in Macduff, Cromarty and Wick. In May 1884 a steam trawler from Shields was attacked by boys in Wick with stones as the crew were mending their nets. A correspondent in the *John O'Groat Journal* tried to maintain that the boys stoned the crew because they were repairing nets on a Sunday and the assault had nothing to do with the fact that the vessel was a trawler. Sensitivity about Sabbath breaking had most certainly reached new heights in Wick if that was the case.

Wick Harbour Trust also charged very high landing dues to trawlers and refused to reduce them in spite of great pressure. All around the coasts things were showing definite signs of getting out of hand and the first whiff of success for the anti-trawling movement, came in 1885 when, in a piece of legislation which was an amendment to the earlier international convention, it was enacted:—

48 & 49 VICTORIA.

CAP. LXX.

An Act to amend the Law relating to Scottish Sea Fisheries and for other purposes relating thereto.—[14th August 1885.]

[Preamble repealed by 61 and 62 Vic., cap. 22.]

Short title. 1. This Act may be cited as the Sea Fisheries (Scotland) Amendment Act, 1885, and shall be read and construed along with the Sea Fisheries Act, 1883.

Application. 2. This Act shall apply only to Scotland, and to the parts of the sea adjoining Scotland.

Definition. 3. In this Act "Sea Fisheries Acts" shall mean the Sea
31 & 32 Vict. Fisheries Act, 1868, the Sea Fisheries Act, 1875, and the Sea
c. 45.
38 Vict. c. 15. Fisheries Act, 1883, and this Act.

Fishery Board 4. When the Fishery Board for Scotland, hereinafter called the
may make bye-
laws prohibit- Fishery Board, are satisfied that any mode of fishing in any part of
ing or regulat the sea adjoining Scotland, and within the exclusive fishery limits
ing any mode of
fishing within of the British Islands, is injurious to any kind of sea fishing
defined areas. within that part, or where it appears to the Fishery Board desirable to make experiments or observations with the view of ascertaining whether any particular mode of fishing is injurious, or for the purposes of fish culture or experiments in fish culture, the Fishery Board may make byelaws for restricting or prohibiting, either entirely or subject to such regulations as may be provided by the byelaw, any method of fishing for sea fish within the said part, during such time or times as they think fit, and may from time to time make byelaws for altering or revoking any such byelaws.

A byelaw under this Act shall not be of any validity until it is confirmed by the Secretary for Scotland.

And for the first time, steam powered fishing vessels are mentioned in respect of carrying registration numbers, presumably because some Smart Alec had noticed that the legislation up to that time referred only to sailing vessels. Fishery officers were empowered to investigate and decide on complaints. Damages could be awarded but the difficulty with proof remained and the obvious solution of separating the inshore and offshore fishermen began to recommend itself in the minds of the legislators.

The first by-law, which is of monumental significance in the history of fishing came on 1st February, 1886, and because of its importance is worth reproducing here. It runs as follows:—

*Bye-law (No. 1) made by the Fishery Board for Scotland, under the Powers conferred on the Board by the Sea Fisheries (Scotland) Amendment Act, 1885.

I. This Bye-law shall extend and apply to (1) the Firth of Forth inside or to the west of a straight line drawn from Tantallon Castle on the south shore of the Firth to the lighthouse on the Isle of May, and thence to Fifeness; (2) St. Andrews Bay and the Firth of Tay, so far as they lie inside or to the west of a straight line drawn from Fifeness to the Fairway Buoy at the mouth of the Tay, and thence to the land; (3) that part of the sea off the coast of Aberdeenshire and Kincardineshire which lies inside or to the west of a straight line drawn from the Cruden Scars Rocks to a point one and a half miles east (magnetic) of Girdleness Lighthouse.

II. Within the foresaid limits, no person, unless in the service of the Fishery Board for Scotland, shall at any time from the date when this Bye-law comes into force use any beam trawl for taking sea fish; and the Master or the person actually in command of any vessel acting in contravention of this Bye-law shall, on conviction, be liable to a fine not exceeding £100; and failing immediate payment of the fine, to imprisonment for a period not exceeding sixty days, without prejudice to diligence by poinding or imprisonment, if no imprisonment has followed on the conviction, all in terms of the said Act.

III. This Bye-law shall come into force on Monday the 5th of April next.

By Order.

DUGALD GRAHAM, Secretary.

Dated at Edinburgh this first day of February 1886.

The foregoing Bye-law having been submitted to me, in pursuance of the 4th Section of the Sea Fisheries (Scotland) Amendment Act, 1885, I hereby confirm the same.

(L.S.)   *DALHOUSIE,*
                                Her Majesty's Secretary for
                                       Scotland.

Dated at the Secretary for Scotland's Office, Whitehall, this 5th day of April 1886.

*[Note.—The foregoing Bye-law was revoked by Bye-law No. 3.]

It is notable that these were the most heavily fished line grounds, obviously because they were the most fertile, and from there the closure of the bays and firths gradually spread. It might be of passing interest to note that Dalhousie was an extremely conscientious man who took a great interest in the work being done by McIntosh. He was very popular and could well be regarded as the best Secretary of State Scotland ever had. In spite of very poor health he often accompanied McIntosh to sea and he had great sympathy for the fishermen, as can be seen from the fact that the legislation was passed from political rather than scientific reasons. Nothing changes. He died a young man in his early forties, followed by his wife within two days. Trawlermen, although it was of little comfort to them, got revenge of a kind when no less a personage than the world famous Poet and Tragedian himself wrote his obituary. Part of it runs as follows, and the location of Dalhousie's estates might be noted in connection with the bye-law.

> Lord Dalhousie was a man worthy of all praise,
> And to his memory I hope a monument the people will raise,
> That will stand for many ages to come
> To commemorate the good deed he has done.
>
> He was beloved by men of high and low degree,
> Especially in Forfarshire by his tenantry:
> And by many of the inhabitants in and around Dundee.
> Because he was affable in temper, and void of all vanity.
>
> He had great affection for his children, also his wife,
> 'Tis said he loved her as dear as his life;
> And I trust they are now in heaven above,
> Where all is joy, peace, and love.

Other signatories of the following 16 bye-laws seem to have got off lightly as far as their obituaries were concerned as none of them attracted McGonigall's attention. Their signatures were excluding trawling from the prolific inshore grounds with increasing regularity, and on 26th July, 1889, under the Herring Fisheries Act of that year the following areas were closed off:—

Wigtown Bay, within a line drawn from Great Ross Point, near Little Ross Lighthouse, on the east to Isle of Whithorn on the west.

Luce Bay, within a line drawn from a point near Port William on the east to Killyness Point, near Drummore, on the west.

Loch-in-dail, within a line drawn from Rudha na Cathair (Mull of Oe) on the south to the Rhynns, near Rhynns of Islay Lighthouse, on the north.

Loch Snizort, within a line drawn from Vatternish Point on the west to Dunlea on the east.

Broad Bay, within a line drawn from Tolsta Head on the north to Tiumpan Head on the south.

Stornoway Bay, within a line drawn from Kebock Head on the south to Bayble Head on the north.

Thurso Bay, within a line drawn from Brimsness on the west to Dunnet Head on the east.

Sinclair Bay, within a line drawn from Noss Head on the south to Duncansby Head on the north.

Scapa Bay, within a line drawn from St. Mary's Point on the east to Houton Heads on the west.

St. Magnus Bay, within a line drawn from Esha Ness on the north to a point near Sandness on the south.

The waters inside a line drawn from Corsewall Point, in the county of Wigtown, to the Mull of Cantyre, in the county of Argyll.

The waters inside a line from Port Askadel, near Ardnamurchan Point, on the west to Ru-Cisteach, near Arasaig, on the east.

The waters inside a line from Ru-geur, Slate Point, on the south to a point near Ru-an-dunan on the north.

The waters inside a line from Ru-na-uag, Loch Torridon, on the south to a point at Long Island, Garcloch, on the north.

The waters outside Loch Tarbert, Harris, from Toe Head on the south to Camus-Huisnish on the north.

East and West Loch Roag, from Gallon Head on the west to Coul Point on the east.

The waters inside a line from Greenstone Point on the west to a point near Meal-Sgreaton, Ru-Cooygach, on the east.

The waters inside a line from Ru-Stoer on the west to a point at Scourie Bay on the east.

Dornoch Firth,
Fraserburgh Bay,
Montrose Bay,
Moray Firth (upper parts of),   } All as specified in the existing bye-
Aberdeen Bay,   laws of the Fishery Board.
Saint Andrew's Bay,
Firth of Forth,

Trawling was banned for domestic as well as foreign vessels from three miles off the coast in general, and after a series of amendments which progressively advanced the limits, the Moray Firth was closed to trawling on 6th August, 1896.

The restriction on trawling did not affect that branch of the industry much. It expanded by leaps and bounds as the skippers exploited the rich grounds in the North Sea, Faroe and Icelandic areas. But it did have the effect of preserving the inshore stocks at a high enough level to make seine netting viable for longer than it otherwise might have been. That in itself was due to the intervention of the Second World War which helped to rejuvenate stocks and prolonging the economic life of the smaller boats into the 1960's. The line fishermen were also assisted because, apart from preventing the considerable loss of gear, their productive life was extended into the 1980's in ports such as Johnshaven, and Gourdon although it will not survive there much longer. As many a now deserted or run down hamlet testifies time was running out for the old ways which had to yield before the pressures of the changing world.

The 34 or so years between 1880 and 1914 were the most prosperous and eventful years the fishing had seen or ever will. Already fewer people were actually fishing but the catching power and size of the boats were increasing to the extent that the decline in numbers made no difference to the quantity of fish landed.

A boat of 1860 was still undecked and could be hauled ashore; by 1890 any fisherman with ambition had a decked boat which had to be taken to the nearest harbour for security in bad weather. All of this meant that the villages lost their most able fishermen to the nearest town with a safe harbour. While they struggled on for a quite surprising length of time in the face of this loss, the changes were ringing the death knell of such as Whaligoe, Clyth, Skateraw, Collieston, Pitulie, Portessie, Balintore and many others. And this was not the only factor by any means.

The traditional methods of processing lined fish, of smoking, or salting them in barrels to keep them edible till they reached the main markets by the sea, were being made obsolete by the railways which could transport fresh or iced fish very rapidly. There still was a large demand for smoked fish but this too became concentrated in the main ports.

1883 was a truly momentous year as far as fishing was concerned as it saw yet another innova-

The areas around the coasts closed off by the various amendments to the Herring Fisheries Act of 1889. There were 17 amendments altogether but they were not all concerned with trawling. The number beside each area is the number of the amendment referring to it. The prohibited area in the Solway Firth is not shown. There were concessions for boats under 40 feet at certain times.

tion in the shape of the first refrigerated railway wagons specially designed to transport fish, herring in this instance, without salt or ice from Wick to London. They were specially built for a charitable organisation which was set up in London, called the Fish League.

The Fish League was created by some well-to-do businessmen and aristocracy in an attempt to reduce the terrible starvation which was so prevalent then in the slum areas around the East End of London.

People, and most of them were young children, were being found dead daily from hunger and the League was created early in 1883 to see if they could do something about bringing cheap fish to London. They arranged for local agents to be appointed in Stornoway, Wick, Buckie, Fraserburgh and Aberdeen who would buy herring, without commission, at the going rate. The secret of being able to deliver the herring to the poor of London, at a price of 2d - 3d per dozen, would be in the fact that they could reduce their freight charges and the wagons were built by the Swansea Wagon Company. They each had an ice tank through which 120 tubes ran and there was a fan, powered by the forward motion of the train, which would circulate air at a temperature of 33°F. There was a charcoal filter to purify the air and each wagon would hold 220 baskets of herring. Six cars were built with the intention of running one daily from each of the ports and they would meet up at Perth for despatch to London. The scheme collapsed because the wagons were built with very poor axle boxes which continually heated up and the bearings seized up. On the way to Wick for the pioneering run on 23rd August, two cars were derailed at Halkirk and on the way back down with their first load they derailed at Kinbrace, Lairg, Blair Atholl and Beattock. The journey which was intended to take 24 hours took three days but the herring were still saleable when they got to London. The League did not persist with having the axle boxes redesigned, possibly because cheap fish was arriving in increasing quantities from Hull and Grimsby, and the scheme was abandoned. But the point about refrigeration was not and on or about Thursday 15th January, 1885 the unique St Clement, A70, was launched from Hall Russel's yard in Aberdeen to the order of Captain Holmes. She had a refrigerated hold, insulated with paper and charcoal, and the cooling plant was worked by the main engine. The hold temperature could be held at -14°F and it seems to have been successful for the first year only and was removed then, because of mechanical trouble. It would be 20 years before another Aberdeen trawler, the 'Princess Louise,' fitted refrigeration.

To compete with, or on, the fresh fish market the outlying districts had to get their catch to the main centres for the best prices and yet another factor in the inexorable drift to Buckie, Fraserburgh, Peterhead, Aberdeen, Lossiemouth, and Macduff was the fact that fishing vessels were beginning to fit machinery which required specialists such as foundrymen not available in small villages. Steam capstans, and their boilers, had become indispensable for hoisting the sails and hauling the nets of the large Zulus and Fifies. They required castings, piping, and fittings, which could not be obtained outside the main ports. Of course many fishermen, particularly on the south side of the Moray Firth, where harbours are available every ten miles or so, could continue to live in their home towns and go by rail to where work was being done on their boats, but the inexorable movement which culminated 90 years later with the concentration of boats at Fraserburgh and Peterhead, had begun. In the fullness of time there would be a handful of ports where there had been dozens.

Yet other factors were coming into play, just as obscure as the others in the beginning, but all playing their part in the creation of the seine net industry for all that. And one of these innovations was an apparent boon but which in the long term was to break more hearts than ever it would uplift. That was the steam drifter. Its arrival, and the speed of its adaption by fishermen, was greatly facilitated by yet another event of these momentous 1880's, about 15 years before the drifter made its general appearance and altered the course of Scottish fishing forever.

On the 10th of May, 1883, three months before the Commission on trawling was constituted, the Select Committee on harbour accommodation was appointed to inquire into the "Harbour Accommodation on the Coasts of the United Kingdom having regard to the Laws and Arrangements under which the Construction and Improvement of Harbours may now be effected." As in the Commission on trawling, the quality of the men who were in the public service then, was of the highest and they conducted their inquiries in a very similar manner. They reported back to Parliament in July 1884, having interviewed 168 witnesses, all over Britain and Ireland, and considered 151 petitions from fishing communities for harbour works to be carried out for them. It will be recalled that up to this time all harbour works had been carried out in fishing ports by private organisations or Boards, such as the British Fisheries Society, from, either their own funds, with loans, or meagre grants from the Government through one of its agencies. Harbour Trusts around the coasts had done the same thing but by 1883 the British Fisheries Society had gone and the increasing size of the fishing boats was making harbour extensions or contruction impossible without substantial government grants as well as loans. It was therefore against this background that the Committee set about its task, and it missed nothing. In passing it should be mentioned that this report was completed in one year by a Committee which travelled by train or stagecoach, without typewriters, adding machines, photocopiers, telephones, electrical gadgets of any kind or even a computer. The evidence was probably written by lamp or candle light with a quill. Most of its sittings were held in London and the witnesses travelled there to give their evidence and the list makes interesting reading,

SELECT COMMITTEE ON HARBOUR ACCOMMODATION.   XXXV

EXPENSES OF WITNESSES.

NAME OF WITNESS.	PROFESSION OR CONDITION.	From whence Summoned.	Number of Days Absent from Home, under Orders of Committee.	Allowance during Absence from Home.			Expenses of Journey to London and back.			TOTAL Expenses allowed to Witness.		
				£.	s.	d.	£.	s.	d.	£.	s.	d.
George Mackay	Harbour Master	Fraserburgh	4	4	4	–	6	–	–	10	4	–
Alexander Stephen	Merchant Captain	- - -	4	4	4	–	6	–	–	10	4	–
John Buchan	- - -	- - -	4	4	4	–	6	–	–	10	4	–
James Farquharson	Harbour Master	Macduff	4	4	4	–	6	–	–	10	4	–
John Smith	Vice Chairman of Harbour Board.	Peterhead	4	4	4	–	5	15	–	9	19	–
David Carr	Solicitor	Stonehaven, N. B.	4	8	8	–	5	5	–	13	13	–
Charles Fyfe Morrison	Harbour Master	Burghead, N. B.	4	4	4	–	4	15	–	8	19	–
T. F. Robertson Carr	Gentleman	Berwick	3	3	3	–	4	–	–	7	3	–
George Collin	Master of Fishing Boat	Eyemouth, Berwickshire, Northumberland.	3	1	11	6	4	5	–	5	16	6
T. Leighton	Merchant Captain	Ambles, Acklington	3	3	3	–	2	15	–	5	18	–
G. Bruce	Gentleman	St. Andrews	3	3	3	–	6	15	–	9	18	–
Hugh Bain Macintosh	Bank Agent	Anstruther	3	3	3	–	6	15	–	9	18	–
John Ferguson	Harbour Master	Lossiemouth, Elgin	4	4	4	–	5	16	–	10	–	–
John Coffey	Merchant Captain	Waterford	4	4	4	–	4	1	–	8	5	–
William Kennedy	Pilot Master	- - -	4	4	4	–	4	1	–	8	5	–
W. G. Strype	Permanent Engineer to Wicklow Harbour Board.	Wicklow	4	4	4	–	5	10	–	9	14	–
Captain Hamilton	Merchant Captain	- ditto -	4	4	4	–	5	10	–	9	14	–
James C. Caldwell	Steamboat Agent	Portrush, Antrim	4	4	4	–	5	–	–	9	4	–
Samuel Patton	Harbour Master	- ditto - ditto	4	4	4	–	5	–	–	9	4	–
James Keebles	Merchant Captain	Sligo	4	4	4	–	7	16	6	12	–	6
William Lalor	Permanent Engineer to Harbour Board of Sligo.	Sligo	4	4	4	–	7	16	6	12	–	6
John Bolind	Merchant Captain	Portrush, Limerick	4	4	4	–	5	1	6	9	5	6
John Connick	Gentleman	Dundalk	4	4	4	–	6	3	6	10	7	6
James Doherty	Civil Engineer	Dublin	3	3	3	–	5	3	–	8	6	–
Francis Megarry	Harbour Commissioner	Galway	4	4	4	–	6	10	–	10	14	–
Edward Solly Flood	Gentleman	Wexford	4	4	4	–	6	6	–	10	10	–
William Armstrong	Shipowner	- ditto -	4	4	4	–	6	6	–	10	10	–
Thomas Flannery	Priest	Connemara, County Galway.	10	10	10	–	8	15	–	19	5	–
Francis Fowler	Pilot Master	Galway	4	4	4	–	6	12	–	10	16	–
William Brown	Manager of Anchor Line of Steamships.	Ballina, County Mayo, Ireland.	4	4	4	–	7	15	–	11	19	–
Charles Knox Gore	Baronet	Ballina, County Mayo	4	4	4	–	7	15	–	11	19	–
John Boyd	Gentleman	- ditto - ditto	4	4	4	–	7	15	–	11	19	–

William Kiddle - -	Captain, R.N. - -	Dublin - - -	3	3 3 –	5 3 –	8 6 –
Peter Wilson - -	Fishery Officer - -	Girvan - - -	3	3 3 –	6 5 –	9 8 –
James Wason - -	Merchant - -	Ballantrae, N. B. -	3	3 3 –	5 15 –	8 18 –
Archibald M'Gillivray -	Yacht Captain -	Lochbuoy - -	5	2 12 6	5 7 –	7 19 6
Alexander Macdonald -	Solicitor and Banker -	Portree, N. B. - -	5	10 10 –	9 5 –	19 15 –
Charles Aldred -	Gentleman - - -	Great Yarmouth -	2	2 2 –	1 19 –	4 1 –
John Walker - -	Pilot - - -	Holy Island, North-umberland.	3	1 11 6	4 8 –	5 19 6
John Dawson - -	Fisherman - - -	Newbiggin - -	3	1 11 6	3 9 –	5 – 6
Edward James Bedford -	Rear Admiral, R.N. -	Paignton - -	4	4 4 –	3 8 6	7 12 6
William Spears -	Fisherman - ¬ -	Sunderland - -	3	1 11 6	2 15 –	4 6 6
David M'Clew -	Factor - - -	Portpatrick - -	3	3 3 –	5 10 –	8 13 –
William Hanks -	Gentleman - - -	Filey - - -	2	2 2 –	3 6 –	5 8 –
William Tout - -	- ditto - - -	Filey - - -	2	2 2 –	3 6 –	5 8 –
Samuel W. Smyth -	- ditto - - -	Aldeburgh - -	2	2 2 –	1 13 –	3 15 –
Francis Gell - -	Clergyman - -	Lydd - - -	1	1 1 –	1 9 –	2 10 –
Robert Ovens - -	Gentleman - -	Cockenzie, Preston-pans.	3	3 3 –	5 14 6	8 17 6
Thomas Lakeman -	- ditto - -	Brixham - -	2	2 2 –	3 9 –	5 11 –
Samuel Raby - -	- ditto - -	Babicombe, Torquay	2	2 2 –	3 9 –	5 11 –
Thomas Cornish -	Gentleman - -	Penzance - -	3	3 3 –	5 7 6	8 10 6
John Mathews - -	Lloyd's Agent - -	- ditto - -	3	3 3 –	5 7 6	8 10 6
William Tolmie Tresidder	Clerk to St. Ives Har-bour Commissioners.	St. Ives - - -	3	3 3 –	5 7 6	8 10 6
Henry Stephens -	Carpenter - -	Truro - - -	3	1 11 6	3 – 6	4 12 –
Charles Rawle - -	Ship Builder - -	Padstow, Cornwall -	3	3 3 –	4 14 –	7 17 –
Samuel Allport -	Harbour Master -	- ditto - ditto -	3	3 3 –	4 14 –	7 17 –
Jacob Care - -	Shipowner - -	St. Ives - - -	3	3 3 –	5 7 6	8 10 6
Edward Lewis Mostyn	Master Mariner -	New Quay, Cornwall -	3	1 11 6	3 13 –	5 4 6
James Clemens -	Fisherman - -	- ditto - ditto -	3	1 11 6	3 13 –	5 4 6
James Haynes -	Master Mariner -	Port Isaac, Cornwall	3	1 11 6	3 9 –	5 – 6
Edward Tamlin -	Pilot - - -	Swansea - - -	2	1 1 –	2 13 6	3 14 6
John D. Hall -	Mariner - -	Pill, Somerset - -	2	1 1 –	1 13 –	2 14 –
Edward Parsons, R.N. -	Haven Master -	Bristol - - -	2	2 2 –	2 1 –	4 3 –
Ellis Roberts -	Inspector of Buoys -	Aberdouly - -	3	1 11 6	2 15 –	4 6 6
Robert M'Dowel -	Pilot - - -	Donaghadee - -	5	2 12 6	2 7 6	5 – –
Robert J. Day -	Harbour Master -	Great Yarmouth -	2	2 2 –	1 14 –	3 16 –
				TOTAL - - - £.	546 – 10	

and the way in which the representative from Peterhead made his observations is equally interesting. As in the Commission on Trawling the questions and answers were numbered.

Mr. JOHN SMITH, called in ; and Examined.

Chairman.

818. I THINK you now hold the office of Vice Chairman of the Trustees of the Harbour of Peterhead, do you not ?—Yes, I have done so since 1875.

819. And you have taken a very great interest in the works at Peterhead ?—Yes, I have.

820. Are you in any way interested in the harbours with regard to shipping or otherwise ?— No, I have no personal or pecuniary interest of any kind, except an interest that every citizen ought to have.

821. This being a labour of love ?—Yes, that is practically so.

822. There has been a great question of erecting a large harbour of refuge at Peterhead ?—Yes, I believe there has.

823. Of course if the Committee on Convict Labour that is now reporting, reports in favour of that, Peterhead's difficulties will be at an end ? — No, I do not think so. The harbour of refuge is a national and imperial concern, and I hope to show you that our local harbours require a great deal to be done to them for local purposes, quite irrespective of the harbour of refuge.

824. That is what I want to come to ; I was going to say the national harbour of refuge is outside the inquiry of this Committee ?—Yes, just so.

825. You think if this harbour was created you would still require a great deal to be done ?— Yes, we should require all that I intend to tell you of to be done.

826. Besides ?—Besides.

827. Can you give us some idea of the present state of the harbour of Peterhead ; a short history of it, in fact ?—Yes ; in the first place let me say that the harbours, as they now are, consist of three basins, and to make it more intelligible I shall put in this plan of the harbours (handing the same to the Committee). I was going to say that the south harbour includes about 6½ acres, the north harbour about 10½ acres, and Port Henry about 5 acres.

828. Do these all join one another ?—The north and south harbours are joined, as I shall describe, by a canal or cut as you will see there, which I will describe to you by-and-bye. The Port Henry harbour is not connected with the others in the meantime, but there is a proposal which

has been considered as to the propriety of making a cut through Birnie's Pier joining the two. That work is in contemplation, but has never been executed.

829. I understand these harbours are absolutely hewn out of the solid rock?—That is so.

830. What depth of water have you at the entrance of the harbour?—At the entrance of the south harbour at low water there is 7½ feet.

831. And what depth have you in the two harbours, the north and south?—7½ feet at the very least in the entrance of the south harbour, and in the north harbour it would be about 7 feet at the entrance at low water.

832. Have you got the depth of water at the entrance to Port Henry?—It is dry at low water, except at the entrance.

833. What is there at the entrance?—I am not sure of the exact depth at the entrance. Almost dry at low water.

834. What is the depth of water in these three harbours themselves?—The south harbour has a depth of 6 feet at low water, the inner basin of the north harbour has a depth of 4 feet, so has the channel from the inner basin through the outer basin also a depth of 4 feet, until you come to the entrance, when it may be assumed to

and so on and at paragraph 850 Mr Smith is at pains to demonstrate his fairness towards Fraserburgh, as Wick's crown had fallen and the title was vacant.

850. Is this from a statement in a newspaper or from the Blue Books?—It is taken from a report in a newspaper, and I have compared it with the Blue Book, and the two statements are almost identical: " The harbours of Peterhead and Fraserburgh are competing for the chief share of the herring fishery. Peterhead has been for years waiting for State aid. Meanwhile the Fraserburgh people had built a harbour for themselves at great cost ;" that is the quotation. Now I have nothing to say in disparagement of Fraserburgh. I believe the people at Fraserburgh have done admirably with the means at their disposal, but the statement of Mr. Spencer Walpole with regard to Peterhead is one to which we in Peterhead must emphatically demur. The facts that I have already given show that

the statement that " Peterhead has been waiting for State aid " is utterly without foundation.

851. You think you have really done just as much for your harbour as Fraserburgh for theirs?—We have done as much as we could, as I shall show you. Now let me indicate the outlay which the operations I have named has involved. Port Henry Harbour and the works connected with it cost in round numbers 16,700 *l.*; the deepening of the south harbour, underfounding walls, reclaiming the ground, the works which I have enumerated, cost 34,000 *l.*, and a considerable balance is still due to the contractor, which may be estimated at about 5,000 *l.* ; in all about 55,700 *l.*

852. Since what year?—That is since 1876.

The evidence of Captain Alexander Stephen of Fraserburgh given earlier, is equally illuminating.

559. Supposing that it is decided to make a great national harbour at Peterhead, and that that work is carried out, how would it affect Fraserburgh ; would it affect the trade of Fraserburgh, or not?—I should think it would have a tendency to affect the nearest port.

560. Would it affect the trade of Fraserburgh : would it be hurtful to Fraserburgh or not?—It might be, but it would be a great improvement of the harbour, enabling it to realize its full revenue and security to life and property if the suggested work is finished.

Mr. *Stevenson.*

561. I presume that the construction of a great harbour at Peterhead would not take away the necessity of making all the improvement that was possible at Fraserburgh ; you would still desire to improve Fraserburgh?—I am fully of this opinion ; seeing that there is no shoal water upon the south-east or east, or south of Peterhead, the sea is so heavy with south-east gales, and the tide is so strong with spring tides, that it makes the sea very dangerous, and I doubt the building

would not stand, and unless I could actually take up my true position in clear weather, I would not narrow the distance between myself and the land, and make Peterhead, but make northward, and get the Moray Firth open.

562. My object is to compare the two places as fishing harbours. Supposing that Peterhead were made into a great harbour, as has been proposed, what would you think of it as a fishing station compared with Fraserburgh?—The fishermen now go much more seaward than they did, and with a strong north wind, though the boats are large, they are not able sometimes to make up against it. When you are 50 miles off the Kinnaird's Head, or off Buchan Ness, with a north wind, you cannot fetch it, and you must go further south. Then as to the boats from Buchan Ness, and the places round there off seaward, when a gale comes on from the south and south-south-west, cannot fetch Peterhead, they would have to run for Fraserburgh or the Moray Firth.

563. Fraserburgh would still retain its advantages as a fishing station, notwithstanding the construction of a great harbour at Peterhead?— Yes; we have very often to accommodate the Peterhead boats, because they cannot get up against the south wind, which is the prevailing wind upon our coast, and accommodate Fraserburgh.

I relate the above extracts merely so that they can be considered against the situation one hundred years later.

The Committee had before them statistics on about everything from sizes of boats, earnings, shipwrecks, loss of life and life saving. They asked 12,752 questions and considered petitions for harbours of refuge which even with modern techniques would be on a colossal scale. The proposals ranged from Craigenroan, a proposal which had been made 20 years previously, . . .

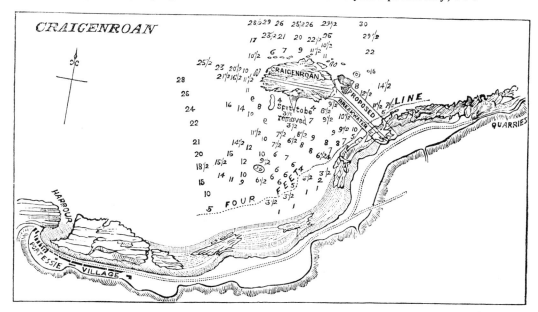

As will be seen, the Commissioners of Supply for the county of Banff, at their meeting on Tuesday, resolved to petition in favour of a boat refuge and a lighthouse for this county. The reasons and necessity for this movement are only too palpable and well known. They are to be found in the losses both last month, when 27 fishermen belonging to the county perished, leaving 13 widows and 42 children, and in 1857, when, in the same district, 42 fishermen were lost, leaving 27 widows and 79 children.

Need we recall what has been done? The losses of 1857 drew public attention, and an official inquiry was made on the subject by the Scotch Fishery Board. The Secretary to the Board, the Honourable B. F. Primrose, and the Messrs. D. and T. Stevenson, engineers to the Board, visited the district, and made the fullest inquiries on the spot. The Messrs. Stevenson subsequently made special surveys of various parts of the coast. The result appeared in an able and carefully drawn up report from the Messrs. Stevenson, bearing date November 1858, in which they recommended that a breakwater, affording a low-water refuge harbour for boats, should be constructed at a part of the coast which presented great facilities, and which even in its present state offers no inconsiderable shelter. A little way from the shore is a rock which would make a good head to the breakwater, and the plan of the Messrs. Stevenson (of which the engraving given above is a sketch), proposed to connect the rock with the shore. The breakwater erected would afford a perfectly accessible place of shelter, not only for boats, but for all craft plying in Moray Firth. The site of the proposed breakwater is called Craigenroan; and the Messrs. Stevenson say of it—

" We are decidedly of opinion that the most certain and the most safe investment of " public money, as well as the most economical method of supplying the wants of the " fishermen of the coast, is to construct the works which we have recommended at " Craigenroan."

. . . to Aberdeen.

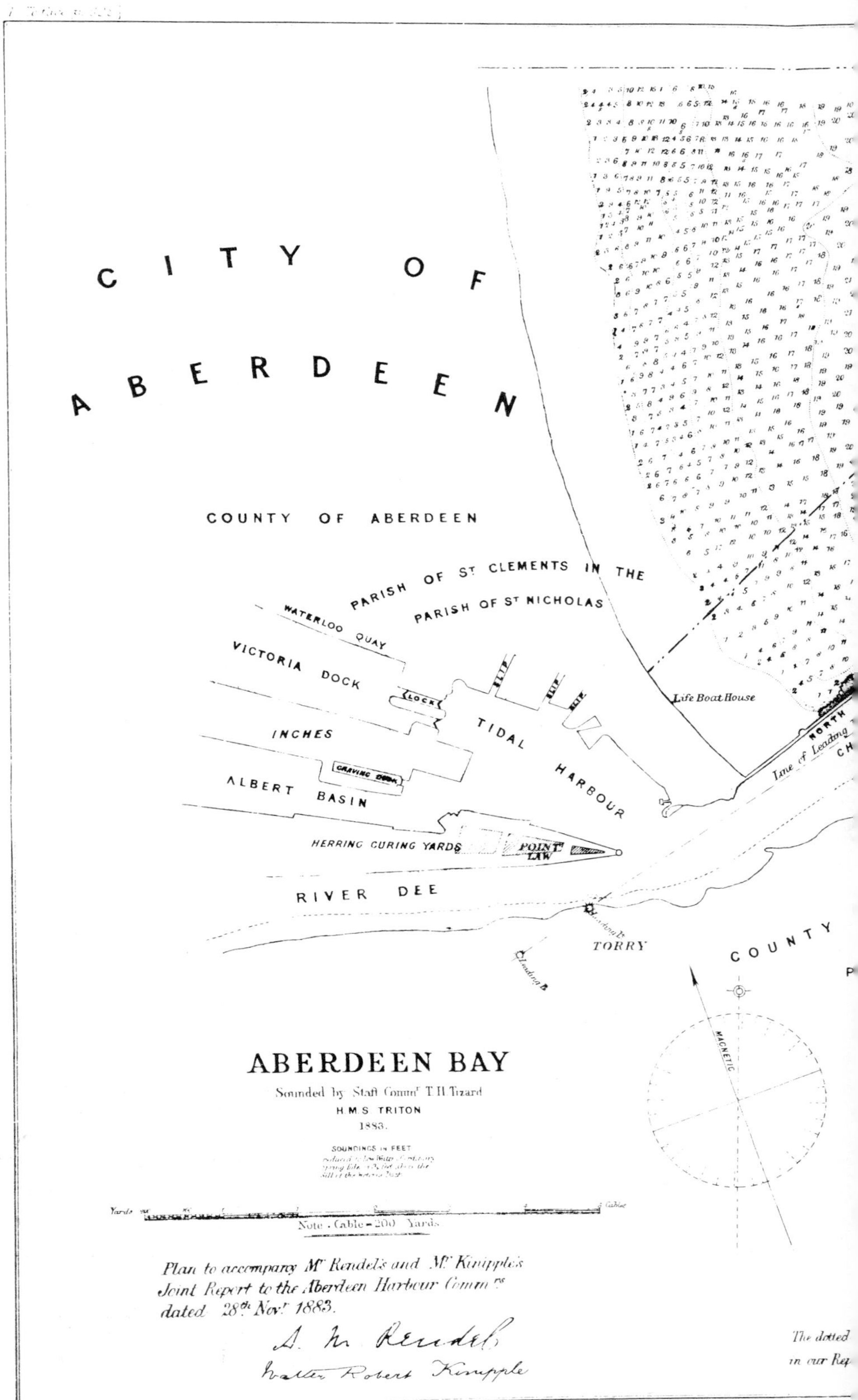

C I T Y   O F

A B E R D E E N

COUNTY   OF   ABERDEEN

PARISH OF St CLEMENTS IN THE

PARISH OF St NICHOLAS

WATERLOO QUAY

VICTORIA DOCK

LOCK

Life Boat House

INCHES

TIDAL   HARBOUR

NORTH

Line of Leading

CH

ALBERT   BASIN

GRAVING DOCK

HERRING CURING YARDS

POINT
LAW

RIVER   DEE

TORRY

COUNTY

ABERDEEN BAY

Sounded by Staff Comm.' T H Tizard
H.M.S. TRITON
1883.

SOUNDINGS IN FEET

Note . Cable = 200 Yards.

Plan to accompany M.' Rendel's and M.' Kinipple's
Joint Report to the Aberdeen Harbour Comm.'s
dated 28.'h Nov.' 1883.

S. W. Rendel
Walter Robert Kinipple

The dotted

in our Re

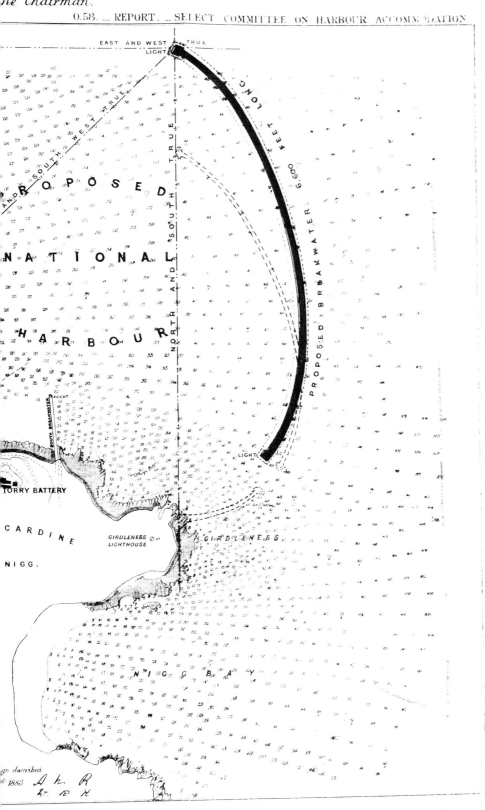

Plan handed in

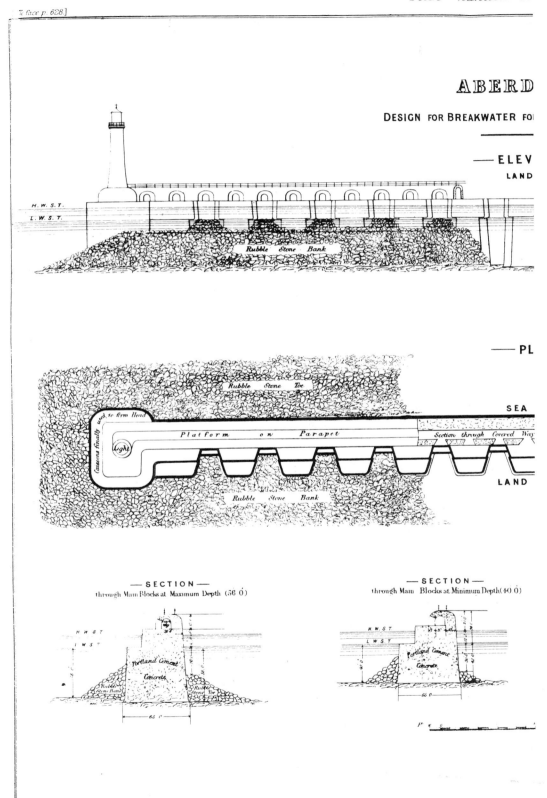

[To face p. 628.]

ABERD

DESIGN FOR BREAKWATER FO

ELEV
LAND

H. W. S. T.
L. W. S. T.

Rubble Stone Bank

PL

Rubble Stone Toe

SEA

Caisson finally used to form Head

Platform on Parapet

Section through Covered Way

Light

LAND

Rubble Stone Bank

— SECTION —
through Main Blocks at Maximum Depth (56 0)

— SECTION —
through Main Blocks at Minimum Depth (40 0)

H. W. S. T.
L. W. S. T.

Portland Cement
Concrete

Rubble
Stone Bank

Rubble
Stone Toe

H. W. S. T.
L. W. S. T.

Portland Cement
Concrete

by the Chairman.

EEN BAY.

R PROPOSED NATIONAL HARBOUR.

ATION—

SIDE

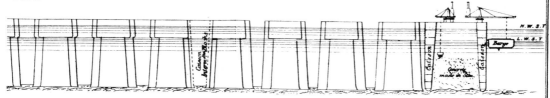

AN—

FACE

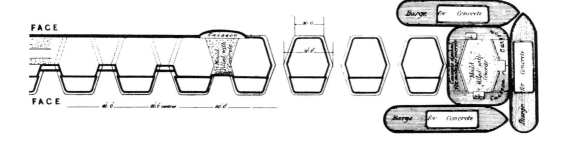

FACE

— SECTION —
through Interm.⁰ Blocks at Minimum Depth (40.0)

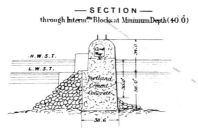

Scale 40 feet = 1 inch.

— SECTION —
through Interm.⁰ Blocks at Maximum Depth (56.0)

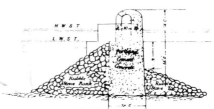

Plan to accompany M.ʳ Rendel's and M.ʳ Kinipples
Joint Report to the Aberdeen Harbour Comm.ᵐ
dated 28.ᵗʰ Nov.ʳ 1883.

A. M. Rendel

Walter Robert Kinipple

Handed in by th

ABERDEE

DESIGN FOR CAISSONS FOR CONSTRUCTION OF BRE

Position of Caisson with 40 Tons of Ballast,

Sectional Elevation

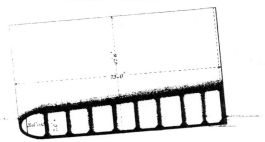

73.0'

Estimated Weight of Iron

Half Plan

Section on line A. A.   *Section B.B.*

High water at Greatest depth

Low Water at Greatest depth
High Water at Lowest depth

Low Water at Lowest depth
Floatation Line of Caisson

Internal Space
to be filled with Concrete
when Caisson is in place

Internal

Junction Line
of Caisson

to be filled w
when Caisson

A

Part Sectional Plan
under upper Deck

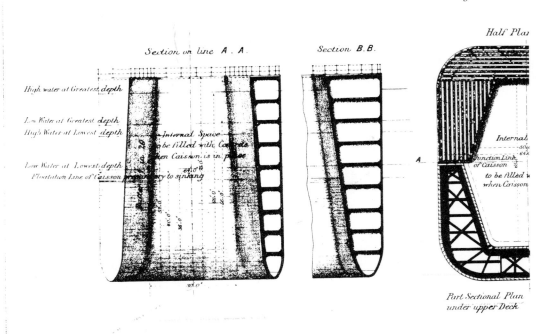

FEET 10   5   0   10   20   30

e Chairman.

N   BAY.

AKWATER FOR PROPOSED NATIONAL HARBOUR.

when being Floated to or from Harbour.

End Elevation

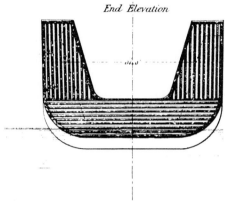

in each Caisson 480 Tons.

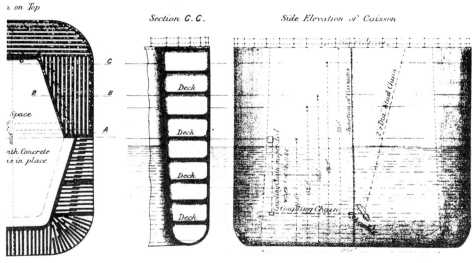

on Top

Space

with Concrete
s in place

Part Sectional Plan
at Bottom.

Section C.C.

Deck

Deck

Deck

Deck

Side Elevation of Caisson

Plan to accompany M.ͬ Rendel's and M.ͬ Kinipple's
Joint Report to the Aberdeen Harbour Comm.ˢ
dated 28.ᵗʰ Nov.ͬ 1883.

A. M. Rendel
Walter Robert Kinipple

By 1899 when the first of the steam drifters arrived for the summer fishing of that year, many of the recommendations made by the Select Committee had been put into operation, many had not, and many had been modified. However, the huge injection of government money whch followed brought investment in this country in harbours to something approaching that being poured into their harbours by the French, Belgian, Dutch and Danish governments. The Select Committee had been at pains to bring to the attention of Parliament the amounts of money that foreign governments had been spending in comparison with the paltry sums of the British. And Peterhead, with its new Harbour of Refuge, was the best equipped of all.

Photograph from the Johnston Collection by permission of the Wick Society.

The 'Content', the first steam drifter in Scotland which arrived in Wick from Yarmouth on 4th July, 1899.

The first steam drifter seems to have been the 'Content' of Wick which arrived there from England on 5th July, 1899 under the command of Skipper Alex Thain OBE. By 1911 there were nearly 800 drifters, most of which were built along the coast between Lossiemouth and Aberdeen. The headlong rush into steam driven vessels had two short-term and one long-term effect. The short-term results were the death of the great sailing drifters and a change in the ownership traditions of fishing boats. A steam drifter cost between three and five times as much as a new sailboat of equivalent size, the last of which was probably launched in 1904, and few fishermen had the capital to buy a steam drifter without borrowing a large part of the purchase price. In the beginning this was not much of a problem because of the general success of the fishings which now were being conducted all year round because of the size of the boats; it was also the most prosperous era that the fishermen would ever see. And there was also the successes that the steam trawlers were enjoying: they were repaying their investors hand over fist. The key to prosperity seemed to lie with steam and every ambitious fisherman needed a steam drifter with its obvious advantages of speed, safety, comfort and manoeuvrability. There was a big difference between standing at a wheel looking through the windows of a steam drifter's wheelhouse and sitting on an unprotected thwart, wearing three pairs of drawers and three ganseys extra, just to keep out the cold at the winter fishings on a sail-boat. Many a skipper had to be lifted from the wheel of a sail-boat once he was in harbour, so numbed was he with the cold.

Photograph by permission of Mrs J. Sutherland, Wick.

Skipper Jim Baikie who sailed the large Fifie 'Alexandra' from Wick to Yarmouth, quay to quay, in 42½ hours. He was publicly awarded a certificate by the Oddfellows for having saved the lives of four men on different occasions. Once he successfully dived in at Cape Wrath with all his sea gear on to rescue Mr Alexander Duchart. He was a survivor of the lifeboat which turned turtle in the river and was a crack shot.

So a new financial structure made its appearance as the need for extra money caused fishermen to approach people outside their immediate family for finance, a process which continues till the present day and was raised to a very high level from the 1960's onward when the arrival of expensive equipment required ever larger sums of money. The attractions to investors at the beginning of the 20th Century were glittering and there was very little difficulty in obtaining finance because of the apparently unending success of the fishings. Not that there ever had been much difficulty with finance over the previous hundred or so years, but the sums required had been much smaller by comparison, and came as a general rule from within the industry. Money had been advanced on the heads of contracts made between fishermen and curers, or, where the fishermen already had their boats and gear, credit was allowed by local traders for household and boat running expenses. This system of credit was used by all, whether they could have afforded to pay their bills as they went along or not, and debts were cleared at "The Back of the Fishing," when the season was over and accounts were squared, from the shops supplying groceries, to the chandlers provisioning the boats. That system began to crumble with the advent of the steam drifter because while a small firm might be able to withstand supplying groceries on credit it could not support a steam drifter burning up to 16 tons of coal a week for months. And hundreds of drifters were coming on to the scene. Oddly the practice of settling at the back of the fishing survived with the herring till the beginning of the Second World War, but not for the seine net men. Their settlements, because of the promptness with which they were paid, were made weekly. White fish buyers did not have to wait months for their money as did herring exporters and thus another of the traditions crumbled.

The British Fisheries Society, that other great source of finance which had put the fishing industry on its feet, had been wound up, as a direct result of the disaster it had suffered in its attempt to build a breakwater in Wick Bay. In modern terms it lost about £10,000,000 between 1863 and 1870 as the sea continually destroyed the construction and with it went the Society's spirit. In a way the Society had drifted from its original aims and had not made much money available to fishermen in its last 30 years or so but that is quite understandable as by that time the industry was charging along under its own momentum — nevertheless few organisations have held higher principles or served nobler purpose. The task in Wick had been too much for a private company and the ill-fated breakwater was to be the last. Thereafter all major port or harbour construction would be undertaken directly or indirectly by the Government, the Harbour of Refuge at Peterhead being the outstanding example in Scotland.

Photograph from the Johnston Collection by permission of the Wick Society.

The 'Content' tows the hull of the 'Elsay' into Wick harbour for fitting out after her launch in the river. Only seven steam drifters were ever built in Wick and steam boats never achieved much popularity there. The 'Content', a classic Pipeshank or Woodbine drifter burnt about four tons of coal a week while the 'Elsay' burnt 12.

In 1886, possibly in anticipation of the increasing costs which were already becoming apparent with the steam trawlers, an Act was passed to control the way in which shareholding in boats could be undertaken, perhaps to ensure that defaulting debtors could be held responsible, and the way in which money could be borrowed for the purchase of a boat, viz:—

49 & 50 VICT.

CAP. LIII.

An Act to amend the Law relating to Sea Fishing Boats in Scotland.—[25th June 1886.]

[Preamble repealed by 61 and 62 Vic., cap. 22.]

Short title.
1. This Act may be cited as the Sea Fishing Boats (Scotland) Act, 1886, and shall be construed as one with the Sea Fisheries Act, 1868, and with any Orders in Council made under the said Sea Fisheries Act, 1868, and in force for the time.

Application of Act. 31 & 32 Vict. c. 45.
2. This Act shall apply to all sea fishing boats as defined in the said Sea Fisheries Act, 1868, and the Orders in Council following upon it, which are or may hereafter be engaged in the prosecution of the sea fishing industry in Scotland.

Property in a boat divisible into shares.
3. The property in a sea fishing boat (hereinafter called a "boat") shall for the purposes of this Act be divided into sixteen shares, and not more than sixteen persons shall be entitled to be registered at the same time as owners of any one boat; but this shall not affect the beneficial right or title of any number of persons or of any company represented by or claiming under or through any registered owner or joint owner.

Joint ownership in a boat.
4. No person shall be entitled to be registered as owner of any fractional part of a share in a boat; but any number of persons, not exceeding five, may be registered as joint owners of one boat or of a share or shares therein.

Purchase and sale of boat.
5. A boat registered in a register of sea fishing boats under the Sea Fisheries Act, 1868, and the Orders in Council following upon it, or any share thereof, shall be transferred by bill of sale in the form contained in Schedule A. hereto annexed, or as near thereto as circumstances permit; but in order to the completion of a valid title in the person of a purchaser or other transferee, it shall be necessary that such bill of sale be intimated and produced to the collector of customs of the port at which the boat is registered, and that it shall be recorded by him in the register of sea fishing boats kept at the principal office of customs there in terms of the said Orders in Council and in the form contained in Schedule C. hereto annexed.

Loan on security of boat.
6. A boat registered as above or any shares or share therein may be made a security for a loan or other valuable consideration, and the instrument creating the security, hereinafter termed a "mortgage," shall be in the form contained in Schedule B. (1) hereto annexed, or as near thereto as circumstances permit; and on the production of such instrument the collector of customs of the port at which the boat is registered shall record the same in the register kept there according to the form contained in Schedule C. hereto annexed, and in the column thereof headed "Mortgages."

7. Every such mortgage shall be recorded by the collector in the order of time in which the same is produced to him for the purpose, and the collector shall, by memorandum under his hand, notify on
Recording of mortgage in register.

the mortgage that the same has been recorded by him, stating the date and hour of such record, and each such mortgage shall have priority according to the time at which it is so recorded.

8. Whenever any recorded mortgage has been discharged in whole or in part, the collector shall, on the production of the mortgage with a discharge for the whole amount of the loan or for a portion of it indorsed thereon duly signed and attested in the form contained in Schedule B. (2) hereto annexed, or as near thereto as circumstances permit, make an entry in the register to the effect that such mortgage has been discharged in whole or in part. *Discharge of mortgage.*

9. The holder of any such mortgage shall not be deemed to be the owner of the boat or of any share therein except in so far as may be necessary for making such boat or share available as a security for his debt; and every mortgagee whose name is duly recorded on the register shall have power to sell the boat or shares or share in respect of which his mortgage is recorded and to give effectual receipts for the purchase money, but if more persons than one are registered as mortgagees of the same boat or share no subsequent mortgagee shall sell such boat or share without the concurrence of every prior mortgagee. *Right of mortgagee.*

10. No mortgagee whose mortgage, or, failing concurrence, without payment or consignation of the amount of any prior mortgage, is recorded on the register shall be affected by the bankruptcy of the owner after the date of the record of such mortgage, and such mortgage shall have a preference over any right, claim, or interest in such boat or any share thereof which may belong to the creditors or assignees of the bankrupt. *Right of mortgagee when owner bankrupt.*

11. A recorded mortgage of any boat or shares or share in a boat may be transferred to any person by an endorsement on the same by the mortgagee duly signed and attested in the form contained in Schedule B. (3) annexed, or as near thereto as circumstances permit, and on the production of such mortgage with the transfer endorsed thereon, the collector shall enter in the registry the name of the transferee as mortgagee, and shall by memorandum under his hand record on the mortgage that the same has been recorded by him, stating the time of such record. *Transference of mortgage.*

12. If the interest of any mortgagee is transmitted in consequence of marriage, death, bankruptcy, or insolvency, or by any lawful means other than by a transfer according to the provisions of the preceding section, the name of the person or persons entitled under such transmission shall, upon a written declaration thereof signed and attested by two witnesses being produced to the satisfaction of the collector, be entered in the registry as mortgagee or mortgagees of the boat or share thereof in respect of which such transmission has taken place. *Transmission of mortgagees right otherwise than by transfer.*

Assistance from Fishery Board. 13. The Fishery Board for Scotland shall give every assistance in carrying out the provisions of this Act, and where necessary shall employ their officers to facilitate its execution.

Power to issue Order in Council. 14. It shall be lawful for Her Majesty by Order in Council from time to time to make regulations for carrying out, enforcing, and giving effect to the provisions of this Act, and every such Order shall be of the same force as if it had been enacted in this Act.

Transfer of mortgages. 15. No transfer, mortgage, or transmission of any boat shall be registered under this Act unless and until there shall have been received by the collector of customs a certificate under the hand of the Registrar General of Shipping and Seamen that such boat has not been registered as a ship under the provisions of the Merchant Shipping Act, 1854, and no boat shall be registered as a ship under the Merchant Shipping Act, 1854, unless and until there shall have been received by the Registrar to whom application to register such boat is made a certificate under the hand of the Secretary of the Fishery Board for Scotland, that no transfer, mortgage, or transmission of such boat has been registered under this Act.

Application of Act. 16. This Act shall apply only to Scotland.

Definition. 17. The term " boat " shall include ropes, sails, oars, and the other appurtenances required for navigation, but shall not include nets, lines, or other fishing gear.

The expression " collector of customs " shall include the principal officer of the port.

A specimen agreement was included with the legislation . . . .

SCHEDULE B.

(1) *Mortgage.*

*" I " or " we."

†" Me " or " us."

‡" Myself " or " ourselves."

§" My " or " our."

* the undersigned in consideration of this day lent to† by do hereby bind‡ and§ heirs or executors to pay to the said the said sum of together with interest thereon at the rate of per cent. per annum on the day of next ; and secondly that if the said principal sum is not paid on the said day*

or§ heirs or executors, will, so long as the same or any part thereof remains unpaid, pay to the said interest on the whole or such part thereof as may for the time being remain unpaid, at the rate of per cent. per annum, by equal half-yearly payments on the day of and day of in every year ; and in security thereof* hereby mortgage to the said shares in the fishing boat named the , of the port of , registered No. , belonging to† ; and* declare that this mortgage is made on condition that the power of sale which by the Sea Fishing Boats (Scotland) Act, 1886, is vested in the said shall not be exercised until the

‖Insert the day fixed for payment of principal as above.

said‖ day of . Lastly,* for‡ and§ heirs and executors, hereby declare that* ha power to mortgage in manner aforesaid the above-mentioned shares, and that the same are free from incumbrances.¶

¶If any prior incumbrance, add " save as appears by the registry of the said boat."

In witness whereof* ha hereto subscribed§ name this day of , one thousand eight hundred and in the presence of**

**Here name and designate the two witnesses.

A.B.

C.D., witness.

E.F., witness.

(2) *Discharge.*

Received the sum of in discharge of the within written security. Dated at this day of 18

A.B.

C.D., witness.

E.F., witness.

(3) Transfer.

I [*or* We]   in consideration of   this day paid
to me [*or* us] by   hereby transfer to   the benefit of
the within security.

In witness whereof I [*or* we]   have hereunto subscribed my
[*or* our] name this   day of   one thousand eight hundred
and   in the presence of [*here name and designate the two witnesses*].
                                                              A,B.

C.D., witness.

E.F., witness.

This legislation encouraged speculators, as opposed to men whose livelihoods were dependent on the successful operation of the boat, to invest and saw the introduction of something quite new in the Scottish herring industry. This was the creation of fleets belonging to an individual or a company. Coupar of Helmsdale, who made his money by acquiring the monopoly of the import of Torrevegan salt, the prime curing salt which was used by the thousand ton every year, owned nine drifters in 1908; 'Pansy,' 'Primrose,' 'Bluebell,' 'Ada,' 'Bertha,' 'Clara,' 'Dora,' 'Ella,' 'Flora;' these all fished from Wick. In Peterhead, while W. H. Leask owned fewer boats outright they either owned or had shares in the following:— 'Resolute,' 'Pioneer,' 'Renown,' 'Mary Stephen,' 'Jeannies,' 'Rosebud,' 'Trustful,' 'Jeannie Leask,' 'Lottie Leask,' 'Rival,' 'Watchful,' 'Hopeful,' 'Lupina,' 'Star of Bethlehem,' 'Comely,' 'Fair Chance,' 'Stately,' 'True Vine,' 'Margaret,' 'Ella,' 'Betsy,' 'W. H. Leask,' 'Jeannie,' 'North Briton,' 'Speedwell,' 'Nellie McGee,' 'J. T. Stephen,' 'The Brae' and 'Pride o Buchan,' 29 vessels in all. That was in 1911.

Photograph by permission of Mrs Shaw, Helmsdale.

Some of Coupars drifters in Helmsdale in October, 1914.

There were other curers and fish salesmen who fleeted in the English sense or took shares in drifters which were skippered by the majority shareholder. This was the advent in Scotland of what was to become an investment company, of the kind represented by the Wood Group, whose primary interest in the fishing industry became purely speculative by the 1960's and 1970's. That kind of phenomenon did not appear till well after the Second World War when spiralling costs, and outlays required the kind of capital which could be supplied by such investors.

The investment of indirect money in many steam drifters at the turn of the century was to have a delayed effect on the industry in the 1920's as we shall see. For the moment suffice it to say that yet another subtle change from the traditions of the previous century had taken place. In a way it was a half step back towards the financing used in the 16th and 17th Centuries where interest in the fishing was taken by the monied only for profit. This time it was more benign but, as in trawling, it was to make more money only, where in the 19th Century, the commitment had been entirely by the fisherman himself and was of life, limb, family well-being and all he possessed. Even in the present day, where a large number of the boats are share held by some or all of the crew, most of the boats have a large presence of speculative money which will be there only as long as the boat remains viable. In the fullness of time finance would not only be available for the purchase of boats but by 1900 events which apparently had little or nothing to do with the catching of fish were taking place. They would lead to an accelerating rate of investment in a range of items which previously had been undreamed of by fishermen. They also ushered out the era where local influences made for local designs in vessels. The process began at a time when the shape of a boat or the set of her sails would identify the very village to which she belonged and who built her. While this evolution has not yet finished it is now difficult to tell the country of origin of a vessel in most instances without reading her registration numbers. Local identities began to disappear with the disuse of local harbours as the requirements of safety, government regulations and the propulsion methods began to standardise designs within fairly narrow limits. These limits became even narrower as design became more scientific and technical. And of course the changes began to arrive at almost breakneck speed in the next 30 years or so. As in all change, it came about as the result of improved communications. And very little of it originated either in Scotland, or with one man, although Scots did play a part in development and were very quick to accept most of the innovations.

Photograph by permission of Mrs Shaw, Helmsdale.

Helmsdale as it was in the 1880's.

In 1888 in Germany, a man called Heinrich Hertz was experimenting with two mirrors made of metal and shaped like thimbles except that they were much larger and facing each other — five feet apart. Earlier, in 1864, a Scotsman named James Clerk Maxwell had predicted that it would be possible to send signals through the air, without wires, and Hertz proved him correct by sending the first deliberate man-made radio signal across the five feet between the mirrors. Hertz's success was followed up by many others but the man who succeeded before the rest was Guglielmo Marconi whose real contribution to science was perseverance rather than genius. In 1901 he sent the Morse letter "S" from Cornwall in England to Newfoundland, nearly 2000 miles, and nothing was ever the same again. Marconi of course broadcast in Morse but the first intelligible speech was broadcast by radio on 6th September, 1902 by an American called Greenleaf W. Pickard. On 25th December, 1906 another American, Reginald A. Fessinden, broadcast Christmas music and readings to the few boats of the New England fishing fleet that had radio receivers. It was to be 20 or more years before the Scottish fishing fleet took an interest in radio but by that time quite a few fishermen had had first hand experience of it. Governments had very quickly appreciated the military possibilities of radio, and it was this that provided most fishermen with their first encounter with the wireless.

Ten years before Marconi sent his signal across the Atlantic Ocean a company in a suburb of Manchester decided to expand its already well established business which manufactured, among other things, dynamos, dentists chairs and moulds for false teeth. It took an interest in a hot air engine and in 1894 introduced a paraffin oil engine which was to develop into the legendary Gardner diesel engine, a byeword for reliability and long life among fishing boat engines. Gardner was not by any means alone in the development of oil engines, none of which were developed for marine use in the beginning. These engines were originally produced to drive land based vehicles and to provide power for generators, farm machinery or factory tools.

Christmas 1904 was less than happy for Mr Walter Bergius as the 23-year-old mechanic had just had the depressing experience of seeing a piston appearing through the cylinder head of the Kelvin car which he had taken from his works in Glasgow.

Photograph by permission of Kelvin Diesels.

A Kelvin Car of the kind which persuaded Mr Walter Bergius that there might be a better future in marine engineering.

Another minor irritation came to his notice when he had re-designed this piston and got back on the road. This was that the width of his car, which had solid tyres, was the same as that of the Glasgow Corporation tram-lines, along which the cars tended to travel regardless of where the driver wanted to go. Mr Bergius was a man of some determination and ingenuity and persisted. In 1906,

Advertisement for Gardner engines in 1911. At first glance it would appear that they had installed 3000 engines but closer inspection reveals that this is the total of the brake horse power of all the engines combined.

Photograph by permission of Kelvin Diesels.

Mr Walter Bergius.

Photograph by permission of Kelvin Diesels, Glasgow.

The launch 'Kelvin' which had the first Kelvin marine engine fitted in 1906.

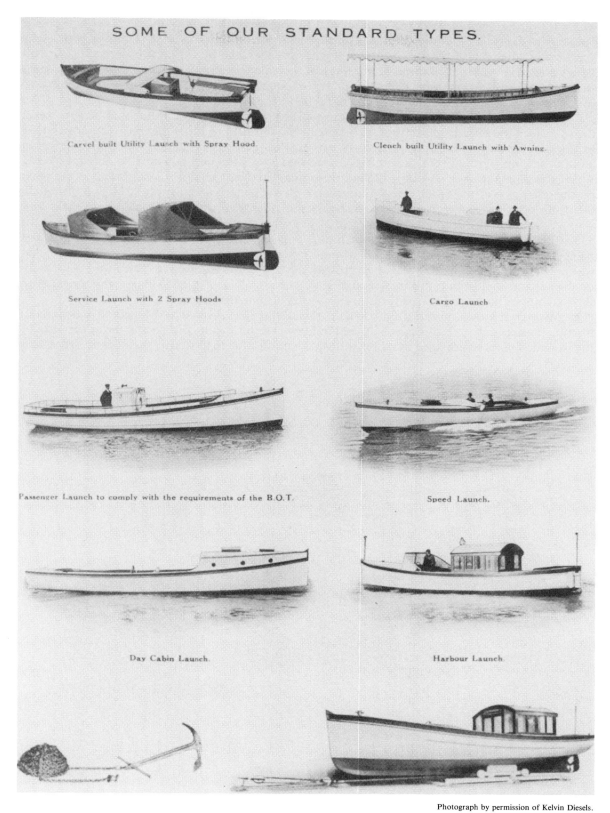

SOME OF OUR STANDARD TYPES.

Carvel built Utility Launch with Spray Hood.

Clench built Utility Launch with Awning.

Service Launch with 2 Spray Hoods

Cargo Launch

Passenger Launch to comply with the requirements of the B.O.T.

Speed Launch.

Day Cabin Launch.

Harbour Launch.

Photograph by permission of Kelvin Diesels.

An example of Kelvin advertising just before the First World War although why they felt it necessary to show seamen what an anchor and chain looked like is not clear.

with a yet further improved design, he installed a 12 horsepower car engine in a 23 foot rowing boat. Success was immediate, she took off like a startled hind, and on 19th July, 1906, he advertised that he was now building marine engines. Another legend was born and by 1919, 3000 Kelvin engines had been installed in vessels all over the world. But that was some time away and the elegance of the great sailing drifters still maintained a dwindling presence for a few years. The last of these, the 'Muirneag' of Stornoway, fished till the outbreak of the Second World War.

The decline of the sailing boat was in proportion with an increase in the numbers of steam drifters which were nearly all constructed between 1900 and 1914. A lot of the construction was done in England but there were busy yards at Aberdeen, Peterhead, Fraserburgh, MacDuff, Ardrossan and Lossiemouth. A few were also built in Glasgow and Wick but only about half a dozen, as Wick, which was slipping into accelerating decline, never adapted the steam drifter on the scale of the ports on the other side of the Moray Firth and beyond. By 1911 there were almost 800 steam drifters in Scotland, nearly all concentrated between Nairn and Aberdeen, with the remainder in Wick, Lerwick, Eyemouth, Anstruther and Kirkcaldy. The investment was immense, well in excess of £300,000,000 by todays standards, and the future looked rosier than it had ever done. The fleet was being modernised at frantic speed, demand and supplies held good for longer than ever before, and the innovations of the past 30 years had brought nothing but more success. There were few clouds on the horizon and the only apparent casualties were the small hamlets and villages which yielded up their ambitious youth to the new thrusting centres of fishing development.

Nearly everything was turning, if not to gold, then certainly to silver. The old method of boats contracting to supply curers had become disused in favour of the auction of fish and the appearance of the fish salesman who provided the boats with an administration to look after their books, settle their

Photograph by permission of Mrs M. Morrison, Campbeltown.
Robert Robertson of Campbeltown who was one of the most imaginative and progressive fishermen in Scotland. He is seen here pictured on an outing with his wife, in the centre, and his sister on the left.

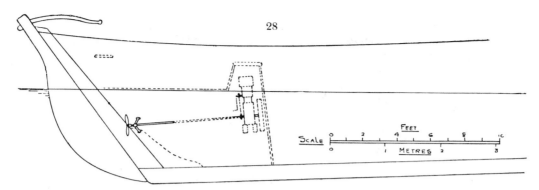

28

7-8 H.P. SINGLE CYLINDER KELVIN AS INSTALLED IN CLYDE FISHING FLEET.

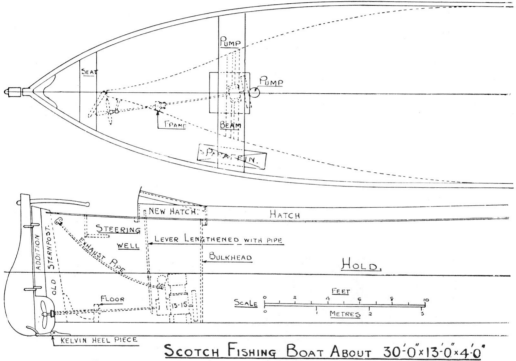

SEAT

PUMP

PUMP

FRAME

BEAM

PARAFFIN.

NEW HATCH   HATCH

STEERING

WELL   LEVER LENGTHENED WITH PIPE

EXHAUST PIPE   BULKHEAD   HOLD.

OLD STERNPOST.

ADDITION

FLOOR   13-15

KELVIN HEEL PIECE

SCOTCH FISHING BOAT ABOUT 30'-0" x 13'-0" x 4'-0"
SHOWING BOTH CENTRAL AND SIDE INSTALLATIONS.

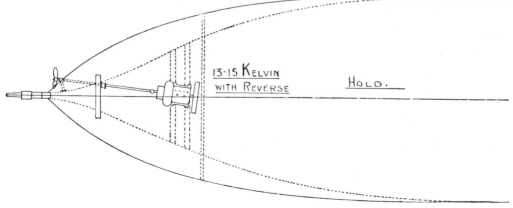

13-15 KELVIN
WITH REVERSE   HOLD.

Illustration from the Kelvin Catalogue No 4 about 1913.

debts, collect their payments from buyers, in return for a fixed amount of commission of their gross earnings. And the characters involved ranged from philanthropists to brigands. The sale of white fish was nearly always conducted in an open market but occasionally a boat would arrange a private sale of its fish, a practice which became more prevalent after the Second World War, from the 1960's onwards.

Till the arrival of the steam trawler the earnings of the crew had always been based on a share of the catch, and net earnings if they were shareholders. On steam trawlers the cook and the engineer were on a guaranteed wage, regardless of how the vessel fished, but at the same time it was nearly always profitably. This practice was carried over to the steam drifters when they began. Trawling had also opened up, in conjunction with the railways, sections of home markets which brought payment in cash rather than extended credit, and prosperity spread in some places in spite of themselves. The development of the propulsion of fishing vessels still had some way to go and the news of oil engines was spreading among fishermen.

Interests in oil engines began just at the turn of the century when inventors paid all or part of the cost of installing their engines in demonstration vessels for publicity. These were usually called after their products and there was a Gardner, National or Nat, Kelvin, Invincible and a Peck. The Peck was the invention of Professor Peck of Edinburgh and his engine seems to have been a true diesel, the prototype of which he installed in the Fifie 'Wave'. However the first engine to be installed by fishermen, on their own initiative with their own money, almost certainly was the 7hp Kelvin bought by Mr Robert Robertson and Mr John McIntyre, his father-in-law, of Campbeltown. It was installed in 1907 in their boat the 'Brothers' CN. 97. Gardners were already installing in England and seem to have begun fitting engines in Scotland in 1908 or 1909. The 'Vanguard' of Arbroath was one of the first to have a Gardner.

The original installations were in small boats of up to 30 feet and were required only to propel the vessel to and from the fishing grounds. There was none of the machinery which was to appear on the fishing boats in the 1920's and 1930's and up to 1910 the engines available were only up to 14 horsepower for Kelvins and 55hp for Gardners. What was to give Gardners their ultimate supremacy, apart of course, from the quality of their engines, was the fact that they went in the manufacture of diesel engines about 22 years before Kelvin did. Kelvin persisted with their pioneering petrol/paraffin engine for far too long.

It was a thoroughly reliable engine if the fishermen did what they were supposed to according to the manual. Those who did, swore by them, with good reason, but the petrol/paraffin engine required a source of electricity to fire the mixture in the cylinder. This came from a small generator attached to the engine called a magneto which only performed at its best if properly maintained and kept dry. These gave a great deal of trouble and very many fishermen, particularly on the smaller boats of up to 15 horsepower used to take the magnetos home every day to ensure that they would be dry for the morning. And if the engine stopped at sea for any length of time re-starting was not always possible. There also was the added nuisance of the petrol/paraffin method. It was called that because petrol had to be injected into the cylinder head before it was started, as petrol ignited more easily than the paraffin which the engine normally ran on. It was much more expensive and the principle was that when the engine had been started with the starting handle it was allowed to run on petrol for about half a minute till it was hot and then the fuel was switched over to the paraffin on which it ran for the rest of the day. To stop, the fuel supply was switched off so that the engine ran dry, thus leaving the cylinder empty for the next injection of petrol to start again. If the engine stopped with unburnt paraffin in the carburettor, then starting could be difficult, if not impossible without draining.

Diesel engines, which relied on high pressure on the oil vapour to make it burn, and not electricity, had none of these problems but before the arrival of the electric starter it too had problems all of its own. It was much more expensive than a petrol/paraffin engine and originally was started by heating the fuel with a blowlamp. There was a sealed metal container on the top of the cylinder through which the fuel was led. This chamber, to be called a "hot bulb" because of its shape, was then heated with one or two blowlamps until it was red hot which meant that the temperature was high enough for the engine to fire when it was turned over. This was done with compressed air, from a tank which the engine pumped up when it was running. If the pressure in the tank was too low for any reason it could be pumped manually. Full diesels, without Hot Bulbs, had to be started manually before electric starts were introduced and Gardners up to 112hp had handles which fitted on each end of the engine. These were turned furiously without the full pressure on, otherwise it would have been impossible for them to be moved, and when they were revolving fast enough full compression was engaged by closing a valve and off she went. There were many fires aboard boats in the early days because of the blowlamps igniting rags or the usual oils which were to be found in engine rooms which often were very cramped and difficult to work in. The official name for a Hot Bulb, or Semi-diesel engine, is a Surface Ignition Engine.

Another method of starting an engine before the introduction of the electric starter, which is still in use today, was the Cartridge Start engine. The Petter engine company manufactured them by the thousand, for marine and other uses. Petter introduced their cartridge start in 1923. Most of their production was for uses other than marine but many vessels were supplied with them in spite of the fact that Gardner and Kelvin had a head start on them.

The cartridge itself was made of paper which had been treated with chemicals to make it burn or smoulder for a short time, long enough to ignite the vapourised fuel. The paper fitted into a metal plug which was quickly screwed into the engine as soon as the cartridge had been lit, in the manner of the spark plug. This was left in place as long as the engine was running and removed for the next start when a new cartridge was fitted.

Gardner introduced their first full diesel, as opposed to a semi-diesel, in the 1930's. This could be started from cold by turning the engine with compressed air until it was going fast enough to fire without any form of heating. It was a great step forward, particularly as far as safety was concerned, but it also meant that full diesels could now be easily started, as the electric starter had not yet arrived

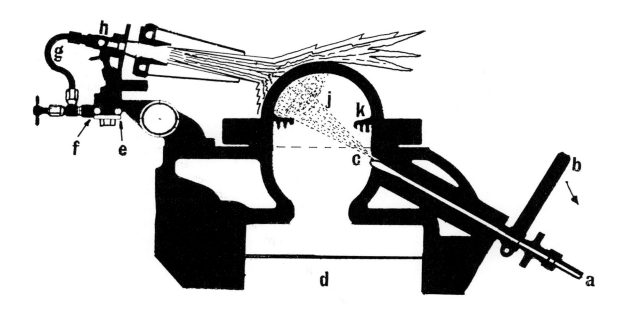

Illustration based on a drawing from "Marine Diesel Engines" by W. MacGibbon
and reproduced by permission of the publishers J. Munro & Co., Glasgow.

The starting method for a Gardner "hot bulb" or "semi diesel" engine c 1920.

(a)   Diesel oil supply to engine.

(b)   Handle for adjusting the direction of the fuel spray inside the cylinder. The fuel was directed into the cylinder once the engine was running.

(c)   Fuel nozzle.

(d)   Piston.

(e)   Paraffin supply pipe to the blowlamp which ran along the length of the engine.

(f)   Compressed air supply pipe which led air through pipe (g) to blowlamp.

(h)   Paraffin supply to blowlamp from pipe.

(j)   Fuel spray directed into "hot bulb" to be preheated by blowlamp.

(k)   Grid which ran around the inside of the "hot bulb" to which the fuel spray was directed at starting and slow speeds as it maintained a higher temperature than the "hot bulb". The engine was turned by compressed air or manually to create the fuel spray after the blowlamp had turned the "hot bulb" red hot.

on board fishing boats. The difference between a full and a semi-diesel, apart from starting them, was that a semi-diesel worked at a lower pressure producing less power, size for size.

The fact that full diesels worked at a higher power made them harder to start and they too required compressed air to get them started.

Kelvin produced their first diesel in 1932 but seemed to have some sort of fixation about petrol because this was a diesel version of the petrol/paraffin engine which was by now used in huge numbers all around the coasts. It too was started on petrol through an ingenious system called a Venturi Box which was fixed on top of the engine. When the diesel itself started the engine sounded as if it had exploded but once that noise passed the engine proved very reliable and numbers were bought by the Navy during the Second World War for use in small landing craft.

When engines were first installed, a 30hp engine was quite adequate for a large Fifie or Zulu and among the first of the large sailing boats to be converted was the 'Crystal River' of Wick which had a Gardner 55hp fitted in 1911. The installation was carried out by Fleetwoods of Lossiemouth and

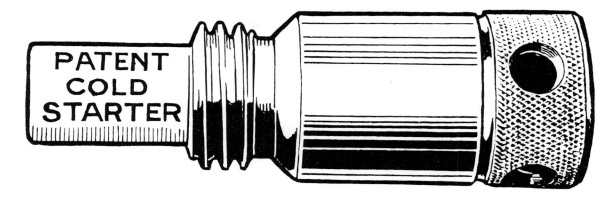

Illustration reproduced by permission of Mr D. W. Edgington, editor, "Stationary Engines".

A Petter cartridge used to start diesel engines. The section marked "Patent Cold Starter" was absorbent paper impregnated with chemicals which burnt like the fuse on a firework when lit. The cartridge was then screwed into an aperture on the cylinder head where the cartridge burnt long enough to ignite the fuel vapour and once it fired compression kept the engine running as normal. The cartridges, one of which was fitted to each cylinder, were left in position until the engine was stopped, when they were removed and recharged. Some mechanics made their own fuses from blotting paper and saltpeter.

Photograph by permission of Mr G. Mackay, Halkirk.

A "hot bulb" engine for a pump with the blow lamp in operation.

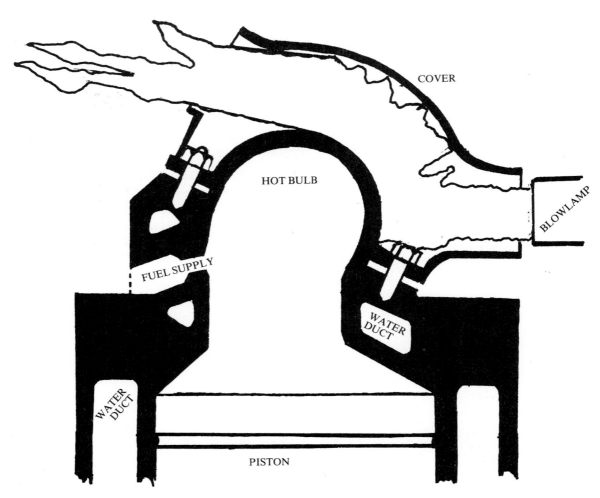

COVER

HOT BULB

BLOWLAMP

FUEL SUPPLY

WATER DUCT

WATER DUCT

PISTON

Illustration based on a drawing from "Marine Diesel Engines" by W. MacGibbon
and reproduced by permission of the publishers J. Munro & Co., Glasgow.

Section of the cylinderhead for a Beardmore "hot bulb" engine.

Henry Fleetwood lived with the Rosie family for two weeks in Wick while he checked that the installation had been successful. The demand for oil engines grew steadily and by 1911 became very brisk. Various ports seemed to identify with a particular engine, Lossiemouth with Gardner and Mac-Duff with Kelvin and so on, depending on which of these companies had an agent nearby. If demand was such that a fisherman could not get the engine he wanted first, then he would take two of smaller horsepower and install them both. Many boats would have two Kelvin 30s or two small Petters when they had originally wanted a 45 or 60 horsepower engine. Where two engines were installed they would have two shafts and propellers and there does not seem to have been an instance where both engines were connected to one shaft.

And it was not uncommon for a boat to have engines of different horsepower, and even different kinds side by side, a situation which came about by fishermen having to fit what was available in the next ten or 15 years when there was a headlong rush from sail.

Boats converted from sail to motor in Wick harbour. In 1902 Macdonald Brothers of Portsoy succeeded in connecting drives from the steam capstan of a large sailboat to a propeller. I have not been able to establish details of how this was done but it seems to have been a system of belts which operated a kind of outboard motor arrangement. A Portsoy boat worked at Stornoway that year with this device, satisfactorily according to newspaper reports.

Photograph by permission of Mr J. Rosie, Thurso.

The large converted Zulu 'Humility' showing the classic white exhaust of the Gardner paraffin engine. There was a considerable thump, or knock, as the engine fired and to offset this, a drip of water was let into the cylinder, timed to the firing stroke. The drip acted as an hydraulic cushion which greatly reduced the knock and was converted to steam by the explosion. The steam had the unintended side benefit of acting as a de-carboniser, which prolonged the working periods of the valves, and was vented through the exhaust, hence the white cloud. The 'Humility' was built in Macduff in 1903.

These installations also hastened the end of the construction of steam drifters and very few were laid down after the First World War. The last steam drifter was to be fitted out in 1932. Ironically enough, the converted sailing boats well outlasted the steam vessels that had caused their downfall originally, and converted Zulus were still fishing from Lerwick long after the last steam drifter burnt her last shovelful. Their longevity, like that of the English sailing trawlers, was due to superb construction.

By 1910 progress had been made with radio to the extent that an aircraft had managed to squeeze one aboard and it was commonplace in passenger, cargo and warships. It was operated by a morse key and all ships with radio had to carry a specialist operator, a luxury that a small fishing boat, particularly one crewed by the owners, could not afford. But the advent of the radio in fishing vessels took its first step on 11th June, 1913 when the steam trawler 'Othello' of the Hellyer fleet of Hull sailed in company with the carrier 'Caesar,' both of which were equipped with Marconi radio sets.

Photograph reproduced by permission of Mr A. G. Credland,
keeper, Town Docks Museum, Kingston upon Hull.

The trawler 'Bardolph' one of the first English vessels to have radio, showing the height of her aerials. The first attempt in European waters at using radio for fishing purposes was by a Dutch trawler in 1905 and two Germans in 1910.

A carrier was a vessel which was used to take the fish, caught by the English trawling fleets, ashore and thus the fishing was not interrupted. There were several reasons why the experiment was carried out in this way, between a trawler and a carrier. The first was that Marconi, who were on the verge of signing a large government contract wanted to test their sets, one of which was a Naval model and the other was military. Hellyers wanted to improve their communications between the trawlers and the carriers because carriers often had to waste time after it had landed the fish, usually in London, finding the fleet again. As often as not it had moved away from the ground they had been working and carriers could be over a day looking for them on the vast grounds of East Anglia.

Both the 'Othello' and 'Caesar' had specially lengthened masts installed to carry the aerials, up to 100 feet in the case of the 'Caesar' and special generators were installed as neither had electricity aboard. Both were lit by carbide lamps. It was hoped that contact could be made at up to 90 miles and radio stations around the coasts of the North Sea were alerted. In the event the maximum range was over 270 miles and the Admiralty station at Cullercoats picked up the contact between the boats clearly. Within three months, 60 sets had been installed, all in English trawlers or carriers and the installation of radio stands as a milestone to the fact that developments in the fishing industry were now clearly no longer going to be based on the knowledge and experience of fishermen, but the training and calculations of scientists. And the minds of these scientists were to be wonderfully concentrated by the events of the following five years, and advances in knowledge were made which were to be to the long term benefit of the fishermen.

The scientists were, of course, working towards the short term detriment of the enemy but among other things they established was that a hydrophone, a kind of radio receiver, could pick up the sound of a submarine engines. This discovery was taken a step further and they found that it was possible to actually send out a radio signal and pick it up again with this receiver as it bounced back from a solid object, like a submarine or the sea bottom. As with all experimental equipment it was very crude by comparison with its successors. In the beginning the equipment could only be used if the vessel was stationary, as the noise of the bubbles travelling along a moving hull made reception impossible to interpret. The operator had to wear a pair of headphones to pick up the return signal and he had to have specialist radio training to make sense of what he was hearing. Before long the London instrument makers, Henry Hughes and Son, were able to improve on this apparatus and made an instrument which was to revolutionise fish finding. No longer would fishermen have to hang piano wires over the side to feel for herring or find the grounds with a lead line. Hughes had made the echometer, but its widespread use was still some time away.

Photograph by permission of the Imperial War Museum, London.

Normally drifters steaming with their mizzens set meant that they were proceeding to the fishing ground. This is the British Drifter Flotilla in the Straits of Otranto in 1917. The equipment in the foreground is an early hydrophone.

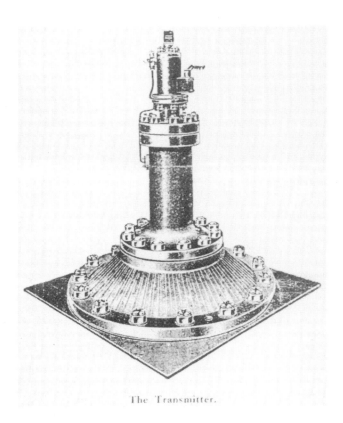

The Transmitter.

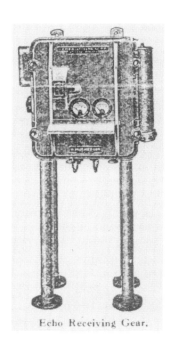

Echo Receiving Gear.

The Echo-sounding gear manufactured by Kelvin Hughes, fitted to the 'St Endelion'.

In 1916 American navy wireless operators succeeded in improving on the work of the Reginald Fessinden when they managed to transmit and receive the spoken word at sea. Radio had come a long way in ten years or so and in the same year the German Army began forces broadcasts to their troops on the Western Front. The enormous significance of this achievement soon became apparent. An operator did not need to know the morse code, which could easily become difficult to follow with the interference of those days. The interference was of course just as bad for speech but at least a man with no training could make sense of what was being said. There was no possibility of that happening with Morse transmissions. The installation of the new radio telephone was delayed for another 12 years or so because the early sets were very bulky and required either battery or mains power to operate them, and neither were aboard fishing vessels till nearly 1930.

During the First World War Scottish fishermen served by the thousand, with 3591 men from the fishing industry entering the forces in 1914 alone. In total 1249 fishing boats were either volunteered or requisitioned, comprising 302 steam trawlers, 838 steam drifters and 109 motor boats, all of which had been converted from sale. Twenty thousand fishermen were on duty, either on active service or on general service at naval bases, out of a total of 25,000 from the fishing industry who were in uniform. Conscription had been introduced in 1916 to replace the horrendous losses in the trenches but most had volunteered by then. Even English sailing trawlers were fitted with small guns for anti-submarine duties and they succeeded in sinking at least two U-boats.

Fishing boats were stationed all around the coasts with large concentrations serving the battle fleets at Rosyth, Invergordon and above all Scapa Flow. Huge minefields were laid in the North Sea and were never properly swept at the end of hostilities. The result was a heavy toll of men and boats for some years after the war with hardly a month passing without the news of a fishing boat

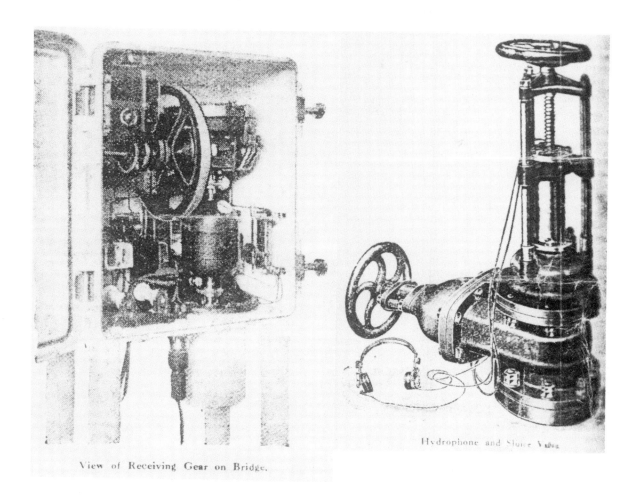

Hydrophone and Sluice Valve

View of Receiving Gear on Bridge.

disappearing, always to a mine. Although most of the Scottish boats were stationed at Scapa and Invergordon quite a few were as far away as North Africa and the Mediterranean Sea.

In the autumn and early winter of 1914 a large number of fishing boats, both drifters and trawlers, had been entered into service at Scapa Flow and there they served in various capacities. Among them were anti-submarine, ferry, minelaying, minesweeping and gunlaying duties. The gunlaying involved acting as spotters for the heavily armed ships during gunnery practice, much of which was conducted using the rock of Suil Sgeir as a target.

Ten days after hostilities were declared a flotilla was in position and one of the drifters was ordered to circle the rock to see that there were no vessels in the line of fire. It did so and returned to signal that all was clear when one of the crew, Mr George Simpson, of the well known Wick shipping and curing family thought he saw a movement on the rock itself. A check revealed that there were men from Carloway in Lewis collecting gugas and they did not know that there was a war on. They had been within a blink of an eye of being blown to pieces.

On the night of 22nd/23rd November, 1914 the U18, under command of Kapitänleutnant Heinrich von Hennig was on station east of Kirkwall trying to find a way into Scapa Flow where the Grand Fleet was, with a view to sinking as many ships as possible. As he proceeded south on the flood tide towards the mouth of the Pentland Firth he decided to attempt an attack through the southern entrance to the Flow, through Hoxa Sound, and he calculated that he would arrive at the Pentland Skerries just as the tide turned to ebb west through the Firth. He was on the surface,

Photograph by permission of the National Maritime Museum.

The U18 which ran ashore after collision with the 'Dorothy Gray'.

replenishing his air and charging his batteries when the lighthouses came on, indicating that the Fleet was sailing. In wartime, lighthouses were extinguished unless friendly shipping was passing, which knowledge U-Boats put to deadly use in both wars. He navigated to the Skerries Light, submerged at slack water and turned into the Firth.

The Pentland Firth is one of the most hazardous seas in the world for surface ships, in daylight, who can see clearly as they navigate among the islands so the dangers to a primitive submerged submarine trying to go round the islands are hair curling with all the eddies, cross tides, swirls and currents. These were increased by the fact that the waters were patrolled and kept under observation from shore stations.

He reached Swona, which was inhabited by the Rosie family at the time, at dawn, and entered Hoxa Sound at 11 am to see only a few destroyers and trawlers through his periscope. None of these offered him a target worth risking his boat and crew for so he turned at 11.20 to position himself to attack two destroyers which were coming out and would be in his line of fire shortly, further south in the relatively open waters of the Pentland Firth.

However, his periscope had been seen by the steamer 'Tokio' and she had given the alarm. The destroyers that Von Hennig had seen moving were actually the first of the flotilla coming to attack him. They were followed by other destroyers and several trawlers, among which was the Peterhead trawler 'Dorothy Gray', PD 533, under the command of Skipper Alexander Youngson. There are two versions of what happened. The official one is that the 'Dorothy Gray' proceeded with the flotilla and pursued the U18 at eight knots. The unofficial version, given to me by an eyewitness was that the trawler had been in Longhope having her engine repaired and most of her crew were ashore when Action Stations were given. She sailed with only five men aboard, limping along at about three to four knots, rapidly falling behind the rest of the flotilla, which were doing seven or eight.

Course of U18 on the night of 22nd/23rd November 1914 based on information provided by Mr R. M. Coppock, Naval Staff Duties (Foreign Documents Section), Ministry of Defence, London.

The U18 lay deep as the anti-submarine patrol rounded Switha and fanned out across the open water in a general south-westerly sweep, passing over her. Von Hennig waited patiently till the noise of their propellers faded into the distance, coming to periscope depth now and again to check both where the flotilla was and where the tides were putting him. He was about 1¼ miles south-west of Hoxa Head, came up yet again to periscope depth, when the U-Boat was struck a tremendous blow which knocked her on her beam ends and bent her telescope at right angles. She had come to the surface under the stem head of the 'Dorothy Gray' whose slow turning propeller no-one had detected. The 'Dorothy Gray' ran into the U-Boat rather than rammed it deliberately and the shock dislocated the hydrophone motor and the reserve steering gear. According to Youngson's report he chased the U-Boat for 12 minutes before ramming it, but there is no explanation officially why the other vessels did not join in the hunt, as Youngson would have been duty bound to report that he had detected one. Nor is there an explanation why the flotilla was so far away from him. Whatever happened, Von Hennig was now submerged in a blind, disabled U-Boat in the Pentland Firth, while on the surface the 'Dorothy Gray' was blowing her siren to attract the attention of the others who were mostly at Dunnet Head. She succeeded and as the leading destroyers raced back Von Hennig tried dead reckoning navigation to get him to the east and the relative safety of the Moray Firth. He hit a rock at a depth of 160 feet, shot to the surface, was rammed by the trawler 'Kaphreda,' which damaged the deck slightly and he dived again with the whole flotilla gathered round him. Somehow he shook them off and must have thought he was clear when he ran into the Pentland Skerries. This time her hull was breached and Von Hennig had to surface, flying a white flag to prevent attack. The flotilla was three miles away and took some time to notice him. Two destroyers rushed over and Von Hennig and his crew surrendered. The Admirality Prize Court awarded the skipper and crew of the 'Dorothy Gray' £500 as opposed to the £200 normally paid for sinking or capturing a submarine. The money was divided as follows; Master £70; mate £20; CPO £20; £16 to each of the four Petty Officers; £8 to each of the four Able bodied seamen; £6 each to the two deckhands, two engine hands and the coal trimmer.

Photograph by permission of Mr R. More, Wick.

Rab More of Wick in a typical pose taken of naval recruits. When this photograph was taken in March 1915 he was 17 years old. He later became skipper of the 'Alert' and rarely did a man have a vessel so suitably named both to her appearance and his character.

The following summer 16 Peterhead drifters were fishing on the Shetland grounds when a U-Boat surfaced among them. The captain ordered them all to take to the lifeboats with the exception of the drifter 'Archimedes' whom he instructed to follow him as he sunk the fleet in turn by gunfire. As each sank he allowed the 'Archimedes' to pick up the crew before turning his attention to the next drifter. The 'Archimedes' picked up 160 men of whom only one had been slightly injured by shrapnel and the U-Boat commander apologised for sinking the boats before leaving the scene. All the survivors were taken to Lerwick where they were landed.

Photograph by permission of the Imperial War Museum.

The drifter 'Belos' on active service flying the white ensign and with her foremast removed. She appears to be acting as a ferry.

Photograph by permission of the Imperial War Museum, London.

Battleships exercising in Scapa Flow during the First World War. It was for vessels such as these that the many fishing boats acted as tenders and ferries.

Ilustration by permission of Mr J. Gatt, Fraserburgh.

The special permit issued to Mr Benjamin Noble of Fraserburgh to fish in a prohibited military area during the First World War. It was subsequently cancelled towards the end of the war.

Less than two years later the drifter 'Gowan Lea,' under command of skipper Joseph Watt of Gardenstown, was on patrol in with the Drifter Line in the Straits of Otranto. The Drifter Line was a flotilla of about 30 drifters which carried out patrol or minesweeping duties. On the morning of the 15th May, 1917 this line was attacked by a group of Austrian destroyers and two light cruisers. One of the cruisers came within 100 yards of the 'Gowan Lea' and ordered skipper Watt to stop and abandon his vessel. Undeterred by the fact that the Austrians could have blown him out of the water with their secondary armament, in reply to which he might have been able to break their wheelhouse windows with his three-pounder, skipper Watt rang full speed ahead, ordered three cheers and a fight to the finish.

The cruiser was then engaged but after one shot had been fired the 'Gowan Lea's' gun either jammed or was hit. Under very heavy fire the gun crew tried to get it operational again but the cruisers superior speed carried her away to the rest of the fight in which 14 drifters were to be sunk. Skipper Watt, unable to take any part in the actual fighting then went among the damaged and sinking drifters to recover the surviving wounded and the dead. The arrival of the British Cruisers 'Dartmouth' and 'Bristol,' put an end to the one-sided battle and Skipper Watt was awarded the Victoria Cross for his courage.

The exploits of the Scottish fishermen, in both world wars, would fill two books the size of this, by themselves, but for the moment the matter has to be rested with the comment that they contributed as much in life, limb and suffering as any section of the population involved in the wars. They were blown up, mined, torpedoed, shelled, rammed, machine gunned, and always gave as good as they got, often from very disadvantageous circumstances because of the incredible way in which the navy was managed. Those who served in the large ships, such as battleships and cruisers, suffered along with the rest of the crew, the very poor accommodation, the arrogance of the officers and in-

Photograph by permission of the Imperial War Museum.

The Austrian cruiser 'Saida' one of those which attacked the drifter line at Otranto in May 1917.

different catering facilities. Food had to be snatched as the opportunity presented itself and there was no guarantee when the next meal would be served if a ship was on patrol or in action. When action stations were sounded for the Battle of Jutland Mr Marcus MacIvor of Wick was about to have a meal and, not knowing when he would eat again, quickly scooped it into his hat and fought the battle with two fried eggs on his head.

The First World War introduced social and industrial upheaval of a kind that the world had not seen before, either on such a scale or in such a short time. And in that short time the world had shrunk to the extent that where previously new ideas used to take generations to spread among whomsoever it might affect, information was now passing around in months or a couple of years at most. Slow by modern standards but still at very high speed in comparison with conditions that had existed ten years before. Everything was changing, politically, socially, industrially, and commercially. Industrial change was everywhere. Cars, lorries, even electricity was beginning to spread across and out from the large cities, and fishermen returning from the large naval bases had seen the convenience of such developments at close hand.

The social change was equally widespread. There had been a revolution in Russia and people were hearing this word "socialism" for the first time, as opposed to the old "liberalism" to which so many of the fishermen had been attracted. Because of war, the fishing communities had come in contact with the world outside their industry in a personal way that otherwise would not have been possible. Till then, in spite of the far flung range over which fishermen travelled, from Shetland, even Iceland, to Holland, their contacts had all been within their trade and about their trade. That, in a changing world, was now in the past. New ideas, or old ideas in new guises, began to find expression in the years immediately after the war, and these ideas were a curiously mixed lot.

Photograph by permission of Mr J. G. Addison, Cullen.

The 'Gowanlea' with which Joseph Watt won his Victoria Cross.

Photograph by permission of Mr C. Dey, Fraserburgh.

A group of Fraserburgh veterans of the First World War taken with Skipper Joseph Watt, VC. They are, from the back row, left to right: W. Addison, W. Wright, A. Mair, J. Summers, J. Noble, A. Noble, J. Finlay, A. Colvin, A. Barclay, J. Watt, J. Milne. Middle row: J. McHardy, G. Walker, A. Davidson, J. McLeman, J. Barclay, F. M. McLaughlin, A. Watt, J. McMaster, J. Noble. Front row: J. Fraser, W. Duthie, J. Mitchell, H. Pressley, A. McGee, Lord Saltoun, J. Sim, J. Watt, VC, J. Carle, W. Ingram, S. Gordon.

Photograph by permission of Mr J. Mackenzie, Wick.

The three pounder gun installed aboard the Wick motor boat 'J D Fletcher' about 1916. The crew had not yet been issued with uniforms and are Jim Farmer, Wick; William Mackenzie, Wick, sighting along the gun; and Jim Miller of Keiss with the shell. Lieutenant Hopkins is the officer and the double row of balls are the parleys which ran up the mast as the sail was hoisted. An ammunition box lies open.

Photograph by permission of Mrs W. Sutherland, Wick.

All kinds of small vessels were used by the Navy as ferries, tenders, minesweepers and examination vessels. Here the whale catcher 'Ramna', on patrol in Scapa Flow, has gained the unenviable situation of being stranded on another ship. She is perched on the German Battle-cruiser 'Moltke' which had been scuttled shortly before. The 'Ramna' was successfully refloated.

Photograph by permission of Mr R. More, Wick.

Lord Kitchener, watched by Admirals Madden and Jellicoe, boards the 'Mayberry'.

Photograph by permission of Mr R. More, Wick.

The Wick drifter 'Mayberry' comes alongside the 'Iron Duke' to take Lord Kitchener on his fateful journey aboard the 'Hampshire'. She was skippered by James More of Wick, father of Rab More.

Among them were a religious movement, the creation of a national association and prohibition, and above all, a variation on a well known theme, which was to change the fishing industry for all time coming.

The end of hostilities saw a large number of men and boats coming home in 1918 and 1919 and the Admirality returned the boats in one of two ways. Either a refit would be carried out by the Admirality at shipyards in Peterhead, Fraserburgh, Wick, Inverness, Ardrossan or Buckie or the owners were given a cash grant to carry out the refit themselves. As replacements for boats which had been lost the Government had built a number of drifters, both in this country and Canada, which were for sale to bona fide fishermen who had been in the war. They could be bought on hire purchase, repayable over 12 years at 5% if required. Some of the original pipe shank drifters, small by comparison with the big Standard drifters, so called because they had been built to a Government standard, had also been bought by the Government, and converted to oil for sale in the same way. The opportunity to buy vessels on hire purchase was something new for Scottish fishermen who till then either paid cash from their savings, with a balance coming from a bank loan for which their homes were put up as security. There was a very high percentage of home ownership among fishermen, the highest of any section of working classes, and they could borrow from the bank at ½% less than the usual rate to buy a boat.

Illustration by permission of the editor, "Fishing News".

Advertisement in the "Fishing News" of 22nd June, 1929.

There had been a loan scheme for the purchase of motor engines to be installed in sailing vessels and this was extended in 1920 to include the purchase of engines for new boats but there was comparatively little new boat construction in the black and unsettled years of the 1920's. In fact the industry was to remain in a state of uncertainty for the next 20 years. 1919 saw the resumption of the East Anglian fishing after an interruption of five years and in October of that year the Marconi company announced the resumption of wireless transmissions to the fishing fleet after it had been suspended early in the war. In modern times the price was at the rate of about £5 a word but this only affected the English trawlers as no Scottish vessel is recorded as having a radio before 1920.

The number of men fishing from Scotland in 1920 was about 36,300 with the vast majority of them herring fishermen concentrated in 854 steam drifters and 1947 motor boats. Of these motor boats 816 were white fishing and nearly all were engaged in small line fishing in the vicinity of their own ports. And with the exception of the large Zulus and Fifies which had been converted to motor, they were mainly between 18 and 35 feet long. There were also 4658 sailing vessels with no engines but again they were nearly all yawls apart from a few die-hards who struggled on with the big boats which were now 20 years old or more.

Fig. 73.   Scottish Drifter Owner inspecting a 160 B.H.P. Atomic Diesel

Photograph by permission of Petter Diesels, Middlesex.

An advertisement from the Petter catalogue of 1932 showing a Scottish skipper inspecting one of their 160 BHP Atomic Diesel engines at their Yeovil works. It was supplied with a telegraph for communication with the engineroom. Under the terms of the Merchant Shipping Act of 1894, section 413, a certificate of competency was required for men in command of vessels of 25 tons and above. Men who were skippers when the legislation was introduced were automatically awarded one.

With the majority of fishermen still concentrated in herring fishing, the market soon fell apart for a variety of reasons and the Government had to step in in 1921 and buy up about 250,000 unsold barrels of herring to prevent a large number of curers, and thence fishermen from being ruined. In spite of this was considerable unemployment but it was not as bad as it might have been without the intervention. The main reasons were that of the two main pre-war customers, Germany had been crushed economically and was being further humiliated by France's demands for war reparations or compensation. Russia was in a civil war and was in such a state of disorder that traditional trade links with Scotland were either severed or debts not honoured. In 1919 the trawler 'John Jefferson,' serving as a cargo vessel, put into Riga with 1700 barrels of herring from Scottish curers when a Bolshevik force arrived, took all the herring and departed, leaving the crew congratulating themselves that their lives had not been taken. The herring of course was never paid and through this and other incidents, curers began to go out of business at an accelerating rate in the next two years. And in 1920, stuck away in a corner of the Fishery Board Report for that year, was something that was hardly worth mentioning when set against the scale of the herring, trawl and line fishings. It was that in 1919, 5000 cwt of seined fish, all plaice, had been landed in Scotland. They had not been caught by a seine net as it is known today, but by the traditional method of using a net without a bag in it.

Photograph by permission of Lossiemouth Museum.

A dog skin buoy of the kind used by the thousand. Farms specially bred terriers, collies and labradors for use on lines and herring nets.

The winter of 1919 was one of mixed fortunes and the *Fishing News* ran an editorial recommending that a fishing college along the lines of that which had been established in Seattle in the United States, would be a great boon to the industry. It could see that the new technology, although it was not calling the innovation that, required a more formal approach than the traditional father to son training. Some time was to pass before any attention was paid to that suggestion. The fishermen themselves had been occupied with getting nets out of stores, boats, some of which had been lying for four years, reconditioned and generally adjusting to civilian life after the hair raising experiences of the sea or in the trenches to which many had been drafted to make up the losses incurred during the slaughter of the major battles. The first of their troubles came with a coal famine in Wick, just as the winter fishing started in January 1920, which came about because the Highland Railway Company did not have enough trucks to move coal north and many drifters from the south, particularly Buckie, Banff and Peterhead were stuck at Wick. A situation which was made worse by the knowledge that the winter herring stocks were good as the few motor boats and sailing boats able to get to sea were demonstrating. Men who had just been through four years of war, and had seen the mismanagement of that at close quarters from a class whose social position above them they had rarely questioned before now, took a different attitude. As was to become more noticeable in the next half century, the fishermen saw that organisation was necessary of a kind that they had not created before; and one which would bring pressure to bear on the Government.

There had been fishermens organisations for at least 50 years before but they had been a form of mutual associations and, until the advent of trawlers, who were not in them, they worked fairly well as self-regulating bodies. Their main purpose had been to create a forum where fishermen could discuss their problems, provide assistance to widows or orphans and their activities were usually confined to their own fishing districts. One very important aspect is that they regulated the fishings in times of heavy landings by limiting the amount of herring nets a boat would use to prevent large catches remaining unsold. Governmental bodies usually ignored their existence in a formal sense but did occasionally invite spokesmen to give evidence to inquiries such as the Commission on Trawling. These invitations were few and far between as a rule and the fishermen, apart from localised protests to curers whom they knew, took no part in the marketing side of the industry in the sense that they had automatic access to decision-making at government level. They have very little now, but at least the modern methods of communications means that they are noticed more than they were in the past. From what I have seen, letters to press and evidence given to various inquiries and boards by fishermen in the 1880's who generally left school when they were 11 or 12, had a dignity and logic far superior to anything in the last 20 years. One such is as follows and it must be borne in mind that when this was written there was no state welfare of any kind and families fed or starved according to what the fishing was like.

To the Editor
Northern Ensign
Wick

Dear Sir,
    A meeting of fishermen was held here this evening to consider the system of trawling and the evil which follows from all kind of trawling. It is well known to all concerned that trawling is only in its infancy on this coast yet, and if it continues much longer we cannot tell what may be the result. At this date in former years we have sent hundreds of barrels and boxes of fresh cod to the English market, besides many hundreds of barrels of pickled cod. While, as at this date, this season, there has only been one and one half barrel of cod cured on the Latheron coast, and not one fish sent away in a fresh state. The reason is that we cannot put a line into the sea on account of trawlers of every description being at work on our fishing grounds and we ask where are we going to get redress for our grievances. To the legislature we need not apply for they are already aware of what destruction has been done to net and line fishing on every coast where trawling has been prosecuted. I think it is worse than useless to apply to our MP for giving us any support in our difficulties as he recommended Sabbath fishing a few years ago. Steam trawlers suit his purpose. It is shameful and degrading to see, as we see from our doors, the Lords Day being desecrated by these people, a sight unseen and unknown to us heretofore. We wonder have the rulers of our land can boast of their Civilisation and Christianity when such nefarious work as trawling is allowed to be carried out on the whole of the Sabbath day. The heathen whom we despise can do no more.

    It is well known that it is from our fishings that we pay our high rents for our crofts and homes and supporting and bringing up our families. If we are to be deprived of our July and August fishings by trawlers, as we have been of our winter fishings, there is nothing else to be looked for but wholesale pauperism and starvation. We cannot give any other name to trawling as far as we have seen of it yet, but the besom of destruction.

    Hoping Mr Editor, you may give this a corner of your first issue or whenever space allows.

We are yours etc,
Forss Fishermen,
Forss, Lybster, Latheron. 22nd February, 1884.

It might be noted that 1000 people emigrated from that district between 1899 and 1910.
    Letters such as these, and in similar vein, were still being written in 1920 because although domestic trawlers had been banned from inshore waters foreign trawlers had not. However, the protests had come either from individuals, or district associations, which did not have a central organisation or purpose. The Fraserburgh and District Fishermens Union realised that one voice to represent fishermen in these unsettled times was necessary and took the initiative by inviting all the local

associations around the coast to attend a conference in Aberdeen on 18th March, 1920. There the Scottish Drift Net and Line Fishermen's Association was formed and it took the historic step of appointing a full-time secretary in the person of Mr James McIntosh at a salary of £350 a year.

The conference had come about as a result of a dispute, originally, among fishermen about when to start the herring fishing the previous year, the result of which it had been delayed by two weeks. The Fraserburgh men had realised that a national organisation might prevent this sort of thing happening again and would also allow views to be heard on such things as the price of coal, boats, quotas, foreign trawling, the landing of west coast herring on the east coast, thus upsetting the market and above all, the prices themselves.

As has been said the markets in Eastern Europe for herring were very uncertain, and in fact were to get worse. The Government had introduced a price support scheme guaranteeing the curers a price of 45/- per barrel for any herring that they were left with. This of course did not help the fishermen all that much as the curers bought the herring on the assumption that they would only get the government price and so kept their price to the fishermen low to ensure that they made a profit. And if they got a higher price than the guarantee so much the better. The fishermen wanted this changed so that the guaranteed price was raised to 60/- a cran and paid to the fishermen rather than the curers. It was not till the Second World War that a controlled and guaranteed price was paid for fish.

Scottish fishermen were not alone in their objection to foreign trawlers, as the week following the conference news arrived that lumpers, or fish handlers, at Grimsby had refused to handle fish landed by Dutch trawlers. The situation regarding foreign trawlers was at the farcical stage because they were allowed to land fish if they had been caught outside British waters. They were permitted to fish inside British limits, closed to British trawlers, but they were not allowed to land any fish taken from

Photograph from the Johnston Collection by permission of the Wick Society.

A typical hull style of Scandinavian vessels on which the Scottish hull of the 1930's came to be modelled. This particular vessel was a Norwegian interned in Wick in 1940 on suspicion of being a German spy.

British waters in this country. Three weeks before the formation of the Scottish Association, the Norwegian trawler 'Brim,' K25, had ominously come into Aberdeen and coaled and provisioned for a fishing trip, which the agents stated would be outside British waters. As she had been the first Norwegian trawler to come into Aberdeen for some years before the war, this was regarded with deep suspicion.

Other signs of how times were moving were visible in the month of March, 1920. On the 24th the drifter/trawler 'Prime' landed trawled fish at Buckie without provoking any trouble. A little earlier and there would have been a most hostile reaction but the general uncertainty in the herring fishing was causing the industry to look again at what else was happening. The numbers are not certain, but there seems to have been about 30 or 40 steam drifters fitting out for trawling and the Peterhead firm of J. Mitchell and Sons acquired a third trawler the 'Inchkeith', in addition to the 'Adventure' and 'Setter' that they already owned.

During the months of February and March Mr Stephen West of Macduff installed 75hp Gardners in 'Racer,' the 'Cedar' and the 'Banffshire,' all of which had been sail powered previously. Fishermen could now choose from a very wide range of makes, horsepower and arrangements. There were the two which dominated the market, Gardner for the larger boats and Kelvin for the smaller, as a general rule. Also available were Gleffifer, which used the slogan "The Fisherman's Friend" presumably without objection from the manufacturers of the throat lozenge because there was very little chance of fishermen mixing up the products; the popular Petter, Hercules, Thornycroft, Ailsa Craig, Atlantic, Alpha, Djinn, Invincible, Beardmore, Vickers, Vickers/Petter, Grei, Wolverine, Tucson, Astor, Kromhaut, Wasp, Bolinder, Penta and Parsons. Quite a few boats were called after the engine in them and there was a Gardner, several Kelvins, a Nat, a William Beardmore, an Invincible and a Kelvin Spark. There were other engines available and they covered a range of fuel from kerosene, to paraffin to thick crude oil and were started by handles, blowlamps, compressed air or slow burning cartridges.

Very few boats had a gear box and the propeller turned at the same speed as the engine, as did the propellers on the steam drifters. They could be put in or out of gear ahead, but to come astern the direction of the crankshaft had to be reversed. In a steam vessel this was a simple affair of reducing steam pressure till the engine stopped turning, throwing over a lever to reverse the flow of steam, and increase pressure again. In a motor boat without a gear box the engine had to be stopped, levers thrown over to change the flow of the fuel and the engine restarted, an operation which might have to be carried out at a high speed in a congested harbour. Signals between the skipper and the engine room on a steam drifter were sent on a telegraph where the skipper turned a pointer to a scale and this was connected to a similar scale in the engine room where another pointer showed his command. On motor boats the instructions were shouted with varied degrees of success from the wheelhouse depending on whether the engine was fitted forward or aft. That too would change for the better in the fullness of time.

1920 was also witness to the first, but regretably not the last, time that Scotland was to imitate something that happened far away and in a manner that was out of character. On 28th October, 1919, the Federal Government of the United States of America passed a law prohibiting the manufacture or sale of alcohol. This had not been by any manner of means a sudden decision as the prohibition movement had been in existence for some 30 years. As indeed the temperance movement in this country had been for even longer.

It was of course a reaction to heavy and widespread drinking among the working classes. Not that they drank any more heavily than legal, medical or religious professions, it was just that there were more of them and in consequence were more obvious.

The temperance movement received a great boost from the American decision and succeeded in having a referendum held under the Temperance (Scotland) Act. This allowed a poll in the 563 districts of Scotland to be held among electors, and if 35% or more voted in favour of prohibition then all licensed premises would be closed from May of 1921. Of the districts, 36 voted for "No Licence" from the choice that they had of "No Licence," "limited licence" and "No change." In the Moray Firth area on 14th December, 1920, Wick, Buckie, Cullen and Findochty alone voted to go dry. The size of the vote surprised everybody and delighted the support.

A huge thanksgiving meeting was held in the Breadalbane Hall in Wick and they cheered on a large platform party of ministers who proceeded to regale the audience with three hours of prayers and hymn singing. Telegrams of congratulations came from all over the country, especially from Thurso and Lybster who were both going to make a fortune in the coming 27 years from thirsty Wickers. Of course illicit distilling and shebeens sprang up before the ink on the order was dry and they soon outnumbered the 29 pubs, hotels, clubs and licensed grocers that had been prevented from selling drink, legally. The shebeeners and distillers displayed an ingenuity in the manufacture and sale of their products which would have made Chicago gangsters stand back in amazement, but that is another story. The claims of those in favour of retaining the licence, that abolition would affect trade, did have a little credence, as many fishermen from both the other side of the Moray Firth, and pioneer Danish seiners went to Lybster in the 30's where they knew they could get a drink. As a foot-note to this episode it might be added that Buckie did not stay dry for long. The sharp eyed, and no doubt public spirited, Mr J. B. Ross of Low Street noticed that the poll was 98 votes short of the required total and had the Buckie decision reversed in the High Court. This was in the face of opposi-tion from prohibitionists who maintained that he should have challenged the results within the statutory period, and not waited till July.

But 1920 was also the year in which Scottish fishing was to change direction for ever, although it was not apparent at the time. When the Scots went to Yarmouth that year, they followed their usual custom of fishing their way down, and had got into the habit of putting into the great English ports between Shields and Lowestoft. There they saw the strange looking Danish fishing boats, which the English called "snibbies" because of their canoe shaped bow, mainly in Hull and Grimsby. They were using a new concept of an old idea, and were catching their fish with a seine net which had been altered by the addition of a bag, very like that of a trawl net. It was very similar in all respects to a trawl except that it was smaller, lighter and did not need the boards or beams that trawlers used to keep the net open as it fished. The beam held the mouth of a beam trawl open, and the other boards were like the wings of an aircraft and kept the mouth of the otter trawl open, as if two otters swam alongside holding it. Seine nets were so light in comparison, and had more buoyancy from the corks and buoys on the top lip of the net, that they would stay open even when they were being hauled very slowly, as they were in the beginning. The strength of the tide flowing through them was enough. But they had an even greater attraction than that, inasmuch as they could be shot and hauled in an hour, something that could not be done with a trawl. This required up to five hours between hauls and the point was not lost on the men who had encountered the Danish seine for the first time. Till then, when they had not been herring fishing, they had only been trawling. The Danes had made them aware of the potential.

And if they were to believe all they read, there was potential everywhere. Earlier that year in March the *Fishing News* carried a long story about a Captain Lybeck of New York who had con-ceived an entirely new approach to fishing. He was going to build a ship with three decks and hollow masts, although it was not clear what they were for. It would carry a spotter plane to locate fish shoals and guide the ship to it. Once it had made contact with the shoal it would steam through it and scoop up the fish on to a conveyer where they would travel inboard to be sorted and processed by the crew. About ten tenders would be alongside at any given moment to speed off with the catch to the nearest market where it would be sold cheaply to the unemployed and would in fact help to create work. Nothing would be wasted as the skins would be cured and made into hatbands. The only snag was that Captain Lybeck needed £10,000 and the *Fishing News* gives no hint of the reponse he got.

Things were not much better for those at home either, as bad weather had made seining from yawls, which was exclusively for plaice from Aberdeen and the surrounding villages, almost impossible. The only fishings which were holding their own was trawling. This was being conducted either by purpose built Aberdeen trawlers or by drifters who had had a poor season and the owners were struggling to keep going. There was a steady stream of prosecutions, and convictions, in Aber-deen Sheriff Court, of trawl skippers for illegal fishing, the most of whom came from Peterhead. The price of white fish was good and much steadier than that for herring and with the uncertainty of the times, offered the prospect of a much better living to fishermen. However, the traditions died very hard indeed and it took another 40 years before the last of the traditionalists either admitted defeat or retired from the herring fishing.

In November 1920 there were 27 yawls seining from Aberdeen but already there were hints of agitation against them because, small though their boats and nets were, they were beginning to clash with the line and creel men in places such as Johnshaven, Gourdon and Ferryden.

Most of the trouble grew from the fact that there was no clear legislation to cater for seine net fishing in this manner as the existing laws all dealt with trawling. Trawlers were banned from the

The 'White Wing' of Gourdon, so typical of the kind of vessel which began the seine net fishing along the east coast in the early 1920's.

An oil mast headlamp used before the advent of electricity.

coasts but the legislation specifically stated beam or other trawls and a seine net had neither. Nor did it have a bag, for this was not to appear until about a year later when the first Lossiemouth fisherman to take an interest in seining after the Danish fashion, brought one back from Grimsby. Dissatisfaction from both seine net and line fishermen grew over the closing months of the year and representations were made to the Fishery Board for Scotland, particularly by Arbroath and Johnshaven men, to do something. They, through pressure both from the local associations and the rapidly expanding Association, announced on 4th December 1920, that an enquiry was to be held into the possibility of opening Carnoustie and St Andrews bays to seine flouder net fishing. Co-incidentally or not, a branch of the Fishermen's Association was formed in Anstruther on 18th December, one of the last areas to be so organised. And so the year which most people were glad to see the back of, closed. 15,000 cwt of seined fish, all plaice, had been landed in the 12 months.

A line hauler aboard a Gourdon boat. 1985.

1921 opened to find an enterprising Mr Dudleigh offering fishermen a choice of 300 different designs of boat, ranging from 14 feet to 65 feet, at very reasonable prices. What was new about Mr Dudleigh was that he was offering them in kit form for the fisherman to assemble himself. He also guaranteed to refund all money within seven days if the customer was not absolutely delighted with his boat. The *Fishing News* mused that perhaps fishermen would be as well to consult with a naval architect before rushing to buy from Mr Dudleigh. 1921, and the following 15 years was not a good time to try to sell boats.

The winter fishings were poor and this soon made itself known in the shape of unemployment. At the end of April there were 16,200 coopers, fishermen, carters and other trades looking for work, and this figure did not take account of gutters.

As early as January ominous signs were flying, not from the event itself, but from what it implied to those concerned. On 14th January, Buckie fish curers and merchants had sent 30 wagons full of kippered and fresh herring to London with the purpose of it arriving on Saturday 15th. For some reason the railway company missed connections and the train did not reach Billingsgate till 12 hours after it closed, with the result that the consignment had to lie till Monday morning in unrefrigerated trucks. Most of the fish was unsaleable and the merchants incurred a huge loss. They called a special meeting in Buckie to see what could be done about improving the railway service and recovering some of the loss, but do not seem to have achieved anything. The loss remained and became another straw on the camels back. Herring, by the way, were retailing in London at 2d per lb., which was lower than the price in 1913.

In February, the month by which time the traditional cod net fishing was usually in full swing,

Photograph by permission of Mr J. G. Addison, Cullen.

Hauling cod nets. The great cod grounds were between Sarclet in Caithness, and Golspie; off Aberdour Bay, Troup Head, and Troup Knock Head. Cod were sold by the score, 20, and were marketed fresh, salted, pickled or smoked.

there was a great deal of trouble between local boats and foreign trawlers. In some ports no start had been made at all because the fishermen were afraid of suffering serious damage to their nets, or even losing them altogether, as had happened to the 'Glenlossie' in March of the previous year. The foreign trawlers, French, German, Danish, Dutch and Belgian mainly, with a handful of Norwegians, paid absolutely no regard to signals or marks and did as they pleased, safe from any prosecution. This was yet another burden as many of the herring fishermen relied on the winter cod fishings to see them through increasingly difficult herring fishings. The level of activity by foreign trawlers was now exceeding that of the pre-war years but then the herring fishings had been prosperous and there was not anything like the amount of Scottish vessels fishing in the Moray Firth as there was now. And the loss of gear was quite ruinous. On week ending 12th February there were five steam, 61 motor and ten sailing vessels at the cod fishing in the Moray Firth and they made 189 landings.

Things were little better for the herring fishermen who held a conference in Aberdeen about the state of the industry in general and what could be done to help dispose of the increasing amount of unsold herring, now lying in barrels all around the country. Suggestions ranged from halving the fleet, which failed because nobody wanted to be in the redundant half, to disposing of the stockpile herring by giving it to the unemployed. In April there was yet another miners strike and 60 vessels, mainly trawlers, were laid up all over Britain as a result.

Yet in the middle of all this gloom there were two events, neither of which attracted the attention of the vast majority of the fishermen but both of which were to be of immense long-term significance.

The 'Falcon' which introduced a completely new design in Scottish fishing craft. Apart from steam drifters, which were modifications of the English sailing trawler hull originally, she was the first new design since Wood Brothers of Lossiemouth built the 'Nonsuch' 40 years before for William Campbell.

In March the venerable firm of James Miller of St Monans launched the 'Falcon', the first new concept in hull design in Scotland since the 'Nonsuch' in 1879. She was built to the order of Mr Robert Robertson, one of the most innovative and progressive men ever to go to sea in Scotland, and was destined to work from his home port of Campbeltown as a ring netter in conjunction with her sister ship the 'Frigate Bird.' The hull itself was a modification of that used by Danes but had an elegance and cleanliness of line that they lacked. She had two Gleniffer engines of 22hp each and was the first large boat to be specifically designed as a motor boat, inasmuch as earlier boats had merely altered existing hull shapes slightly. She was new in every aspect even having acetylene lighting fitted which, while nearly all steam boats had it, was a great novelty in a motor boat, as till then lighting had been by paraffin lamp. Acetylene was created by allowing fresh water to drip into a container of the chemical carbide and the resulting gas was held in a tank. In exactly the same way as a town's gas supplies were distributed from a gasometer, a copper pipe ran all round the boat from this tank. There were various branches from this to the light fittings and there were also connections where a travelling light could be attached with a rubber tube. Acetylene lamps served fishermen very well. There were very few problems, the most common of which was that the carbide would oxidise and become useless in its hundredweight drum if it lay for a while, but the fishermen prevented that by pouring paraffin into the opened drum so that the lumpy material was submerged.

The carbide lamp dismantled to show the water tank on the left and the chamber for the carbide. There were larger lamps which had two much longer burners opposite each other on the gas chamber.

Photograph by permission of Mr D. Garden, Lossiemouth.

A portable carbide lamp.

The Gardner engine which was the favourite of the fishing fleet.

While they were not intended to be, the 'Falcon' and 'Frigate Bird' are unquestionably the prototypes of the thousands of boats which were to be built later, either as dual purpose or seine net boats. They were about 50 feet long and maintained the traditional varnished hull finish, which was rarely to be found other than on west coast ports.

Meantime the Fishery Board had been carrying out its promise to hold an inquiry into Seine Net Flounder Fishing and on 23rd April, 1921 issued this historic statement.

1. It is lawful to use the seine net or flounder net in the capture of white fish in the waters lying between the line drawn due east, true, from Red Head, Forfarshire, and a line extending three miles from the low water mark due north, true, from Babbet Ness in Fifeshire, to westward of a line joining Buddon Ness and Trentsmuir Point or within one half mile of the mouth of any river, or within one half mile of any stalk, fly or bag net, provided that no other boards are used.
2. That no boat using the net shall exceed 40 feet overall and shall not be propelled otherwise than by sails, oars or motor engine.
3. That in working the net only one boat shall be employed.
4. That no net shall be used between sunset and sunrise.
5. That the net shall be hauled as soon as its ends have been brought together and not be trailed or be dragged across the sea bottom.
6. That the total length of the net shall not exceed 200 yards.
7. That the size of the mesh of the wings of the net shall be such that the square gauge of 2½ inches measured along each side of the square will pass easily when the net is wet and that the size of each mesh of any bag attached to the net shall be such that a square gauge of two inches will so pass.
8. That no flat fish under eight inches in length will be landed.

This bye-law takes effect from 22nd April, 1921. . . .

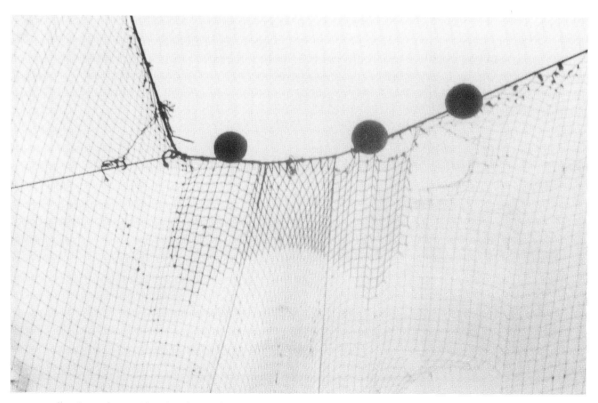

A cotton seine net showing the reinforcing at the mouth where the strain of the wings became heaviest.

Photograph by permission of Mr P. McCabe, Peterhead.

William Stewart's boat 'Rival'.

There are several points of great interest to be observed in this bye-law, the most important of which is that when the Board referred to seine net they meant it in the traditional sense of the sweep net. The kind that in fact was being used by the yawls at that time. A bag is obviously considered to be an addition and the net was intended for the capturing of flat fish as only they are mentioned. Clause 5 specifically says that the net cannot be trailed or dragged across the bottom of the sea in the

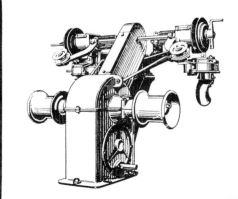
Illustration by permission of the editor, "Fishing News".

Advertisement in the "Fishing News" of 22nd June 1929.

area set aside for seining. This meant that only the Danish method of seining was permitted and implies that some of the more adventurous fishermen were already attempting to drag the net to improve its efficiency. The Danes at that time, and still do for that matter, anchored one end of the rope and steamed away from it, turning when the rope ran out, to shoot the net. They then returned to the anchor, shooting the ropes on the other side of the net having followed a course similar in shape to a teardrop. The loose end was picked up, the boat itself anchored, and the net was hauled to the boat over the broadside. The Danes did this either by hand, with a hand winch, a capstan or a motor winch. In the small Scottish yawls of 1921 the net could easily be hauled by hand and the absence of net hauling machinery did not matter. Events were already in train, however, in which net hauling machinery would be essential, and when the time came that machinery was available.

In the *Fishing News* of 2nd April, Messrs Sam Chapman & Sons had an advertisement saying that they had now become agents for Danish warp coilers and winchers for steam drifters and motor boats. Haddock and plaice nets, mending twine, rollers and all necessary gear could be supplied from stock. By 21st September the giant of the netmaking industry in Scotland, Stuarts & Jacks of Musselburgh were advertising that they were now manufacturing Danish seine from their own twine. Fishermen in Scotland had been dealing with Stuarts & Jacks for 100 years almost, and their name was a by-word for quality, so when they advertised nets it was to them that most of the pioneer fishermen turned once they began seine netting. And over the years the observations of the fishermen were sent back to the manufacturers and the shape of the nets were altered until they have become as effective as they could possibly be.

On 14th May a new breed of fishermen made their first appearance in the shape of three skippers, one from Johnshaven, one from Aberdeen and one from Arbroath. They were lined up in front of Sheriff-substitute Patullo at Dundee Sheriff Court charged with illegal seine netting off the Forfar coast, and were each fined £1, the first men ever to be convicted of such an offence.

The lookout station at Collieston whence some of the first poachers to be fined were observed by the Coastguard.

It was pointed out in court that while the offence had been committed on 7th April, the Secretary of State had issued a bye-law on 23rd making seining in that area legal. The Sheriff-substitute said that really made no difference as they deliberately fished there, knowing that it was illegal at the time. He was unmoved by one of their statements that he had gone to the Fishery Board's Office in Aberdeen to ask if he could fish in the area, that very day, before he went to sea, and he had been told that it would probably be all right. While he could recall the conversation quite clearly he could not remember with whom he had it.

Further north in Aberdeen things were being viewed much more severely. The following day the skipper of a Gourdon boat was accused of illegal fishing and of concealing the boats number. Collieston coastguards had observed him, and other boats, all fishing with their numbers covered by nets and canvas. The wind blew up the net that had accidentally covered the number of one of them, thus allowing it to be identified. Sheriff Laing said that this sort of thing was becoming far too prevalent and imposed the very severe fine of £50 or 60 days and the skipper was heard to mutter that some people further south were only fined £1. Thus a long and tiresome tradition was established, the character of which lay between the highly comic and terribly tragic and would fill this book by itself.

But what these men were doing, with their tiny vessels and small nets, was neither here nor there and matters were quite different elsewhere. The tempo of poaching in the Moray Firth was gathering momentum and trawlers with foreign registration numbers, but with British names and ports such as Hull, Grimsby, Granton and Aberdeen on their sterns were fishing regularly. Foreign trawlers were, of course, still permitted to fish in the Firth and fishermen who lost gear as a result were having great difficulty in identifying the vessels. However, there were more burdens being piled onto backs that were slowly becoming incapable of supporting them.

By June the *Fishing News* was reporting regularly that Danish and Norwegian seine net boats were landing good shots steadily at Grimsby and that local English owners were thinking of investing in the kind of motor boat that their fishermen were using. One Dane had landed 400 boxes for a seven-day trip, by modern standards, considering the net and boat sizes, the equivalent of 1000 boxes

Photograph by permission of Mr C. F. Baldry, Framlingham, Suffolk.

The Lowestoft drifter 'Girl Norah' coming into Lowestoft with her winch and coilers clearly visible. Mr Baldry took this photograph on 2nd May, 1932. The 'Girl Norah' was lost with all hands in December 1936 near Calais.

in a day or so. On 21st June, the company of James Irvin sent the trawler 'J Burn' to sea from Yarmouth to fish with a seine net, the first English vessel to use the Danish method. She met with immediate success and within four weeks her example had been followed along the English coast as far as Scarborough. The 'J Burn' seems to have had a special steam winch installed and shot her net about every hour. She did not have a rope coiler however, and the famous capstan makers of Elliot & Garrood developed a steam coiler in about six weeks from her first trip. This was fitted to the drifter 'Carpe Diem.'

Photograph by permission of Mr J. Gatt, Fraserburgh.

Two pioneers of the Fraserburgh seine net fishing. Mr Benjamin Noble, left, of the 'Comfort' and his lifelong friend John Buchan, skipper of the 'Victoria'. Another very early Fraserburgh pioneer was Mr John Duthie.

Photograph by permission of Miss M. Watt, Gourdon.

Charlie Moir of Gourdon, one of the pioneers of seine net fishing on the Kincardine coast in 1921. He is probably aboard his yawl 'Comrades' ME 37.

The Scottish summer herring fishing was reaching full swing about the time that these reports were coming in. Not a great deal was done about imitating this kind of fishing in Scotland because the fishermen were trying to recover their winter losses in the only way they knew how. They nearly all had a number of herring nets and nobody really believed that you could make a living with one net between a crew and a net which only cost £10 at that. It was also difficult to believe that this little net, which only required three or four to operate, could do better than a drifter with a crew of eight or nine aboard, carrying 80 to 100 nets and all the mending that went with them. Mending, that to a large extent was done by the wives, retired fishermen, and mending contractors if damage was particularly heavy. The seine net by comparison, was merely taken off if it was torn and another laid on in its place. It could be patched up while the boat was still at sea; serious damage was, of course, repaired ashore. And the greatest attraction of all took a little time to become accepted. If nothing was being caught in a seine net after a couple of hours, the boat could shift to other ground. Once the drift was shot for herring the size of the catch was only discovered when the nets were hauled perhaps six hours later. If bad weather came on, a drifter could be lying to her nets for more than a day and with luck might get them hauled more or less intact. A seine net boat would have gone home at the first sign of broken weather. The drifter of course, held out the prospect, that if it did strike herring it could catch enormous quantities which could gross the kind of money early seine net skippers could only dream about, with their small but steady fishings.

But 1921 began an era when there was no guarantee that a drifter could sell its catch and men who had sweated most of the night hauling herring could spend an equal amount of time dumping it in the afternoon because it could not find a buyer. And the herring might not have found a buyer for one or all of several reasons. In late 1920 the Secretary of State had called fishermen's respresentatives together and told them that the industry must finance itself. The main reason was that the market was in complete turmoil because of the Great War. Germany was on its knees and Russia was in a civil war. In 1919 and 1920 the Government had agreed to help the industry by buying unsold herring, and had bought over one million pounds worth in 1920. By 1921 it had only managed to sell one third of it and announced in June 1921 that there would be no more subsidies in the form of buying unsold herring. Indeed, as Mr Jones, chairman of the Fisheries Board, said at a banquet to celebrate the extension to Macduff harbour in May, no Scottish fishermen wished to live on the dole if he could find a market without government assistance. The sooner they could do without the grant the better. There was a Dr Murray, MP for the Western Isles who was claiming that the Government were spending 37 million in Mesopotamia and offered no help to those who had served in the war, but nobody listened to him.

Before the war 80% of the catch of herring had gone to the continent but now there was great difficulty in selling any there because, apart from the ruined German economy, Norwegians were undercutting the price at which herring from this country were being sold. Any herring that was sold there that year was at a loss, and this in turn meant curers either going out of business or reducing their labour forces. Either way unemployment increased rapidly, often enough leaving emigration as the only possible alternative, which thousands took. All this of course, came on top of poor fishing, both at home and in Yarmouth and the summer fishing of 1921, the following year, followed the same pattern. There was a scarcity of herring, low prices because of the glut from the previous year, and most curers noticed nervously that the Mark had fallen from 450 to 490 to the pound by October. That was to come, for the little herring they did sell was on their own initiative, because the Government officially closed the German and Russian markets on the 1st June, before the herring season had even begun, leaving the industry to its own devices. It has to be stated that the Government had similar problems with the agricultural, railway and mining industries, and the latter two of which were organised by trades unions and capable of co-ordinated actions in a way in which the fishermen could not copy. So with most of the Government's attention directed elsewhere the fishing industry embarked on a period of almost unrelieved depression, particularly as far as the herring fishing was concerned. Due to the combination of poor fishing and low prices the result was that most of the boats did not clear their expenses. It was estimated that 75% of the Lossiemouth fleet, in other words about 52 boats of its 72 boats, made a loss, the effect of which was making itself felt as early as September because the boats could not settle up with their suppliers. By October, four of their steam drifters had had trawling gear put aboard and two more arrived during the month bringing the total to six. It was not as large a fleet as Buckie now had, and Buckie had taken some considerable steps towards refitting to trawling earlier in the season. On 13th September a large meeting had been held in Buckie fishmarket and a petition prepared to have the Moray Firth opened to seine net fishing. Such had been the disasters that had befallen many owners that in the same week the *Fraserburgh Herald* carried an advert offering a large motor boat and 60 nets for sale at £500. So seining, which had not attracted much attention at the beginning of the herring season now seemed to be a much better prospect because of the difficult season.

Exactly why Buckie, of the major ports, took the initiative towards having the Moray Firth opened to seining is not clear and seems to come from a variety of reasons. The poor season apart, one explanation might be quite a few Buckie men had gone on contract earlier in the year to fishing on Yarmouth drifters which had been converted to seine net. In the small print of their contracts, and unnoticed by them in the relief of getting work, there was a clause which committed them to working on Sundays, something that they were not aware of until it actually happened. This, of course, was deeply offensive to men who mostly were of strong religious conviction and a number of them returned home as soon as they could without breaking the contract. The penalties for that were severe.

The Mark note which, along with its successors of much greater face value, bankrupted so many curers in Scotland. One curer in Wick, Mr Gordon Dower, papered a room in his house with the money which had put him out of business.

The 'Ebenezer' and the 'Crest' careened for painting in Wick river.

However, they had been seining long enough to see what was involved and inform others. Another reason of course was the increasing activity of trawlers, legal or otherwise, and English boats which were coming to the Moray Firth in increasing numbers, using the Danish seine or snurrevaad. There was also a strong body of option that the herring fishings would take three or four years to come back again. Something would have to be done in the meantime, and seine netting might be a part of the answer. Finally, Buckie fishermen have always been among the more enterprising and more than one fisherman recently has expressed the view that if there was water on the moon the first thing the American astronauts saw would have been a Buckie boat.

The month of October found fewer Scots boats than usual at the East Anglian fishing as many had either been laid up or were trawling. Seventy fishermen from the Lossiemouth area were on Aberdeen trawlers and another 40 had been to Canada to bring back drifters and trawlers which had been built by the Admiralty to replace war losses. The industry did not exactly need these extra vessels which were being sold at £4875 for a new steel drifter and £3750 for a wooden one. There was also one Lossiemouth motor boat at the seine net, but nobody was sure if seining was legal in the Moray Firth. The *Fishing News* thought that it was, outside the three mile limit, and said so on 15th October. There being no challenge from the Fishing Board, who till now had only formally agreed that seining could be legally carried out as explained earlier, the paper then published a description of how the method worked on 26th November.

SEINE   FISHING.

How the Net is Worked.

THE METHOD EXPLAINED.

Seine fishing has recently come much into favour with drift net fishermen, who have found it a more profitable occupation than the herring fishing. In the article printed below the method of using the seine net is described

On account of the failure of the herring fishing, both at the Scottish and the English ports, and the consequent loss to the fishermen, many of them have turned their attention to seine net fishing. This they have found to be very profitable and less expensive than either trawling or drift net fishing.

Seine net fishing is quite distinct from trawling. The net is not pulled after the vessel as is the otter trawl. The net consists of two arms, provided with a bag in the middle, and the method of working it can best be likened to that practised by the salmon fishermen on a river like the Dee. One end of the warp (or rope) is held by a salmon fisherman on the bank of the river, while another member of the crew rows into the middle of the stream and drops the net, which spreads out lengthwise, the warp attached being paid out all the time. He then rows back to the bank again, paying out the warp attached to the other end of the dropped net. When the bank is reached, both warps are steadily hauled in by the crew, who are now on the river bank, and who walk towards each other. By this means the net is gradually closed, and when both parties meet, and the net is brought ashore, it is absolutely closed.

Curve Round a Buoy.

The same method is adopted in seine net fishing, the difference being that instead of the warp being held by a man on the river bank, which, of course, is impossible at sea, it is attached to a buoy. This buoy is kept in position by an anchor. The vessel then steams ahead in a great curve, paying out 960 fathoms of the warp. The net, which is 202 feet in length is then dropped. The vessel proceeds to steam back, paying out the other 960 fathoms of the warp towards the buoy where the two ends of the warp meet. They are then taken aboard the vessel through the rope rollers on to the winch, and thence to the coiler, which automatically coils the whole length of the rope on board the vessel.

The same pressure, or pull, is maintained on both ends of the warp so that the net is being steadily drawn together, and when it arrives at the side of the vessel it is closed.

During the hauling aboard of the net, the vessel is lying stationary. After the net is hauled aboard, and the catch emptied into the vessel's hold, the same procedure is again gone through, the length of time occupied in doing so being one hour. It is essential in laying the gear to place it so that the net is hauled in dead against the tide.

Three Kinds of Net.

The net used is a light cotton one. There are three kinds of nets — plaice, haddock, and cod. One of the greatest disadvantages of the seine net fishing is that it requires to be prosecuted in rather fine weather. Up till now it has not been practiced in the dark, owing to the fact that collisions might ensue, as the vessels are so frequently sailing in such a big sweep when laying the net. Another disadvantage of this method of fishing is that it cannot be prosecuted with success in waters where the sea has a rough bottom.

Gear Required.

This particular method of fishing has been largely used by the Danes for a good number of years on the Dogger Bank with tremendous success. Motor boats and steam drifters can be easily adapted for the seine net fishing. Drifters do not require to be changed in any shape or form. All that is needed is a special winch, a rope-coiler, rope rollers, and the laying of a steam pipe from the engines to the winch. The whole gear can be either laid aft, amidship, or just at the back of the foremast if there is the necessary room. The cost of installing the gear, including net, etc., is about £350, as against about £700 in converting a drifter into a trawler. Less power is required for the seine net fishing than for trawling, and it is much less expensive. It is these facts that have commended its adoption by the Scottish fishermen, some of whom are at present agitating for permission to be allowed to fish within the three-mile limit.

The Net.

The meshes of the net measure from 3½ inches down to 2 inches. For flat fish, plaice, etc., it measures 40 fathoms in width between the arms, with the bag 5½ fathoms in depth. For round fish, such as haddocks, etc., the measurements are 30 fathoms and 8 fathoms respectively.

The *Fishing News* was at that time produced in Aberdeen which explains the references to the River Dee. The official description which appeared in the manual issued to Fishery Officers in 1925 by the Fisheries Board read as follows:—

APPENDIX R — *cont.*

Danish Seine Fishing — In 1921 a number of British vessels adopted a method of seine fishing which has been in use in Denmark for many years. The two principal areas are on and around the Dogger Bank and in the Moray Firth. One of the essential requirements of seine fishing is a comparatively weak tide. Unlike trawling, seining gives the best results the more exactly the net can be hauled against the tide. The seine net has a great initial spread of 36 fathoms and a height of six or seven fathoms. But it is claimed that it is the two warps, each about 1,000 fathoms in length which do the fishing. Expert fishermen consider there is still much to be learned in the art of laying the net. The procedure is as follows: A buoy is anchored on the selected fishing ground and a warp is attached to this. The vessel steams at full speed about two points off the tide, running out the warp from coils on deck. When seven ropes (840 fathoms) have gone over the side the course is altered about ten points so as to run directly across the tide, and two more ropes (240 fathoms) are paid out. The vessel is then eased down whilst the net, in line with the rope, is shot from the platform aft. On the same course, two more ropes are laid, whereupon the course is altered another ten points, or so, back towards the starting point. When the buoy is reached the vessel is made fast to it and both ropes are passed to the winch. As the warps are being hauled they are coiled by a special coiler, one fisherman dragging the coils to a position from which they will readily run when the next haul is made. From the moment hauling commences the two wings of the net begin to close and there comes a point in the haul when it is claimed that the closing walls drive the fish back down the funnel of the net. The net being brought alongside, the cod end is rolled over in the water, the cod-line secured and untied and the fish dipped out with a large landing net until such time as the weight has been sufficiently reduced to permit the light netting and its catch to be lifted bodily.

The last sentence about how the net was emptied shows that the development of the seine net had some way to go.

So 1921 drew to a close with the fishing industry in a state of upheaval and hesitancy. The East Anglian fishing had been worse, if anything, than the Scottish summer fishing and some Fraserburgh men had come home more than £40 in debt, the equivalent today of about £3-4000 each, for the ten week season. This was on top of other losses and there was great uncertainty about the future in most, but not all, minds.

Among the minds returning from the Yarmouth fishing which could see the future with great clarity were those of two young coopers and a fisherman. It is not clear exactly who felt the spirit move first during that fitful fishing in Yarmouth, but move the spirit most certainly did. In style the movement was very similar to that which had began in the U.S.A. by the quite unusual Mrs Aimee Semple McPherson. She founded the Church of the Foursquare Gospel, which was getting on like a house on fire, in spirit at the time, but later in fact. Mrs McPherson, who soon have 45 lawsuits against her, had many imitators, mostly in the U.S.A., but the three young men were the first to embrace her religious style in Scotland.

Style it certainly had, and so had the men who heard the call here. They were Jock Troup, from Wick, Willie Bruce from Fraserburgh and Dave Cordiner from Peterhead. Jock Troup had a strong voice, personality and a sharp sense of humour, exactly the kind of character this form of religion seems to nurture. Willie Bruce had similar qualities but Dave Cordiner was a much quieter, deliberative man.

Photograph by permission of Mr A. Cordiner, Peterhead.

Mr Dave Cordiner the evangelist who made so many conversions during the revival of 1921 and the following years. After he had addressed a meeting in Dundee in 1922, he was approached by a man called Willie Taylor who showed him a revolver with which he had intended to kill him. Dave Cordiner had converted his would-be assassin during the meeting with the intensity of his preaching.

The movement began about the middle of November, by whom is not exactly clear. Jock Troup had not originally been selected to go to Yarmouth and only went after a month or so to replace a cooper who had fallen ill and had to come home to Wick. Dave Cordiner was already there, cook on the drifter 'Energy,' as was Willie Bruce. It was after Jock Troup's arrival, and his association with Willie Bruce that the movement gathered its incredible momentum. Within a couple of weeks meetings were so large that even by shouting the speakers could not make themselves heard in the Yarmouth Mart and a religious fever gripped thousands of men and women to the extent that work became neglected so that they could attend the meetings.

The hall, with the Congregational church on its right, where Jock Troup and Willie Bruce held their huge meetings in Fraserburgh. The overspill from the church filled both the hall and the street outside.

The meetings were held in the classic American hot gospel style where the audience, or the congregation, were warmed up with stirring declarations of faith, and some fairly harmless confessions, which were roared at them by either Jock Troup or Willie Bruce, or both. Jock used his sense of humour to great effect and there would be singing of the catchier hymn tunes, none of which were to be found in the Church of Scotland hymnary. Then it was back to the speakers and an invitation to the aroused audience to come forward to purify their souls by confessions and commitment. There frequently would be a rush to the platform and some quite interesting sins were confessed. In their anxiety to bleach their souls a few thoughtless lassies made their sins even more interesting by confessing with whom they had been sinning, sometimes to the chagrin of some of the others in the audience. More than one man fled from a meeting to face condemnation rather than the salvation he had been seeking. But these were minor details and when the fishing closed the evangelical movement transferred with it to Fraserburgh, on the crest of a wave.

Dave Cordiner returned home to Peterhead where his long evangelical career might be said to have begun when he had addressed a huge meeting in Broad Street there. Jock and Willie came to Fraserburgh, as they were to tell an enormous gathering in the Congregational Church there, because, while they were in Yarmouth, they had seen the Broch every time that they had prayed, and this was a sign that Fraserburgh was next for salvation. The scenes in the church had never been experienced before or since. The building was crammed to the door, with people sitting in the aisles and on the steps right up to the pulpit. Hundreds were ouside and the meeting was continuously punctuated by cries of "Hosannah," and "Halleluja" and "All Hail to You," and prayers being recited in loud voices from all corners. Jock and Willie, along with three or four ministers, addressed the gathering and when Jock announced that he had to leave town to carry his work further, there was widespread wailing and grief.

The *Fraserburgh Herald* took a very cynical view of the whole thing, one of the only papers to do so, and said that Jock was angling for control of the missionary movement in China, which at that time was every good missionary's aspiration. They also forecast that the movement would be very short lived. In a way the editor was right, but there are still remnants of the revival of 1921 active to this very day, in one form or another, in most of the ports of the Moray Firth. It certainly was a strange incident inasmuch as its character was so unlike the grim, humourless, dour religion of Scotland generally. Whether it took on so quickly because it was such a contrast is hard to say, but it also receeded as quickly as it came. Jock, however, kept going, and eventually went to the United States where evangelism of this kind is, if not more enduring, certainly renewed with great frequency. Dave Cordiner emigrated to Canada where he died in Winnipeg in 1979.

The month of December was to encounter yet more innovations before it ran out and among them were the first of the Lossiemouth steam drifters which had converted their deck machinery to allow them to fish with a seine net. When the Yarmouth fishings had proven so unrewarding a few had left early and called in at the port of Grimsby, among others, where the Great Grimsby Coal, Salt and Tanning Company Limited could supply all that was needed for a boat to follow seining. By 6th December this would also have been available from the Northern Engineering Co. of Fraserburgh but, for the moment, the pioneers outfitted in Grimsby, Yarmouth, Hull or Scarborough. Seine netting as it was going to alter the character of Scottish fishing out of all recognition, was poised on the brink of its entry into the lives and times of ports all around the coast.

The arrival of the Lossiemouth drifters back home with their new equipment and nets coincided almost to the day with an apparently unconnected event taking place about 120 miles to the south in the ancient town of St Monans in Fife. There in the yard of the venerable and famous company of James Miller & Sons, work was going ahead on number 408, to become the 'Falcon' of Campbeltown, the prototype of the classic ring net hull and indirectly the pioneer shape for Scottish vessels until the 1960's.

Miller's, founded in 1747 and still building boats in 1985, had been pioneering in boatbuilding for nearly two centuries since John Miller opened his doors for business in the hamlet of Overkellie, a few miles inland, probably as house carpenters. They actually arrived in St Monans by way of St Andrews in 1779 just as the great Fifie hull was taking on its distinctive shape and Fife men were beginning to travel, and sometimes row, the 200 miles to the North of Scotland where the herring fishing was beginning its meteoric rise to prosperity. This hull style, with local variations, was imitated all around the coasts and remained the major influence on design till well into the 20th Century when Miller introduced the 'Falcon.' Miller's were also pioneers of first the half decked, and then the fully decked Fifie, long before the Washington report on 1849 recommended that all fishing boats should be so constructed.

Miller's had also been involved with Professor William Peck of Edinburgh when he installed a diesel engine that he had invented in the 65 feet Fifie 'Wave' in 1905. Either this vessel, or the 'Pioneer' ML 30, was the first fishing boat in Scotland to have an engine installed but they were almost certainly used for experimental or demonstration purposes. The first fishing boat to have an engine installed by working fishermen, on their own initiative, was the 'Brothers of Campbeltown' in 1907. These men were Robert Robertson and John McIntyre, his father-in-law. By 1922, only 15 years later, 25% of the fleet, or 2020 boats out of a total of 7545 were motor driven. They landed 17,600 cwt. of seined fish that year as opposed to 46,700 by steam vessels.

At the beginning of 1922 the seine net, and the grounds on which it could be conveniently used, if not exactly a mystery to the pioneering fishermen, certainly involved them in mental gymnastics that they did not encounter with herring or line fishing. These grounds, and the tides which ran over them, they had known for generations, and as far as great and small line fishing was concerned they knew to within a fathom or two, where they could shoot. As the gear lay on the bottom, and usually was hauled along itself, obstacles were rarely encountered. The seine net was totally different as it now became necessary to know where every outcrop of rock, wreck or fissure in the bottom began and ended. For this knowledge to be of use, very sharp landmarks, or mise, as the northern creel men called them, had to be found and remembered. Landmarks were of course not always available, either because of poor visibility, or distance, in which case dead reckoning on the compass, where the speed of the boat and tide carry had to be taken into account. Some of these factors had, of course, already applied to the great liners, who frequently found the grounds with a greased lead line, but again they did not have to heave across the grounds.

The net itself came in a variety of lengths and sizes but generally fell into three categories. There was the smallest, the fluke net, the haddock, known as the intermediate and the cod, which had a bag. The fluke net as used by the yawls which did not have a bag, but many were to have them fitted to them as the fishermen came to understand how they fished. Fitting a net with a bag was by no means a new idea, as some inquisitive souls had made the following law-making necessary 115 years earlier:—

XII. And be it further enacted, That from and after the first day of June one thousand eight hundred and nine, no person shall use in any river or lock or at sea, in or on the coast of Great Britain, any herring net, or any traul net, drag net or other sea net for the taking of herrings, which hath a mesh of less than one inch from knot to knot, or any false or double bottom cod or pouch, or shall put any net, though of legal size, behind the others to destroy the small fish, and that every person offending herein shall forfeit

No net to be used that has a mesh of less than one inch from knot to knot.

every such net as aforesaid, and
the sum of forty pounds for every
such offence; and it shall be lawful for the Commissioners for the
herring fishery, to be appointed
pursuant to this act, to cause every
such net to be burnt.

There was no legislation against setting a bag in a seine net. From the beginning nets could be bought more or less complete, in either hemp or cotton and with buoys on the head rope and lead weights on the footrope. The fishermen altered these according to their ideas of what local conditions required, as indeed they do now. Early nets did not have a fish trap to prevent the fish coming back out when the strain came off, but the first of these were being fitted by 1923. Fluke nets seem to have been among the last to have them and seine nets were used without traps till into the 1930's. The ropes could be sisal or manilla, and many were made in the local ropeworks, as most sizeable ports still had one.

The yarn of the net itself was heavier than that of a herring net but not as heavy as that of a trawl. It was not reinforced in any way because its original conception of being hauled to the boat did not put it under the same strain as fly dragging. For preservation it was barked, in the same way as herring nets, and usually at the same time as nearly everybody with seine nets had herring nets as well. Any patches were made of pieces of other nets or woven from already treated twine. By comparison with today there was a lot less mending, in spite of the fact that the grounds were unfamiliar, because of the low power and the fact that there was comparatively little fly dragging.

Different ports had different styles of design of net and even in the way that the ropes for towing the net were laid on. These ropes which were manilla, suffered considerable wear as they were dragged across the sand, wore out quite quickly. It was the custom in Wick to lay the new rope nearest the boat and gradually work them down as the older rope below wore out. Buckie men worked the other way. Nets were mainly supplied by Stewart and Jack, Low's of Elgin and Marshall's of Buckie.

The rigging of the nets themselves was also done in a variety of methods. There were no purpose made buoys for them at first and fishermen used whatever they had. This often was the glass balls that they used for cod and haddock drift nets, or corks such as were used for herring fishing or the lozenge shaped corks used by salmon fishermen. There was a great deal of work with both these methods as the glass balls were frequently broken when the net came alongside or the lozenge shaped corks tore in the lift of the water pressure at depths for which they were never intended. An aluminium float was produced but it was never a success either, as it collapsed with the pressures below 40 fathoms and became pressed around the head rope. It was not until the development of the galvanized float, to be followed after the war by one made of plastic, that the top of the net was conveniently held up as it fished. And by 1923 it was not fishing in the way that the Fishery Board had intended on the 23rd of April, 1921, because the fly drag, or dragging seine net behind the boat on the fly when the fishery cruiser was not looking, had come into its own.

Several ports claim to have begun fly dragging and they all could have done so quite independently of one another because in 1923 there were no radio transmitters on Scottish boats and each white fishing fleet kept its news pretty well to itself unless they met at the herring fishings. There are several versions of how fly dragging came about and two follow.

Lossiemouth men began fly dragging inside the three mile limit in late 1921 or early 1922 because if the fishery cruiser appeared the ropes could be hauled in quickly or even cut in a real emergency. Till then the boat had hauled the seine net over the broadside, the same way as herring nets were hauled and was anchored as she did so, which meant that the cruiser would be almost upon them before all that was sorted out and the boat got under way. This all made plausible explanation difficult, so towing the net behind a moving boat was much preferable, apart from the fact that more fish were caught that way.

Photograph by permission of Mr W. Thain, Wick.

Mr William Thain mending nets at Wick harbour. He is accompanied by Mr William Mackay.

Fly dragging began in Wick for quite a different reason. A crew member of the 'Zoe' had slept in thus delaying their departure by about an hour. When he got to the grounds Skipper William Thain, shot his dhan, without checking the state of the tide, thinking there was enough ebb left to get in one drag. By the time he returned the flood was on which meant that the net was now facing the wrong way. If he anchored and tried to fish the tide would carry the net underneath the 'Zoe' and everything would become tangled up. So when he lifted the dhan and his anchor he put the 'Zoe' astern and

Photograph by permission of Mr W. Thain.

The 'Zoe' entering Yarmouth in 1923. The mast and derrick are stowed because "Smith Dockies" had shallow holds which made hauling herring nets very uncomfortable as the crew had to stoop under the mast if it was stowed to the wheelhouse. One Wick drifter, the 'Drift Fisher' shot a seine net only once, in an unsuccessful attempt to find the body of Mr William Bruce who had fallen overboard from another drifter the 'Morven Hill'.

towed the net after him. He towed with one hand on the telegraph to the engine room in case the net caught an obstacle and he could ring her ahead to take the strain off before too much damage was done to the net. It was a much more serious matter to catch on an obstacle, or fastener, with a net under tow than one which was being slowly hauled to the boat, as the damage was much greater. As it happened he had been fishing on a clean sandy area and got the net aboard without mishap and with a good shot in it.

A couple of years earlier on the other side of the Moray Firth in the winter of 1921, Mr Benjamin Noble of Broadsea, now a part of Fraserburgh, had been conducting experiments in his boat the 'Comfort'. He had towed a creeper back and fore on the line grounds north of Gamrie and Rose-hearty looking for fasteners so that he could mark them and avoid them with the seine net that he had bought for £4.10/- in Grimsby. He was also having trouble with it on the line grounds known as the Dirty Face because it was digging into the mud there to the extent that he could hardly haul it. In an attempt to prevent the net from digging in he attached the wooden balls normally used to run sails up the masts of the large sailboats, called parrels, to the foot rope, so that they could run along the mud in the same way as trawl bobbins did on a trawl.

WK 164, the 'Owners Delight' a Keiss Fifie alongside a large Scaffie in the crowded Wick harbour about 1890. Much imagina-tion was used in naming boats, with many of the names reflecting the owners outlook on life. Names such as 'Wha Wad Thochtit' (BK1), 'Mine and Thine' (LH 868), 'Try Again' (ME 445), 'Peace and Plenty' (KY 1907), 'Anchor of Hope' (KY 419), 'Fishers Friend' (KY 294), 'Queen of the Fleet' (AH 220), 'Pride O' Fife' (KY 1929), 'I Love May' (KY 569), 'We'll Try Our Best' (A7), 'Prospects Ahead' (KY 257), 'Belle of the Ocean' (INS 1364), 'Catch Me If You Can' (CY 63).

All around the coasts fishermen were meeting yet other problems, sometimes afloat sometimes ashore. Afloat it could be an embarrassment of riches and often a net would come up with a quantity of fish that was difficult to handle. Large catches of most kinds of fish were common and these brought their own problems. Early seine nets had no reinforcing ropes along them, and many did not have a trap to prevent the fish from swimming back out when it came to the surface. Not that fish were particularly difficult to keep in a net without a trap but so heavy were the catches that it did not matter how many escaped. There was no lifting gear to swing fish aboard originally and the first adaption in the steam drifters was to lay a wire rope between the funnel and the mizzen mast and sling a single or double fall tackle from it. The strop was then hooked to that, the fish in the bag separated until there was a quantity small enough to be hoisted manually by the crew without tearing the net. This could take a long time with a large shot. Big shots were often towed ashore, beached on the high tide and ebbed dry, especially if it was of flatfish. Not all flatfish attracted a price and in the beginn- ing only lemon soles and plaice could fetch a price with the result that witches, megrims, dabs and brill were shovelled wholesale over the side. One Lossiemouth boat towed a bag of megrims ashore thinking they were lemon soles and had to then dispose of about 70 boxes of worthless fish. There was often difficulty in selling other kinds of fish as well. Monks, catfish, whitings, haddock and small cod were rarely bought in any quantity, and often not at all, as at that time the fish selling organisation was primarily geared to herring outside the trawling ports of Peterhead, Aberdeen, Dundee and Granton. Of course, there was a small market which was mainly satisfied by the inshore line vessels for good quality cod, haddock, ling, hake and large flatfish like turbot, halibut and skate, but this was not prepared to cater for the sudden increase of fish available by the change to seine net. Even good sized cod or haddocks, by todays standards, sometimes had to be sold two for one. This meant that under the old system of selling cod, haddock, hake etc by the score, or 20, two medium sized fish would only count as one so that as many as 30 or 35 would be sold as 20.

Sometimes a port would have a buyer who had a contact for a particular fish for a specialist market and fish could be sold there when no other port would take them. Buckie was always a good outlet for hake and Macduff for haddock. The only things that Wick buyers were interested in were good lemon soles, plaice, hake and occasionally the good large haddock, known as the black haddie. But all interest in white fish sales ceased when the herring drifters arrived. At a time when a bag full of fish was common, and fish of a quality and size that modern fishermen can only dream about, there was a very heavy destruction of the highest quality of fish. Due to the efforts of Lord Leverhume, who was expanding his retail fish selling shops, MacFisheries, and probably above all, to the thousands of people who were opening fish and chip shops, a market gradually was created for this kind of fish, the quality of which was superior in every way to that landed by trawlers. The chip shops introduced housewives to fish that till then they had not bought because they were not readily available and expensive. They created a peculiar fish eating pattern across the country, probably because the merchants supplied them that way. Roughly speaking whiting and haddock predominates in Scotland and the north of England, with skate, cod and dogfish in the southern half of England.

In the eyes of the biologists, the Scottish grounds in 1922 would be regarded as underfished and capable of exploitation to a far higher degree than they experienced till then. In 1913 the Scottish fishing fleet had stood at a total of 8512 vessels made up of 298 steam trawlers, 884 steam drifters and liners, 523 motor boats and 6807 sail boats, most of which were yawls up to 25 to 30 feet. They employed about 33,000 fishermen, the majority of whom, with the exception of the East Anglian and Irish fishings, took their livings from their native coasts. The fleet in 1922 was about 1000 vessels fewer, a decrease of about two a week in the nine years or so, largely of sailing vessels. Many had been converted, and 800 were fitted with engines during the war with the result that the number of motor vessels exceeded steam in 1915. That year also saw the highest number of steam drifters and liners ever when the number stood at 923. In this period of nearly a decade there was very little new building, outside of the construction of yawls and government vessels. With a notable exception, or two. What scientists would consider underfishing by this number of vessels and men, would be that they were not catching the quantity of fish that they were capable of, but would correct this imbalance as time went by. A comparison of the numbers employed in the 1980's with those of the 1920's would indicate that the imbalance has been over corrected but at the same time the standards of living of the eras have also to be compared. Hindsight is a wonderful thing, but even it is not always fully conclusive.

In the Spring of 1922, the French attitude to the German failure to pay war damages hardened considerably and the occupation by them of the best German coal fields sent the Mark into a crazy spiral of devaluation which accelerated as the year wore on. The exchange rate in January 1922 was 600 marks to the Pound Sterling. By November 1923 the rate was 16,800,000,000,000 — an exchange rate which defies imagination, but it was true. Mr George Simpson of Wick, who was in Hamburg trying to see how to get paid for his herring, was offered a large department store for £100. He, like hundreds of other curers, had sold herring to Germany in spite of the government refusal to guarantee prices. There was after all, little alternative, as the Germans, because of widespread starvation, had bought a fairly large quantity of herring and nobody dreamed that inflation would reach the levels it did. The fishings in 1921 and 1922 were comparatively poor and there was nothing like the supply available in 1920, but there was still a lot of money at stake.

1922 saw landings of seined fish increasing from 15,000 cwt in 1920, to 64,000 of which 46,700 was landed by steam drifters. In the two districts which predominated the seine net fishing, the Buckie area had 212,800 square yards of seine net, valued at £5472, and the Findhorn area,

Photograph by permission of Mr T. V. Thomas of Preston and Thomas Ltd., Cardiff.

A Preston and Thomas fish-frying range of 1915, one of the best friends that the inshore fisherman ever had. In 1982 the 10,000 or so fish and chip shops in Britain went through approximately 190,000 tons of fish, one third of all landings, for human consumption. They had to use at least 30,000 tons of imported fish because of a shortfall in the landings by British boats. Cod is far and away the most popular fish with their customers.

Lossiemouth really, had 139,300 square yards, worth £3980. At a time when a seine net cost £10 - £12 it meant that these districts had about 500 and 370 nets each. The herring fleet was using 144 million square yards of nets, nationally, and the liners 32 million yards of line. Herring nets could, and did, suffer considerable damage.

Seine nets of course, suffered damage as well, but it was of a much more complicated nature than herring nets. A herring drifter could have 80 or 90 nets shot and damage to even half of them meant she could still fish. Damage to a seine net meant that it had to be replaced at once and the damage repaired at the first opportunity, whether afloat or ashore depended on the extent. A seine net of course, is not as straightforward as a herring net which was a simple curtain of netting in which all meshes were the same square size and shape. It has to retain its conical shape when under strain and this required fishermen to learn how to make the three legged meshes which were worked along its length to narrow the cone towards the cod-end. The net has to be kept tight mended both in its length and out in the wings which guide the fish into it. There is also a trap which keeps the fish inside when the net stops moving behind the boat.

Very few nets had a trap in 1922 and there was much experimenting in the various ports to perfect them. It took about 15 years before all seine nets in use had traps but fluke nets seem to have been the last to have them. A lot of the delay was of course, due to the fitful way in which seine net was undertaken in the first few years as it was regarded as only a supplement to herring fishing. Another was that there was not a market for a lot of fish and it did not matter too much if many escaped. The fishermen were also used to seeing fish escaping at the herring fishing and did not concentrate on preventing this at first.

Photograph by permission of Mrs J. Begg, Castletown.

The 'Westward' on the slip at Wick. The Begg family carried out their own repairs of all kinds, and were regarded as being highly skilful in everything they undertook.

Photograph by permission of Mr D. Robertson, Aukengill.

The 'Westward' beached for overhaul at Aukengill, where she belonged. She was one of four identical boats built in Thurso in the 1920's for line fishing in the mouth of the Pentland Firth and west towards Strathy. Her sister ships were the 'Northward', 'Eastward' and 'Streamlet'.

The few nets which had traps in the beginning had them inserted the opposite way from modern nets, in as much as they were attached to the bottom rather than the top, of the bag. As far as Wick was concerned, it was the skill and observation of William Thain that caused this apparent oversight to be rectified. Wick was about 12 months or so behind Buckie and Lossiemouth in the adaption of the seine net and the first Wick boat to use it was the 'Fairy Hill,' under Skipper William Waters. He fished from Grimsby in the autumn of 1922, and in early 1923 the drifter 'Spectrum' went there because her skipper William Stewart could not get a sale for seined fish in Wick. William Thain was a member of the crew and shortly after their arrival in Grimsby he noticed a man putting a trap in a seine net. He went over, said nothing but saw what he considered to be a serious mistake. The trap was attached to the bottom of the net and the open flap to the top. The logic was obviously that when the fish entered the net, particularly flatfish, once they had passed through the trap, they would try to escape by nosing the bottom. He realised two things. Firstly if the bottom of the net was torn, then the trap would be torn also, and useless. The logical place to fit it was at the top because the fish only tried to escape when the boat stopped towing and the strain came off. Till then they were all packed in the cod end. When the strain came off for hauling the net aboard, they swam forward to escape, but by that time the trap had fallen over the entrance under its own weight, closing it off and making escape nearly impossible. Without a word, on the grounds that he did not want to interfere with the man, he came back to the 'Spectrum' and fitted traps into their nets, which did not have any, and he fitted them the way he had reasoned. The loss of fish was cut dramatically and he returned home shortly

The drifter on which William Thain first fished with a seine net in Grimsby. She is carrying the larch fenders which were used by all sizeable boats, sail, motor, or steam, before the rubber tyre proved such a convenient substitute. Also visible is the old fashioned "7" in her number and her crest on the bow. Most drifters skippers had their own crests, always on the funnel at least. This is a practice that has also almost disappeared.

afterwards to take charge of his father's drifter 'Zoe'. Soon he was conducting other experiments with rigging and achieved notable success by extending the hood of the head rope, first by one foot and then another. The contribution that he made to the fishing abilities of the seine net was considerable and for 60 years until his death in 1984 he was regarded as the leading authority on seine nets construction in the North of Scotland. Other men elsewhere were also experimenting but by 1930 the shape of the seine net had evolved, albeit with local variations, to the net that is used today.

Innovations during the coming 15 years were made to many other aspects of fishing foreby hull shapes and nets, and in spite of the restrictions imposed by these difficult times the whole future of the industry was shaped between the wars. The first improvements which required to be made once the seine net had been adapted, was to the handling equipment. Men were working from the very small yawls without any mechanical means at all, to the largest steam drifters and motor boats, nearly all of which had steam capstans, primarily designed to haul a bush rope and discharge herring. A few had winches, fewer still had winches and coilers, and most were doing their best to haul seine net ropes round the capstan barrel and hand coil them either on the deck or in the rope hole. Both methods were back breaking and, with the net being shot hourly, coiling could be continuous for eight hours or more. This meant standing bent and keeping your balance while in a most unnatural position, with a break of only a few minutes as the net was shot again.

Photograph by permission of Mr G. J. Addison, Cullen.

Mr George Addison and Mr Alec Finlay of Cullen hand-coiling aboard the 'Procure'. The capstan has the double chock necessary to keep the ropes seperate. Here they are coiling on deck but many boats coiled straight into the rope locker which was situated near the base of the capstan. The introduction of the mechanical coiler led to the ropes being spread more evenly along the deck as was the practice till the introduction of rope bins in the 1960's.

Where the ropes were being hauled by the capstan, whether it was over the broadside in the Danish method, or latterly over the stern in the fly dragging method, they had to be kept seperately. Often enough they would get entangled in the capstan barrel as it is difficult to keep to ropes turning seperately, particularly as the shape of the barrel tended to guide them together. The first attempt to prevent this was the introduction of a capstan barrel which roughly resembled two modern winch barrels bolted vertically together. There was a ridge in the middle which successfully kept both ropes apart, but that was really a stop-gap measure. Although the vast majority of the capstans had been made by the famous English firm of Elliot and Garrood in Beccles, replacements were often made in local foundries such as the Rose Street in Inverness and the Aberdeen Foundry.

The future obviously lay with winches and coilers and a few of the pioneering drifters had already had these fitted in Yarmouth, Grimsby and even adaptions of trawler gear in Aberdeen. These came with a variety of drives but the early winches were either steam driven or by a series of shafts which connected to the main engine. It did not take long, however, before the native ingenuity of local blacksmiths, engineers and mechanics took over and within 15 years Miller's were making the Fifer winch and coiler, The MacDuff Engineering Company had developed their famous machines, Main and Sutherland were turning out their winches and coilers by the score and they were available with belt or shaft drive connected to the main engine.

Photograph by permission of Mr D. Robertson, Aukengill.

The 'Westward' with her owners, the brothers Begg, lying at Aukengill pier. She was built in Thurso by Messrs Allan as a line boat in the 1920's. The influence of the styling of steam drifters can be seen in the shape of her stern and several boats were built in both England and Scotland to this pattern. Two yawls were built on Stroma with the same kind of stern.

Many of the large motor boats had a steam capstan which had been kept on board after they had been converted from sail and either a steam winch was installed or the steam boiler was removed and a small donkey engine was fitted to run the winch and coilers only. There was a wide variety of ways of doing things and it took some time before the system reached its most efficient. Apart from the above winches there were also Hollands, Belfast, Beccles manufactured by Elliot and Garrood, and a variety of lesser known and foreign machines available, particularly from Denmark, the home of seining.

Early winches were of very primitive and dangerous design, consisting only of the uncovered drives and gears held up on a stand. Even today care has to be taken when working around a revolving winch but in the 1920's and 30's there were many terrible accidents where men had their oilskins caught and lost arms, legs and their lives. None of the machinery was covered and it was only about 1930 that the first of the enclosed winches were manufactured, probably by either Miller or the MacDuff Engineering Co, but Lybster boats continued to use the original winches till after the Second World War. In March, 1932, Mr Robert Duthie, of Inverallochy, a member of the crew of the 'Golden Feather' was caught in the bight of a rope and whirled round the winch barrel. His boots flew off and landed beside another of the crew who noticed his plight. He rushed, stopped the winch and Mr Duthie was taken to the Bignold Hospital in Wick where it was discovered that some of his teeth had been knocked out and he had dislocated his shoulder. His was a very lucky escape. Mr Tommy Reid of Thurso had his leg torn off and the crew prevented him from bleeding to death by sticking the stump into a bag of flour which staunched the flow. He survived but there were many tragedies and indeed they occur to this day.

An Elliott and Garood hydraulic winch and coiler of 1948. It is difficult to believe that this famous company no longer exists.

But time was proceeding and by the 1930's a totally enclosed winch such as the Belfast, was available which had coilers attached to the top of the winch. They could be turned to whichever direction the net was being hauled. In October 1934 a hydraulic capstan, the Hyland, was on offer and it could be converted into a great line hauler very simply. The hydraulic capstan, and its direct descendant which was of great importance to the seine net fleet, did not achieve widespread popularity till well into the 1960's. They were made of quite different materials and to a higher tolerance than the engineering and foundry companies around the Moray Firth were used to in the 1920's.

Nearly all the metalwork then was cast and suffered many breakages, particularly of pinions, which could be broken by a sudden jerk, especially on a cold day. This was supplemented by the fact that a large percentage of the fishermen who looked after the engines and mechanical apparatus on the boats never seemed to believe that grease was good for moving parts and rarely used it. This in itself explains why the mechanics who had to repair the results were among the most accomplished and stylish users of strong language that could be met anywhere. And these mechanics had to be familiar with the natures of 20 different kinds of engines, a wide variety of winches, capstans, coilers, gear boxes, belts, shafts, chains. They had to be able to take out a broken pinion, or a completely smashed drive, take the pieces to a foundry if a spare was not available, have a new one cast, take it back to the workshop, machine it, often to a very high standard, and above all, get that boat back to sea. This usually involved crawling around in the bilges, working unprotected in rain or snow on the deck, or twisting themselves like acrobats to get around or underneath an engine. Sometimes they

Photograph by permission of Mr J. Rosie, Thurso.

Mr John Rosie, Wick, in his boiler suit, so typical of the hundreds of engineers who kept the Scottish fishing fleet at sea. They would turn out day or night, regardless of time or occasion, to get a boat, which had broken down, back to sea, and mended, invented, re-invented and improvised with startling imagination. There were many small engineering shops around the coasts without whom the fleet would not have survived.

would go to sea with the boats, travel to the west coast or even the Western Isles, stay away from home till the job was done and do whatever was necessary. And no matter what was necessary the boats were always charged a fair price, something that is rare today. From the 1920's, even before, until the boom of the 1960's the old established firms, many of whom have now gone, always asked only for what they honestly considered to be a reasonable price, which by modern standards seems ridiculous. Today fishermen are inclined to be charged according to how their boat is fishing, and usually at the rate at which the most successful in the fleet is fishing. There are hundreds of stories from 20 years ago and more, of how the engineering firms helped the fishermen, but very few today. In the bitter years of the 1920's and 30's the engineering firms took as heavy losses as the fishermen in their efforts to keep the fleet, particularly the herring fleet, at sea. These men, and companies, nearly all of which were family owned, are worthy of a book to themselves.

Among the early experimenters was Mr Alex Middler, engineer superintendent with Irvins of Fraserburgh. In 1922 he had been developing a creel hauler which was like a miniature capstan driven by a 6hp engine. It was not until 1924 that he finally got around to installing it in a yawl, to the great satisfaction of the owner, as the back breaking work of hauling a creel from ten or more fathoms disappeared. He seems also to have tackled the problem of gearing the barrel to turn at the correct speed for hauling. Others were later to experiment by fitting car and lorry gearboxes to winches to give a variable speed as the early machinery turned at the same speed as the engine. The only way to control the revolutions on the early winches was to run the main engine at the required speed. As early as 1924 Mr Middler was forecasting that the future lay with hydraulics and heavy oil engines, and this was at a time when the vast majority of engines were either paraffin or steam driven.

Elsewhere other matters which were to influence events, were coming into play. The Torry Research laboratory was becoming increasingly prominent and moved to new premises more suited to its needs in 1923. Out at sea, on which everything depended, things were slowly and surely getting worse due to a mixture of bad fishings, bad weather and bad politics.

Bad fishing seasons and bad weather the fishermen could take, and they had seen these often enough in the past. The whole economy and system of the herring industry, which still predominated Scottish fishing, was organised around a process of gradual payments and settlements which a poor fishing now and again hardly affected. That time, which had existed for over 120 years was swept away in 1914, although it was not apparent in the first year or so after the war. It was replaced by influences from outside, over which the fishermen had absolutely no control, but could only struggle against. Matters previously beyond their experience such as the deteriorating social situation at home and political conditions abroad, came into play with devastating effect.

The country was slipping towards the General Strike of 1926 and there were bursts of industrial unrest as it approached. Although the Strike itself only lasted about a week, the miners were out for six months with a serious effect on the coal burning fleet which numbered about 750. Apart from the strikes there was gradually increasing unemployment, which reduced demand for kippers and herring although white fish sales were increasing to the effect that by 1926 landings had risen to 56,000 cwt and the motor boats outgrossed steam seine netters for the first time by landing 39,800 cwts of the total. This may have been partly due to the fact that coal was difficult to obtain but landings by motor boats would only once again fall below those by drifters.

Photograph by permission of Mr J. McDonald, Wick.

The 'Whiteheather' with her drifter stern. She had a 60 Kelvin engine.

What really did the damage to the herring industry above all else was the loss of the foreign market. Three hundred and fifty thousand barrels of herring, out of a total of 551,000 went to Germany, creating a serious overdependence on that market which was to go seriously wrong the next year. In 1913, 2,442,000 barrels of herring had been exported, nearly all to Germany and Russia, which at that time included Poland, Estonia, Lithuania and Latvia.

Poland, and the other three Baltic States had achieved independence in 1919 and 1920 in the aftermath of the Russian Revolution and had begun buying herring in their own right. But the Government was becoming increasingly antagonistic towards trade with Russia which had taken 1,000,000 barrels of herring a year before the war. The Governments of the 1920's actively discouraged trade as the decade wore on because they saw no reason why they should help to feed a society which was promising bloody revolution around the world at the first opportunity. It obstructed and cancelled contracts with the Russians with the inevitable result that, on top of their other troubles, the fishermen had to watch while their largest market of all was denied them for political purposes. Large amounts of unsold herring lay ashore and curers were going out of business as a result of the cancellations or having to sell their herring at a loss. As it turned out the Russians bought no herring at all between 1927 and 1932 which were among the worst years the fishermen had ever known.

On the face of things 1926 was a time to batten down the hatches and wait for the storm to pass, yet there were two ring net fishermen from Campbeltown who were prepared to sail into the eye of the economic tempest by ordering a new boat from Miller's of St Monans. She was the 'Crimson Arrow' which was launched in 1927 for Mr John Short and Mr Robert Robertson. With the exception that she did not have a wheelhouse and was ten feet shorter, her hull was identical in appearance

Photograph by permission of Mr N. Short, Glasgow.

The 'Crimson Arrow' lying off Sanda Island harbour in May 1928, after delivering a picnic party to the island. Her ring net can clearly be seen and her horizontal steering wheel is immediately forrard of it at the hatch.

Typical drive arrangements for a fore-and-aft mounted Macduff winch, driven by a 26/30 Kelvin before the introduction of coilers.

Legend
- a.   Engine flywheel.
- b.   Cast iron sliding dog clutch.
- c.   Hardwood bearer bolted to vessel's timbers.
- d.   Cast iron bearing.
- e.   Cast iron crown and bevel drive, so called because of its shape.
- f.   Vertical drive shaft.
- i.   Cast iron bearing.
- j.   Cast iron crown and bevel drive.
- k.   Cast iron pedestal for shaft to barrels.
- m.   Cast iron brake pawl, showing side view in inset above.
- n.   Cast iron winch barrel for hauling ropes.

Drawn by Jean Vandecasteele from information provided by Mr John Rosie.

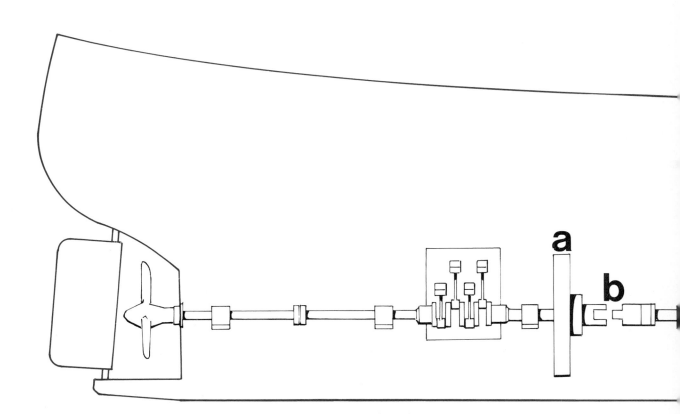

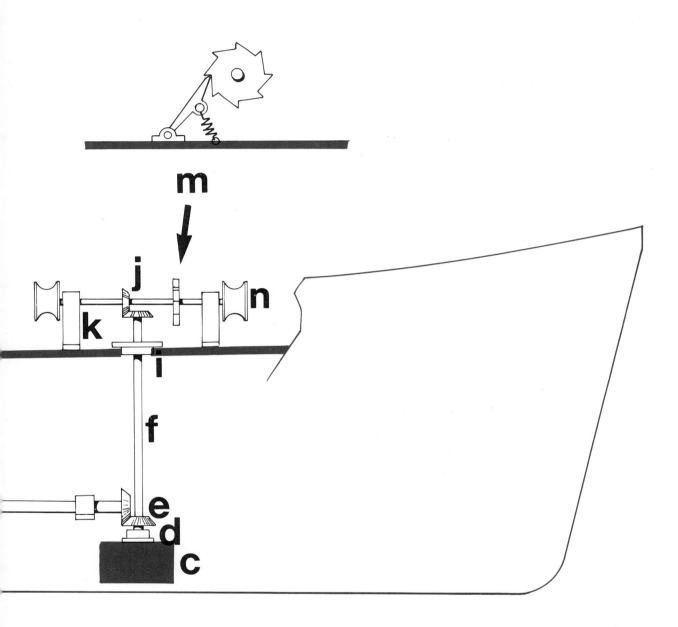

to the 'Falcon' which had been built for Mr Robertson four years before. What is important about the 'Crimson Arrow' is that she was a stepping stone to a boat that was to pioneer the use of many of the innovations which were beginning to appear. Her name was the 'Nil Desperandum,' a particularly appropriate one for the times, and she was launched for the same men, from the same yard, in August 1928. Only three other vessels have been launched with so many innovations, and they were her contemporaries. She was 46 feet long, had her wheelhouse forward of the hold and was the first boat to have her engine controls in the wheelhouse. Previously instructions had been shouted or telegraphed if the boat was too large for the skipper to reach the controls himself. She also had bulwarks, higher and safer for the seine net than the traditional sailing build which consisted of the frame ends with a shallow weatherboard attached. Her winch was the latest Miller design which would swivel on its mountings to whatever direction was required. This in itself had another novelty in the form of a two speed gearbox, one speed for hauling and the other for discharging the herring. The winch also had Miller's protected clutch which would disengage the drive automatically if the boat yawed and the strain came on from an awkward angle. Another novelty was a power lifter to empty the ring net and this was a great improvement on the old method of using a basket on a pole to skim the herring aboard. She had a newly developed Kelvin-Ricardo engine and carried a set of sails for emergencies. The 'Nil Desperandum' was specifically built for ring net fishing, but she was by no means the only vessel built at that time with a novel approach to fishing in mind.

Photograph by permission of the Fisheries Museum, Anstruther.

The revolutionary 'Nil Desperandum' launched for Robert Robertson and John Short of Campbeltown by James Miller and Sons in August 1928. She is seen here at St. Monans.

Photographs by permission of Mr N. Short, Glasgow.

Mr John Short at the helm of the 'Crimson Arrow' with the engine-man beside him. In the photograph on the right he is shown later in life mending, and wearing a beautifully knitted gansey.

About a year earlier the man who has to be regarded as the pioneer of seining from vessels designed specifically and solely for that purpose, in the face of great criticism and sarcasm, launched the 'Marigold' INS 234. He was John Campbell of Lossiemouth who began his fishing career under sail and was skipper of the 'Miss Campbells' when he was 18. From there he progressed to the 'Glengynack', a steam drifter which he had built with partners, but by 1912 was becoming convinced that the fishing fleet was becoming too large for the demand. The 1920's and 1930's were to prove his foresight only too accurate. He sold his 250 herring nets, with the intention of taking up fish curing, but the outbreak of war shortened his career there when he joined up in 1914. It was more than likely that his wartime observations helped him to firm up his ideas and he bought a drifter, which he renamed the 'Marigold' in 1920 and immediately went trawling with her. It was not until the following year that Lossiemouth men were to see the seine net in Grimsby and it is not clear if he was among them but he certainly adopted the seine net at the end of that year. He persisted at the seine net with the uneconomic 'Marigold' till 1926 and during that time he had been weighing up the possibilities of having a motor boat built specially for seining alone, even to the extent of having his family using their school mathematics to do calculations on power output, engine speeds and gearings so that he could formulate in his mind the kind of vessel and power he would need. By 1926 he was ready and on the heads of a promise from an old associate to put up half the money he went to James Wood, manager of the firm of William Wood in Lossiemouth, and explained his requirements. He agreed, quoted a price, and John Campbell returned to his associate to find that he had taken cold feet, with the excuse that he could not put money in a motor boat because they lost half their value whenever they were launched. By now committed, and with insufficient capital of his own, he persuaded his nephew John West, to take a share and work proceeded. And as it proceeded, so did the criticism and the attempts to dissuade him, with people even trying to get Mrs Campbell to influence him. Fortunately for thousands of fishermen who were to follow his example, he ignored them, and even though he was nagged by doubts and worry about the step he was taking, he proceeded to the sea.

Photograph by permission of Mr A. Campbell, Lossiemouth.

Mr John Campbell, Lossiemouth, the first Scottish fisherman to fully commit himself to seine net fishing.

Photograph by courtesy of Mrs H. Brownlee, Lossiemouth.

Mr James Macleod of the 'Briar' in later life.

Photograph by permission of Mr A. Campbell, Lossiemouth.

The 'Marigold', built by Mr John Campbell solely for the purpose of seine net fishing. The derrick is carried in this position to give room on deck.

Photograph by permission of Mrs H. Brownlee, Lossiemouth.

The second seine net boat in Lossiemouth.

Within two and a half months the 'Marigold' had paid the almost unbelievable dividend of 12½%. This example was not lost on the observers and soon a close friend, James Macleod, made arrangements to have the 'Briar' built along the same lines. The 'Briar', INS 420, had a new design of propeller and a more compact reverse gear which was fitted two frames further aft than the 'Marigold'. This was an important step towards the day when the increasing size of the boats, and advancing engineering, would allow both the crew and the engine to be housed aft. But that would be in the future. Another vessel built about the same time was the 'Vine' which William Slater redesigned with the latest Gardner 48/50 semi-diesel.

Photograph by permission of Mr D. Stewart, Falkirk.

The crew of the 'Briar' empty the net when everything was done by hand. They are, right to left: James Stewart, John Macleod, James Macleod, looking out of the wheelhouse; in front — Peter Stewart, later to be killed during the war and, not clearly visible, is Johnny Mackenzie the driver at the back.

Equally progressive, and almost certainly the first to be launched as a duel, even multi-purpose craft capable of undertaking any of the common fishing methods without alteration, was the 'Cutty Sark'. She was built in the spring of 1928 by J. G. Forbes, Sandhaven, and should hold as prominent a place in fishing history as her illustrious namesake does in mercantile history. She had a 36/42 cartridge start Petter engine, forward mounted, but her capstan which was on the foredeck had its own engine. Her winch and coiler were mounted aft of the wheelhouse, and were driven from the main shaft running from the engine to the propeller. The steering gear consisted of a chain drive between the wheel and the rudder post, in the same style as the steam drifters, but a novelty in wooden boats. These, especially the converted sail boats, all had worm gear consisting of a rod which was attached to the rudder and turned it by being screwed backwards or forwards. The use of the chain caused yet another innovation in the shape of the platform which was built over the rudder post to prevent the net from becoming tangled with it. Hundreds of thousands of seine nets were to be shot from these in the coming years.

Photograph by permission of Mr W. Macdonald, Fraserburgh.

The 'Cutty Sark', built by J. & G. Forbes and unquestionably one of the milestones in the history of Scottish fishing.

Like most of the vessels to be built in the next ten years, and the three trail blazers which were to follow her from the Fife yards so shortly after, she carried a set of sails. The 'Cutty Sark' was ketch rigged and could undertake drifting, seining, lining or ring netting by simply laying on whatever gear was necessary. Thirty-two similar vessels were to be built in 1928, ranging from 30 to 45 feet in length, and seven were over 45 feet, nearly all for Eyemouth. The smaller vessels were for the Moray coast.

The 'Cutty Sark' had been launched at a time when seine netting was beginning to appear as an alternative to herring fishing rather than a supplement to it. After the disastrous years of 1926 and 1927, when landing by drifters had collapsed because of lack of coal, many turned to seine net because it required much less coal and the first three months of 1928 were very successful for all the boats which were seining. Steam boats landed a total of 48,600 cwts and motor boats 47,800 cwts, a total of 96,000 and this was to be the last time that steam seiners outfished the motor boats. Prices were good but even with these it was becoming obvious that the steam drifter carried too many overheads, particularly by comparison with a small motor boat, half her size, but which could fish just as well. As early as 1916 the Government had recognised that the steam drifter was obsolescent, only 17 years after the beginning of its widespread adoption, but it did not seriously do anything, for a variety of more pressing reasons elsewhere, about their conversion to oil until 1928.

About the same time as the 'Cutty Sark' was being launched the Government had bought about 20 of the original "Pipe Shank" or "Woodbine" drifters, so called because their funnels resembled

Photograph by permission of Mrs H. Brownlee, Lossiemouth.

Skipper James Macleod at the helm of the 'Briar'. The 'Briar'
sank during the war after being accidentally rammed by a naval
vessel. This was shortly after she had been circled by a U-Boat
which obviously did not think she was worth a shell.

these smokers comforts in shape. They had been laid up at Lowestoft and Yarmouth because they were too under-powered for seine netting and too small to compete with the large "Smith Dockies" as many of the large modern drifters were called. Their steam engines were removed and 36 horsepower oil engines installed, giving them nearly double their steam power. They were between 45 and 50 feet long, slightly larger than the new motor boats being built by Forbes and Miller, and were offered for sale on hire purchase, with interest at 3%. It is worth noting that when they were coal burners they consumed about four tons a week as opposed to the 15 or more by the largest of the standard drifters, so called because they were built to the government standard design. A motor boat with a paraffin engine could get the same results at the seine net for around 50 gallons at 11 pence per gallon, or if she had a diesel engine for 5½d per gallon. And she did not need anybody to throw the oil into the engine either, oils such as Russian Vapourising Oil, Anglo American Vapourising Oil, Youngs Paraffin, Pratts, Shell, Wakefield Motorine, and many other lubricating oils. They came in different strengths according to the time of year as there was no such thing as a multi-purpose oil.

Engines were very large in comparison to their power and could not be installed aft in the small boats of between 35 and 45 feet because of the lack of room created by the sheer. This problem did not exist with the large converted sailing boats which had enough room below for the cabin and the engine room to be aft. The matter was complicated by the addition of a gearbox which occupied even more room. As the size of the boats grew, or more importantly the engines became more compact, they were able to be mounted aft but the stage where both crews and engines could be housed aft of the hold was some way off in the small seine netters. In the 1930's when an engine was mounted aft it usually meant that the cabin was forward, a condition that was never popular particularly if the fishermen were trying to take a meal on a rough day. And conversely when an engine was mounted forward more often than not the exhaust blew across the deck, choking and covering the crew with soot. It was bad enough with one engine but some boats had two forward, meaning that the exhaust would be blown across the deck except when the wind was held dead astern. This only became a problem at the seine net, because previously the herring nets had usually been hauled with the engine stopped, and lining was done from steam boats whose funnels kept smoke clear of the decks. Although Lossiemouth was now showing signs of her dominance of the seine net industry for the next three decades there were still 29 steam drifters at the seine net there as 1928 came to a close. One very good effect of 1928 had been that during the year share fishermen were brought into the scope of the National Insurance and Pensions Acts from which they had previously been excluded as adventurers. Contributions were still voluntary, but at least fishermen could now take out this form of insurance.

Photograph by permission of Mr J. G. Addison, Cullen.

Cullen harbour in the 1930's. The boats are the Fifie 'Liberty' and the drifters 'Resource', 'Deliverer' and the 'Xmas Morn' at the point. The four motor boats together are from the outside:- 'Glide', 'Tyro', 'Fidelity' and 'Procure'. The 'Gleaner' and 'Quest' are ahead of them.

One other outstanding event which was to have a great influence on Scottish fishing after the Second World War took place about the 4th of August in the English port of Grimsby. There the trawler 'St Endelion' set sail equipped with an echo sounder which had been built to an Admiralty patent by Messrs Henry Hughes, later to become the renowned firm of Kelvin Hughes. The impact it made was immediate and the 'St Endelion's' example was quickly followed by other trawlers because the use of the echo sounder made the time wasting need to find the ground with a leadline, obsolete overnight. Marconi, who had hitherto concentrated on radio, produced a set which was installed in the drifter 'Violet and Rose' in 1930 and this made a great impression on all who came in contact with it. But above all, the instrument which was to really catch the imagination of both skippers and owners was unquestionably the Hughes MS 3, the letters MS standing for Magneto Striction which is a way of converting electrical pulses to acoustic pulses, or simply electric waves to sound waves and vice versa, so that the result can be seen on a dial. Or in the case of the MS series which was introduced in 1933, on a paper strip which showed a profile of the sea bottom.

The reason why the Scottish fishing fleet did not adopt the echo-sounders till after the war was threefold. Firstly the majority was still herring drifters, for whom the state of the bottom was unimportant and secondly the section of the fleet that was seine netting was doubly fortunate. It had vast expanses of sand, mud or shingle such as the Moray Firth to work, where obstacles were relatively few and the grounds were teeming with fish. They did not need an instrument, yet, to find fish. And in the 1930's cash for anything but essentials was non-existent.

As the echo-sounder made its mark so that other instrument to which it was a first cousin, was beginning to find acceptability among fishermen.

Radio had come a long way since 1901 and had begun to take enormous strides after the end of the First World War, by which time speech transmissions had been mastered and millions of people had access to sets across the world. Radio telephony came into close contact with the fishermen when the Royal National Lifeboat Institution began installing sets in 1926 but it was bulky and very susceptible to dampness and expensive. However, gradually, with company vessels such as trawlers leading the way, the fleet did adopt radio, and the vast majority of the sets were receivers only till after the Second World War. As late as 1936, 123 trawlers and liners had radio telephone in the Scottish fleet; 236 had receivers only. Of 428 steam drifters, only one had radio telephone and the rest receivers only, as did the 126 motor boats which were equipped with radio, nearly all of which were battery powered.

The delay in the installation of radio telephone equipment was again that the privately owned vessels did not have the same uses as fleets, and receivers were quite adequate for their needs which mainly centred on the weather forecast. There was nothing in the way of market reports which would send them away from ports which had a glut, and in the 1930's things were generally bad all over anyway. One thing they did listen for, over and above the weather forecast, was that every quarter of an hour a short silence was observed so that weak distress signals could be detected. Trawlers with radio rooms had these periods marked on the clock faces. Generally however, the life saving potential of a radio transmitter was not considered worth the cost till after the war.

January 1929 opened to find that there were now 17 motor boats seine net fishing from Fraserburgh, but most of the fleet was trying to make the best of a very poor winter herring fishing. Ashore the organisation to process the white fish and its by-products had struggled to its feet. The fish were landed either gutted or ungutted, according to custom at individual ports, but generally gutted fish attracted a marginally better price. As in the herring industry, where most of the guts were used as manure, or were converted into a variety of additives to other products, which included boot polish in Wick, so the white fish offal was processed. There were factories in Aberdeen, Granton, Glasgow and Falkirk producing fishmeal, fertiliser, and glue. Cod liver oil was being made in Aberdeen and salted fish skins were exported to Vienna for tanning from the same city. The Marvis factory in Wick was turning out dehydrated fish which could be cooked in a variety of ways and MacConnachies were tinning herring in Fraserburgh.

But exports of the bulk of the catch, herring, were still in a bad way. There had been sporadic attempts to recover the Russian export market and they did begin to buy herring again in January 1928 but this only met with indifferent success because of government hostility to any trade with them.

There was sporadic trade with Germany and the Baltic States, but nothing like what it had been or what the industry needed. But what the industry did most definitely want, and was to acquire in large numbers in the coming years, was already among it. It was cheap, handsome and it had electricity. In fact there were two of them, one called the 'Winaway' built by Mr Alexander Aitken of

Photograph by permission of the Fisheries Museum, Anstruther.

The launch of the 'Onaway' from the famous yard of James Miller and Sons, St. Monans. She has the classic Fifie hull but was referred to as a Super Baldie.

Anstruther and the 'Onaway' was by Mr Walter Reekie of St Monans. The 'Onaway' was 53.6 feet over stems 16 feet in beam and drew seven feet, with a registered tonnage of 26.75. She was powerfully built with oak frames at 13½ inch centres. Her engine was a four cylinder 48hp Gardner semi-diesel and was mounted aft, meaning that her cabin was in the foc'sle and it was the last word in comfort and design. The beds were six feet three inches long by 22½ wide, enormous by the standard of the day; each crew member had a locker or drawer, for his dress clothes and another for his sea clothes. Previously nearly all fishermen had to keep their spare clothes in a kitbag or a kist if there was room. The finish was in mahogany panelling and the table was suspended from the deck above, which gave the crew the luxury of being able to stretch their legs, something that was also a rarity then. As she was primarily built as a herring drifter, although seine net was accounted for in her construction, she had a steam capstan with the boiler set in the forehold. It seems surprising that she did not have a winch and coilers fitted at her launch but this may be due to the owners intention of being primarily herring fishermen. Like the 'Winaway' which was almost a sister ship she had had electricity installed during construction and they are probably the first vessels to be so designed in Scotland. Their running costs were reported at two pence per mile and they were also the first vessels with wheelhouses designed to hold radio receivers. They were not the first vessels to have radio receivers, in Scotland, and several already had them by that time. Most of the radios in use had been fitted in Yarmouth, Lowestoft, Grimsby or Aberdeen as the radio service industry had not developed to the smaller ports. This, in fact, may be the reason why both were launched, and at first fished, without radio which was fitted about six months after they had been in service. They were nicknamed "Super Baldies," the Baldie being a half decked hull which first appeared during the wars of Independence which Garibaldi fought in Italy in the 1860's.

Photograph by permission of Mr J. G. Addison, Cullen.

Mr Adam Addison and a crew member of the 'Procure' gut during a drag.

The Zulu hull, first constructed by William Campbell of Branderburgh in 1879, took her name from the fact that the Zulu war against Cetawayo was going on at the time, and indeed the second Zulu to be built was called after him. Obviously these names were chosen skilfully as at the time they were topical and on everybody's lips thanks to the full way in which the local newspapers were reporting on world events. It was good advertising.

The launch of these two vessels were about the only good thing that happened to the fishing industry that year which was one of unremitting adversity generally. The fishing was very poor and the weather matched it causing heavy losses of gear. It was a time when the few vessels with radio would hear the weather forecast and, if it was bad, would pass it along to those who had none, and they then could all return to port in time. Sometimes, a wrong forecast of a gale would be given and several times in the stormy year of 1929 the herring fleet hauled its nets and returned to port in anticipation of a gale which did not materialise. Of course, there were always one or two bolder spirits who would not come in, either out of bravado or perhaps they had a fisherman aboard who was an expert meteorologist, as some indeed were. Almost invariably they would arrive back in the morning full of herring, to the chagrin of the others. After the third false alarm in as many weeks even the most tolerant of human frailty were provoked. The staunchly Christian Mr George Flett of Wick, who had never been known to criticise anybody in his life, was moved to observe: "That mannie tells a lot o' lees." Men of lesser principle had other ways of expressing their dissatisfaction. Of course the inevitable happened during the East Anglian fishing.

The Equinoxial gales were late and it was generally assumed that, as they had not blown by the end of September, there would not be any until the middle of December. The weather would be variable, as it always was towards the year end but nothing more than that to which the fleet was well accustomed. On 11th November the notorious gale, to be called the Armistice Breeze, took the fleet by surprise. There had been a half-hearted warning broadcast but very few paid any attention after their previous experiences with the forecasts that year. The loss of gear was very great, with some boats losing their whole fleets. Others sustained very heavy damage as the drifts become entangled and it was only the handful of boats which were not fishing that survived unscathed. Normally the season would have had another four or five weeks to go, and desperate though the losses were, the fishermen would have replaced them against the possibility of making some sort of recovery. However, on top of these losses, the Government began actively discouraging any attempt to sell herring to Russia and this made further fishing pointless. Most of the Scottish fleet returned home a month early to record one of the most disastrous fishings in living memory. From then on the construction of small, wooden, seine net boats expanded steadily. The steam drifter still had a quarter of a century's life left, but it was a life that was artificially prolonged by the Second World War. The last steam drifter was to be built in 1932 and by 1938 there were 402 in the Scottish fleet of liners and drifters compared with 854 in 1920.

1930 opened with news that, in spite of their tribulations, many a fisherman heard with more than just a passing thought. It was that their old friend, Scarborough Jeemie, the Welsh eccentric with the English tee-name who lived in Scotland, had altered his helm to put this troubled world astern of him.

Photograph by permission of Mrs N. Leitch.

Scarborough Jeemie outside his hut with Sandy, his dog and Clemenceau, Asquith, Lloyd George and Churchill.

Mr Tudor James was the son and grandson of well-to-do preachers who lived near Mumbles Bay in Wales. As a young man he had gone to Oxford University to study a musical degree, and then follow his father into the ministry, but while he was there both parents died and he inherited the then enormous sum of £30,000. He immediately embarked on a high flown life style and spent his holidays between London clubs and various continental resorts, particularly Monte Carlo. For a few years after graduating he lived on his legacy and travelled around Europe in the company of many well-to-do English families to whom he was related through his mother. However, he had never given up on the idea of being a preacher and about 1890 decided to set up an organisation on similar lines to that which had been created by the Royal National Mission to Deep Sea Fishermen. He chose Scarborough as his base, bought a house there which he converted into a tea room and recreation hall, and called the "Old Ship." To begin with it was very successful and after a few years he was sponsoring football and hockey teams, a choir and an orchestra which gave charity concerts. Unfortunately, he was a hopeless business man and the teas he sold did not even cover their cost which meant that he had to use his money to maintain the building and pay his helpers. After the first five years or so decline set in and, as his money and following went, he began to behave eccentrically. He often dressed up and went about in oilskins and sou'wester but what was worse from the view of the town council, he dressed the "Old Ship" up in an eccentric fashion as well.

By 1905 Scarborough was making, and succeeding with, a bid to become a fashionable resort. Unfortunately, the "Old Ship" which Tudor James had now tarred, hung with old nets, lifebuoys and buoys, and did not have two windows painted the same colour, was smack in the middle of the main promenade, to the great dismay of the council. Threats, pleadings, compulsory orders were of no avail and even visits from his brother, who was a director of Rio Tinto Zinc, failed to dislodge him. Eventually the council ran out of patience, had the building condemned and sent down a labour force to evict him and demolish the "Old Ship". He got several fishermen to help and succeeded in fighting off the demolition squad but it was only a temporary respite. They returned with the fire brigade and hosed the defenders out into the street, and Mr Tudor James had to find a new abode.

He had been in Scarborough for about 20 years and during that time had met hundreds of Scottish fishermen who had put in there on their way to and from the East Anglian fishings. So his choice of abode lay with Scotland and he set up his new home in Wick in 1908 or 1909. At first he tried to begin as he had in Scarborough but did not have the money to acquire property and had to start his mission in a women's rest station. It did not succeed and after a year in lodgings finally went to live in an old gunpowder store on the north side of the bay. From this humble abode, which he christened "The Cabin" grew his real fame and he passed into fishing lore with great affection.

"The Cabin" was only about ten feet square and for the first few years he meticulously whitewashed the step and the floor. Up to 1914 he received many visitors whom he greeted with a caution to mind his marble step and to lower their topsails. In other words to remove their bonnets. Most of them were from the south side of the Moray Firth and attended the open air services which he held in the summer, playing his violin and leading the hymn singing. Every service began with the hymn "Showers of Blessings" which he changed to Shoals of Herring. Sometimes he would hold small private services aboard the boats in harbour but his real claim to fame was his observation of naval etiquette. As the herring fleet arrived each morning, sometimes up to 200 vessels, he would be on the headland waving a flag in greeting to them. Without fail every one blew their sirens in acknowledgement, and the ceremony was repeated in the afternoon when they returned to sea. He was a clever, cultured and witty man who became increasingly hostile towards fishcurers and politicians. In the 1920's as the fishermens difficulties increased with the decade, and he made many enemies by making frequent speeches at street corners about the fishcurers. He had a dog, cats and several hens, all of whom were named after politicians and generals of the First World War whom he did not like. He frequently would select one for a tirade which would last an hour or two.

As the decade wore on, age and the damp conditions in which he lived began to affect him and he rarely went into the town during the last three years of his life. The people nearby kept an eye on him and saw that he was fed but latterly he fell into a state of squalor. Yet his mind did not fail and he retained his sharp wit to the end, by which time he was living in the most abject poverty as his brother had died and all family communications with him ceased.

He thought that he was going to die in the spring of 1928 and decided to throw a party for some of his old acquaintances whom he knew to be at the winter fishing in Wick. So he wrote to a friend in London: "Send me immediately two sprigs of borage, of the finest brandy, a cask of sherry and one of molasses. A wine glass of Curacoa, and another Maraschino. A basket of strawberries. I'd like to make a naval cup with silver braid. I want to make my old friends a bowl of punch before I bid them farewell and a toast to prosperity in this life before I await them in the next."

He later cancelled his order but his condition steadily worsened until latterly he had to be taken into the poorhouse at Latheron. There he died at the age of 75 on Xmas Eve 1929 and was buried in an unmarked paupers grave.

Fishermen, most of whom acknowledged superstition in one way or another, would have been well justified in regarding their old friend's death as an evil omen. If ever they should have burnt the witch, it should have been in January 1930 because that month ushered in almost a decade of relentless and unremitting war with poverty and debt. Many a well-to-do fisherman who had managed to withstand the 20's on his savings, was ruined and broken.

During the 1930's it was not uncommon for a shot like this to be dumped, a process which took as long to complete as it did to haul. This was one of the most demoralising of all the tribulations which befell the fishermen when the prospect of relief from the grinding oppression of debt was dashed from him, just when he thought that he had it within his grasp.

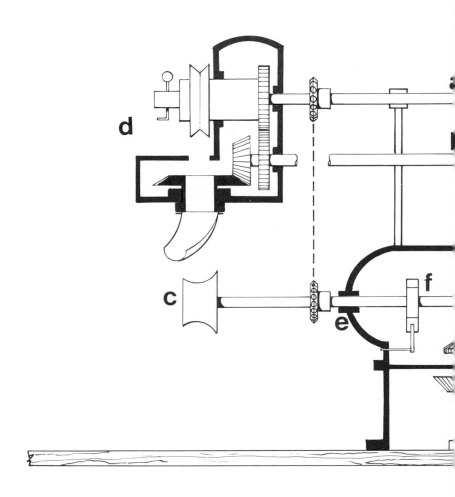

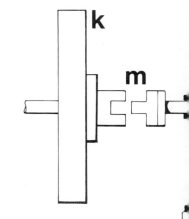

Details of the connections between the engine and a belt driven winch of the kind in use before the introduction of hydraulic power.

Legend
a. Rotating shaft.
b. Fixed shaft.
c. Winch barrel for hauling ropes.
d. Coilers to which ropes were led from winch barrel.
e. Brass bearings.
f. Brake.
g. Jockey pulley handle.
h. Bearing.
i. Jockey pulley for tensioning belt drive.
j. Belt drive.
k. Engine flywheel.
m. Sliding dog clutch to engage drive to winch.
n. Drop drive to allow drive shaft to run beneath floors.
o. Bearings to align and steady drive shaft.
p. Drive pulley.

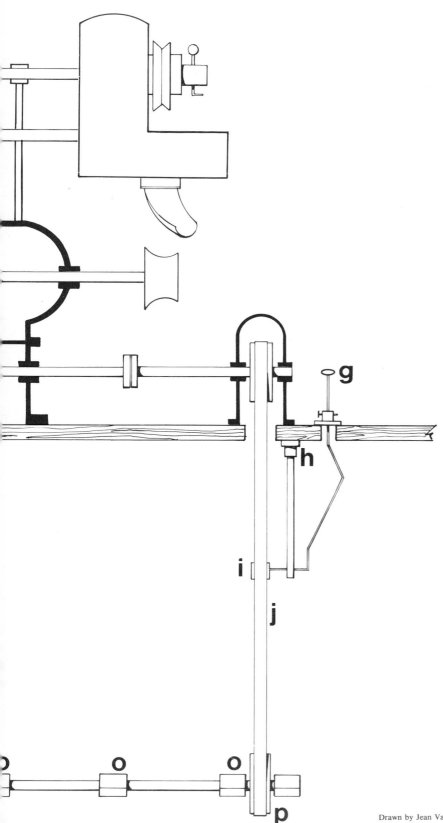

g

h

i

j

o   o   o

p

Drawn by Jean Vandecasteele from information provided by Mr John Rosie.

Wick's herring fleet had been decimated since 1900 and its position had long been superceded by Fraserburgh. It is worth noting that Wick gave in to the adverse conditions after the First World War almost without a struggle, the only major port to do so. It was as if the old town, exhausted by its efforts in the 19th Century, had no reserves of strength left for the fight for existence in the 20th. Emigrations, more often than not to the slums of the cities in the south or abroad, almost reached epidemic proportions as people fled before the economic storm. Only a few of the stouter hearts stuck it out at the sea and Wick found itself with a large curing organisation ashore, capable of processing the catch of 200 drifters, but a fleet of only 30 or so belonging to the town. It was totally dependent on visiting vessels for viability, something for which it was to pay the penalty after the war.

Other ports resisted the economic conditions with much more vigour, if not much more success if they remained at the herring fishing. The Government was still obstructing trade with Soviet Russia but there was some recovery in the German, Polish and Baltic markets. The only sign of any hope in 1930 and 1931 was the increasing number of small motor boats which were being built by Noble's, Jones, Thomson, Forbes, Miller, Irvine's, Macduff Engineering and many others. These names were a guarantee of workmanship of the highest order and several vessels built by these companies are still fishing in the 1980's, nearly 60 years later. The numbers of motor vessels seine netting between 1926 and 1933 grew as follows; 370, 406, 432, 462, 485, 509, 567, and 622. By 1932 the price of seined fish had fallen from an average of 22/9 in 1929 to 17/4 a hundred-weight.

Bad though things were in Wick, not all fishermen had had the fight knocked out of them. The progressive skipper Jimmy Bremner had the 'Fisher Boy' launched on 6th February, 1932 from the yard of D. Alexander. This was the first new vessel of any size to be built in Wick since the drifter 'Chance' in 1907, 25 years earlier. She was 49 feet long, had a 36hp Gardner semi-diesel, a radio receiver, could carry 300 gallons of fuel which she burnt at the rate of 2½ gallons per hour. In Wick this fuel cost seven pence a gallon, but he could get it in Jarrow on the way to Yarmouth for four pence. When he retired in 1962 fuel was 6/8 a gallon. Complete with four nets and 14 coils of rope, she cost £1397 ready for the sea and the first engine overhaul cost £4.10.0.

1932 saw the first experiments with a net called the "Pareja," or bull net, introduced from Spain and so called because its wings resembled the horns of a Miura fighting bull. It was towed between two boats and is called the pair trawl today. Elsewhere things were very bad and it was reported in the local press around the coast that a Yarmouth fishing company had gone bankrupt and its creditors had exposed its 11 drifters for public auction. There was a reserve price of £675 on each but none received any bids. Exports of herring were down from 2,442,000 barrels in 1913 to 880,000 and the desperate situation prompted two of the trade associates to amalgamate to see if any pressure could be brought on a government which displayed an almost complete indifference to the plight of the herring industry, largely for political reasons. In an attempt to force some kind of response the Scottish Herring Producers Association was formed on 26th February, 1932, by the Herring Salesmen's Association and the Scottish Steam Drifters Association. It was designed to represent the interests of all involved, salesmen, boatowners, share fishermen and hired men. An Aberdeen advocate, Mr Eric Brander was appointed chairman and three committees were set up. One was to consider the adoption of uniform wages for engineers, firemen and cooks, who were the only members of the crew of a drifter with guaranteed pay. Another committee was to report on the constitution, administration and formation of local branches in the 14 districts; the third was to undertake the very important task of seeing how markets could be won and to impress on the Government the urgency of pressing the Russians to take more herring.

While the new body did not appear to make much impression on the Government or the Secretary of State, it did plant a seed that bore fruit about four years later. At the time it seemed as if the Government had fallen back on the old political trick of listening with apparent concern and then palming them off with the usual hypocrisy. And not only the British Government were playing the political game in which the fishermen were the ball. The Russians were already antagonised by the attitude of this country but were needing to replace the shortage of food caused by Stalin's massacres of the peasantry. However, they were also well aware of the plight of the fishing industry here and

Skipper Jim Bremner lands fish in Scrabster. He was the first man to install a radio in Wick, the first to build a new boat for 25 years between 1907 and 1932 for the port, the last to pursue the herring fishing in the traditional way, and the last Wick skipper to go to Yarmouth, in 1953. He is seen here with his son John who followed him as skipper and, at the winch, his brother Sandy who by popular consent is considered to have been the cleverest man ever to have sailed from Wick. His brains and speed of thought, particularly his wit, were widely feared and respected.

realised that they could screw the price of herring down to a very low level here if they held out long enough. It was a matter of which government would yield first, the Russians to internal starvation or the British to pressures from their fishermen. Whichever it would be, the compromise was not to come in 1932.

In 1933 there seemed to be an improvement, but it was an illusion. Latvia decided to increase imports from Scotland to 53,000 barrels, a figure which would make it the third most important market. However, once the herring had been delivered, the Latvian Government immediately imposed foreign currency restrictions because of a financial crisis and none of the herring was paid till a year later. The British Government had not guaranteed finance for the deal and quite a few smaller curers were forced out of business, taking a proportionate amount of fishermen with them. Even with the Latvian order, exports were down to 733,000 barrels by the end of 1933. On 20th

Gutted at the rate of 40 a minute, selected into five qualities and plenty more where they came from.

December a small announcement was made by the Government to the effect that a Sea Fish Commission had been appointed, but nobody had much faith in that as the creation of a Commission was another old dodge to keep complaints down.

1934 was about as bad as 1929, and some ways worse, because of the scarcity of herring and the poor quality. The opening of the summer season found the industry in a state of uncertainty unlike anything experienced outside of war. Many curers, who had been carrying losses for more than a year, had reduced the arles to the women gutting crews. The arles were the traditional fee which passed from the hirer to the hired to confirm a labour agreement. By accepting the arles the woman, as indeed did farm servants at feeing markets, undertook to work for the season or term for the curer. The same procedure applied to soldiers accepting the Kings Shilling and to hired men at the fishing. However just before the season started, unemployment benefit was increased to more than the 10/- arles, and many of the women gave them arles back. The result was that the work force necessary to process the herring was noticeably reduced. This and the poor market prospects, was responsible for much of the dumping that took place that summer. The fishings were poor, the quality poor and made worse by a heavy presence of dog fish which made large quantities of herring unattractive to the buyers. Contrary to experience where scarcity usually meant good prices, some of the worst dumping ever experienced took place. One thousand eight hundred crans were dumped in Wick on 19th June, 400 in Fraserburgh on 26th and 1600 in Lerwick on 27th June. Herring came down to the totally uneconomic price of 10/- a cran. A steam drifter needed to gross at least £90 a week to break even, and more if she was buying nets or being paid up under a loan scheme. In 1934 this was an unattainable figure for most skippers.

Photograph by permission of Mr P. McCabe, Peterhead.

BF 361 the 'Boy David' lands a good shot at Aberdeen.

Photograph by permission of Mr A. Henderson, Wick.

'The Rival 11' coming into Wick with her cotton nets hung to dry. She was built as a motor vessel but retained the proportions of the sailing Fifies. She was the first diesel engined fishing boat in Scotland built as the 'Linfar'.

Perhaps some of the Commissions findings were filtering through to the Government by June because, while it was not exactly encouraging trade with Russia it was turning a blind eye to any that private curers could arrange. They had offered a sort of half hearted help a month earlier but there was a catch. There would be a guaranteed subsidy if net earnings fell short of fitting out costs, to a maximum of £50 for a steam drifter and £25 for a motor boat. But this would only be paid if fewer than 1000 boats were at sea on 7th July, and the Fishermen's Association had to regulate the numbers voluntarily. Loans were also made available for the purchase of nets, at 3% interest. In response herring were being landed and something had to be done with it. So the Government looked away while negotiations began with the Russians.

They wanted 70,000 barrels and were in a buyers market. From the beginning of the negotiations they offered a very low price and imposed rigid conditions. They insisted on a second inspection of the herring in October before accepting them and this meant that the curers had to keep them for about three months, with one inspection shortly after they had been packed and another just before shipping, if they were accepted. The way the Russian buyers had of inspecting the herring was to open barrels at random and take a bite out of the back of a few to test for quality.

What the delay of three or four months meant was that the curers would have to tie up their scarce capital for that length of time, plus the delay in waiting for payment. This was on top of a dead loss on the sale in itself, but the deal fell through because of lack of finance. The Government was

Photograph by permission of Mr P. McCabe, Peterhead.
The 'Cairntoul' originally the 'Poppy', one of the large motor drifters built between the wars.

taking nothing to do with the negotiations anyway, so the Herring Trade Association tried to get the Co-operative Society to finance the contract. They, however, asked for impossible guarantees, as did the next organisation to be approached, The National Bank of Scotland, so all the effort went for nothing.

The gloom was relieved in emotional if not physical terms on 24th August when the Commission made its report and recommendations. There was not a lot that was new about it but at least it was a sort of an official report which might make the Government pay attention. Briefly what the Commission said was this:—

If the catch of herring in 1933 had not been so low then one third of the fleet would have been redundant in normal circumstances. It recommended an orderly reduction of the fleet by the control of a government department rather than allowing things to go on as they were with poverty and desperation forcing men out of the herring industry. A Herring Board should be set up in Edinburgh which would oversee all aspects of the fishing. There should be a system of licencing for all, herring fishermen, salesmen, curers and kipperers. Only those with licences would be allowed to pursue whatever line they were in and to qualify they would have to meet certain standards. Credit facilities to assist with boat refits were suggested as were seasons, fishing areas, and close seasons. Legislation to this effect had been passed over 400 years before. They also suggested that imports from Norway should be regulated to assist the home market. One of their most interesting proposals was that the Herring Board should conduct the administration of all exports and arrange shipping, freight, insurance, foreign agencies, credit to finance contracts till payment was received and to promote sales at home by advertising. Curers were at liberty to do the negotiations, with the exception of Russia, but once the contracts had been made the Board would take them over. They would also have the power to force a curer to sell their surplus of herring if there was a danger of their being dumped on the home market. Another interesting suggestion they made was that the brine chilling of herring might be examined as an alternative to the traditional cure.

These of course, were only recommendations to the Government but they were publicised to invite comment. The report was widely approved and endorsed almost without comment by the Herring Producers Association. So with these proposals to think about the industry closed the 1934 season during which only Lerwick made anything like a successful showing. For the rest it was the same sad story which was slightly lifted by the news that a contract had been negotiated with Germany. Adolf Hitler had not yet attracted too much attention.

In December the Scottish Boatowners Mutual Insurance Association, which had been established in 1925, called a special meeting in Buckie to see how it could help its members who numbered 200 steam drifters and 100 motor boats. They paid £12,300 from their reserves to the subscribers, most of whom were in a very bad financial condition. A sign of the times lay in the fact that even the mighty Buckie fleet had gone from 591 vessels in 1920 to 361 in 1934. Lossiemouth disposed of its last steam drifter and now had the most modern fleet in Scotland, and possibly Britain. Her fishermen were beginning to explore the fishing grounds along the north and west coasts, even as far as the Irish Coast. They had been going there for seven generations but this was different, and Lossiemouth asserted itself in the position of premier seine net port as Fraserburgh was the premier herring port. But even Lossiemouth's thrusting enterprise was affected by the general state of the market and landings by motor seine net boats fell by 5%, for the second time only, before the Second World War. The figures for landings by the Scottish fleet are as follows, in hundredweights.

Year	steam	motor	Year	steam	motor
1922	46700	17600	1930	18900	59100
1923	53200	18800	1931	14600	89300
1924	64300	32900	1932	28900	112700
1925	31200	30300	1933	12200	147500
1926	26200	39800	1934	16000	187800
1927	24600	47800	1935	5100	178100
1928	48600	47800	1936	2100	243500
1929	31500	55300	1937	800	323100

About the same time as the Scottish Mutual Boatowners Insurance Association was trying to relieve the plight of its members, a similarly philanthropic gesture was being made on a rainy December night in Wick; the method was different but the principles were roughly the same. Two fishermen entered the premises of one of the more prominent fishsalesmen who was owed a great deal of money, removed the cabinet containing his books, and threw it into the harbour. By the time it was recovered the books were largely illegible and the record was destroyed. Most of the people on the wrong side of the page went to try to restore their debt as best they could, even though they were physically ill with worry, but others took advantage of this quite unique opportunity.

The findings of the Sea Fish Commission had now been on public record for four months and most of the comments were in. To show that they meant business the Government published the Herring Industry Bill in January, 1935. Originally it had intended to pass the recommendations in total as an Act of Parliament but changed its mind and set up the Herring Industry Board in March without waiting for Parliament. They in their turn rapidly made the recommendations which they thought would improve the state of the industry and had all their proposals ready by 5th April, a remarkably short time. Following objections from the Herring Producers Association that the catching side of the industry was not represented on the Board, Skipper William Forman of the Peterhead drifter 'Vine,' was appointed to represent their interest. His appointment was unique in as much as he was the first fisherman to sit on a decision-making body by the Government, as opposed to the previous practice of merely giving evidence before one.

GRILLED HERRINGS

Grilled herrings commend themselves as something easy to prepare, quick to cook and appetising when served.

GRILLED HERRINGS.

INGREDIENTS : *2 herrings, a small piece of butter, parsley, mustard sauce.*

METHOD : Scale and clean the fish, then wipe with a clean cloth. Upon each side of the herring make three cuts 1½ inches apart, cutting down to, not through, the backbone. Remove the heads. Now just brush each with a little butter, as the herring contains its own cooking fat. Grill quickly under a very hot grill till brown on each side. Dust lightly with salt, garnish with parsley, and serve with mustard sauce. (See p. 30.)

GRILLED HERRINGS WITH TOMATOES.

INGREDIENTS : *1 herring and 1 tomato per person, a little butter, parsley, salt and pepper.*

METHOD : Cut the tomatoes in halves and fry in a little butter, taking care not to break them. Grill the fish as before.

Serve surrounded by the tomatoes.

If you prefer, you can grill the tomatoes at the same time as the herrings. Put a bit of butter on each tomato to prevent the skin burning. Turn when ready to cook on underside.

GRILLED HERRINGS WITH LEMON JUICE.

INGREDIENTS : *1 herring per person, a little butter and lemon juice.*

METHOD : Skewer the heads and tails together. Grill as before. Add the lemon juice and serve. I want you to look at the illustration and see the neat little wooden skewers that make herrings bite their tails.

GRILLED HERRINGS WITH PARSNIPS.

INGREDIENTS : *1 herring per person, a few boiled parsnips, a few breadcrumbs, a little beaten egg, fat for frying, salt and pepper, parsley.*

METHOD : Cut the parsnips lengthwise in quarters, egg and breadcrumb them, fry a golden brown. Grill the herrings as

Grilled Herrings.

Extracts from the 32 page booklet produced by the Herring Industry Board to boost the sale of herring on the home market.

GRILLED HERRINGS

before, serve with the parsnips; you have no idea how good the combination of flavours can be.

SPELDERED HERRINGS.

This is a Northumbrian method, and is really only another way of grilling fresh herrings.

INGREDIENTS: *2 or more fresh herrings, teaspoonful of lemon juice, dash of cayenne, a tiny nut of beef dripping for each herring.*

METHOD: Scale and clean the fish, remove the heads and tails and backbone. Lay them on a dish, dust with cayenne, squeeze lemon juice over, put a nut of dripping on each one, then grill over a hot fire. Serve with cut lemon. Very delicious!

What will you do with the roes in such a case? These make delicious savouries, but if you prefer, fry the roes in butter or good dripping, then garnish the speldered herrings with them.

When grilling herrings with roes it is worth while to take out the roes, season each with a little black pepper, salt and a dash of nutmeg, then replace in the herring. If the herrings have been split and boned, the roes are easily put back.

BROILED HERRINGS.

Broiling, which is cooking in front or on top of a clear fire, is a rather slower process than grilling but need only take three or four minutes longer. The broiling pan with its deep sides, as still used on the East Coast, is a most convenient utensil in which to cook herrings. It is essential, of course, to have a clear hot fire, and the bars of the grate free from coal-dust or cinder ash.

The herrings need not be cut on the sides. They are all the better for basting once or twice during the cooking with the fat which runs to the bottom of the broiling pan.

In many places the little Dutch oven with its row of hooks conveniently arranged to suspend the fish while broiling is very popular. In front of a clear fire it is a most desirable cooker, and has one great advantage over any other form—it allows both sides of the herrings to be nicely browned without disturbing the fish.

Broiled herrings taste particularly good with horse-radish sauce.

Grilled Herrings with Lemon Juice.

The only strong complaints came from curers who did not like the clause about a minimum price to be paid for herring intended for export. The other 100 objections were on more trivial matters in the eyes of the Government, and the bill became law on 25th May, 1935 in time for the summer season. Under the main clause, nine, £600,000 was provided to the Herring Industry Board to dispense in the form of loans for refits, new boats, nets, bridging finance for exports and alterations to fishcuring premises. The Board also introduced a scheme to purchase old steam drifters for scrap and many fishermen took advantage of the offer. For example in 1936, 37 Buckie drifters, 21 Findochty, 18 Banff, 17 Fraserburgh and nine Peterhead, two per week, were broken up.

There is no doubt that the industry took confidence and 1935 was a considerable improvement on 1934. It would have been difficult for it to be worse other than by complete collapse. One of the gradual changes which had been taking place lay in the style of the new motor boats and in their size, power, shape and machinery. With these changes a new breed of men were appearing on the edges of the industry, but latterly they were to become central to it.

The introduction of the canoe stern in the Falcon meant a great deal more than the alteration of the shape. In the course of time it would change the whole approach to planning and construction. Till the Falcon was launched by Miller's, boats had been built from half models of the hull, by men of the highest abilities who could make vessels by sheer intellectual application. They did not need detailed plans and there were basically only three main hull styles, the Fifie, the Zulu and the Scaffie, until the arrival of the steam drifter. By 1903 half models were being used only for Fifies, Zulus and steam drifters and the construction of Scaffies was confined to yawls which did not require half models. These were built by fitting the planking around well used moulds and then building in the timbers after the hull had been pre-formed. The practice today is the same and indeed half models are still widely used, but not for the carpenters to work from as they built.

The canoe stern, or cruiser stern as it was to be called by 1935, was something new and meant that a new approach would be required: the use of drawings. Carpenters would have to be able to read them and build from them. Not that this presented any difficulty but for the first time the shape of the boat, both inside and out, was presented before them clearly. Any alterations or suggestions they had could be done merely by rubbing out a line as opposed to taking a model, altering it and then making sure everybody knew what was to be done. At a time when hull shapes were changing, engines and gearboxes were being redesigned annually, it was of considerable importance that hull design kept pace with such developments, and drawings were the answer.

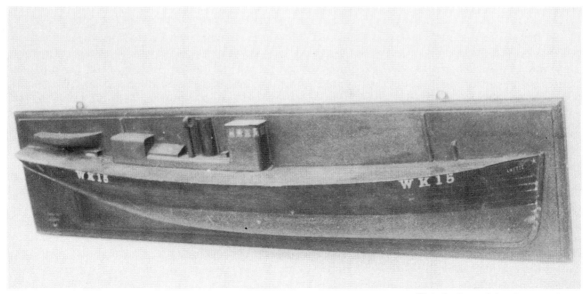

Illustration by permission of the Wick Society.

A half model of the drifter 'Lottie' built by D. Alexander, Wick.

The sturdy 'Kittiwake' taking a few passengers on a run to sea.

Not many yards prepared their own drawings as they were family concerns where the owners were too busy with the administration and supervising the work. Some had sent their sons to Glasgow to learn drawing in the shipyards there, but they were few and far between. In fact, it was when large companies, and the Government, who had drawing offices, began to take an interest in building drifters and trawlers that the use of drawings first entered the construction of fishing boats. But the new hull shape made drawings desirable and many of the companies acquired their drawings from specialist designers rather than set up their own drawing office or train a draughtsman. New boats were being built in the traditional manner, without drawings, till about 1933 or 34 when the last of the motorised Fifies and Zulus were built. Thereafter every boat had a cruiser stern until the square counter stern came in in the 1960's.

So therefrom came the specialist firms of fishing boat designers who were to have such a great influence on the appearance of the fleet. They were in a position to consult with skippers, carpenters and could also incorporate features required by legislation on matters such as safety. And their abilities became increasingly in demand as most family builders made use of their services. Watson of Erskine, who had been yacht and lifeboat designers for half a century, turned to fishing boat design and firms such as McAlister of Campbeltown continue to provide a design service in the 1980's. Millers of St Monans is one of the few to do its own designing and modern skippers have the choice of either commissioning the drawings themselves from the designers or leaving the whole thing to the builder.

In 1935 this was not usually the case. As the new grounds on the north and west were being explored the boats were gradually increasing in size. More attention to comfort became necessary and the counter stern presented the opportunity to do this. It also had a wide flair above and below the waterline which the narrow sterns of the Zulus and Fifies did not have. This meant that there was more room to design for and the slowly increasing size of the boats meant that the day when both cabin and engines could be accommodated aft was rapidly approaching for seine net boats. Seine net boats although they were still fitted with bunks to accommodate a herring crew only needed four or five at the most and as fewer and fewer went to the herring fishing designs changed with them. Fewer bunks, more compact engines and increasing size all played their part and the ideal of having everything aft was reality by 1936.

Photograph by permission of Mrs N. Bremner, Wick.

The 'Sprightly', one of the earliest Wick seine net boats, showing both her steam capstan and rope coilers. She had been bought about 1930 from Macduff where she had been built by several herring skippers for use as a haddock line boat during the late winter when the drifters were laid up. This explains her slim lines.

The 'May Queen' showing her canoe stern. She was sunk by a German bomb which missed the Forth Bridge.

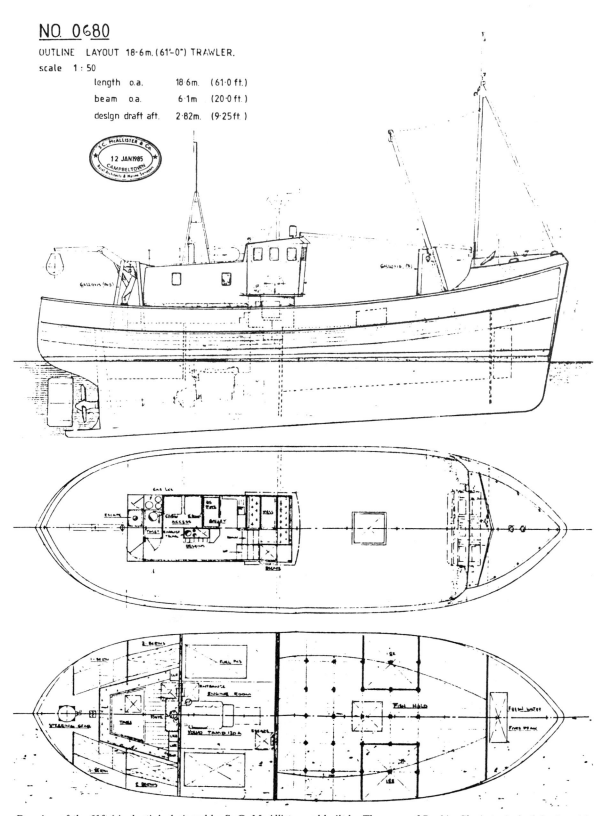

NO. 0680

OUTLINE LAYOUT 18·6m. (61'-0") TRAWLER.

scale   1 : 50

length o.a.   18·6m.   (61·0 ft.)

beam   o.a.   6·1m.   (20·0 ft.)

design draft aft.   2·82m.   (9·25ft.)

Drawing of the 61ft 'Audentia', designed by S. C. McAllister and built by Thomson of Buckie. She is typical of the Scottish seine vessels of the 1970's.

It was the installation of engines in new designs between 1920 and 1934 that had made forward accommodation necessary and this had never been popular. The choice was either having the engine forward, with the resultant fumes on deck, or the cabin with the discomfort. Another modification came about at this time, when cooking facilities were moved from the cabin to a custom built galley behind the wheelhouse, in the same way as the steam drifters had. This added greatly to the comfort in as much as the atmosphere till then had contained a variety of ingredients ranging from sweat to fish, old cooking smells, smoke from the stove, pipes and cigarettes, occasionally engine exhaust and human exhaust. The aromas were usually enhanced by the fact that the stove kept the temperature in the cabin fairly high, and the ventilator could never cope adequately with the results. Many a land-lubber, fancying himself as an adventurer and going out on a fishing boat for a day, had the stuffing literally knocked out of him by the cabin before the boat had cleared the quayheads.

The vast majority of the boats were kept spotlessly clean and the standards, particularly of those along the south side of the Moray Firth, were legendary. It was rare to see a boat in need of a coat of paint and while they were being refitted it was not uncommon for fishermen's wives to come aboard and scrub everything they could reach, from stem to stern. That included lifting the floor boards, at least twice a year. Because of their involvement as herring gutters the fishermen's wives had an even closer concern with their husbands boats than there is today. Apart from bearing six to ten children they usually knitted all their woollen clothing, mended the nets, made the sand bags for the cod nets, and much of the clothing used by both themselves and their families. In the 1930's this work was done either before or after they went to the gutting, by the light of a paraffin lamp and before a black coal range which did all cooking and usually washing. Some had wash houses, but not all. Their day usually began about six and could last till midnight yet somehow, they managed to fit in a social life. The Sisterhood, soirees, concerts, guilds all flourished with their attendances as they never did before or have since.

Photograph by permission of Mrs. J Gatt, Fraserburgh.

Some of the ministering angels to the Scottish herring fleet pause from their labours in Watts yard, Fraserburgh to have their picture taken about 1890. The lady fifth from the left in the front row was Jean Noble, the famous Grannie Jeannagie, whose kindliness to those in the Braidsea district of Fraserburgh less fortunate than herself, was legendary.

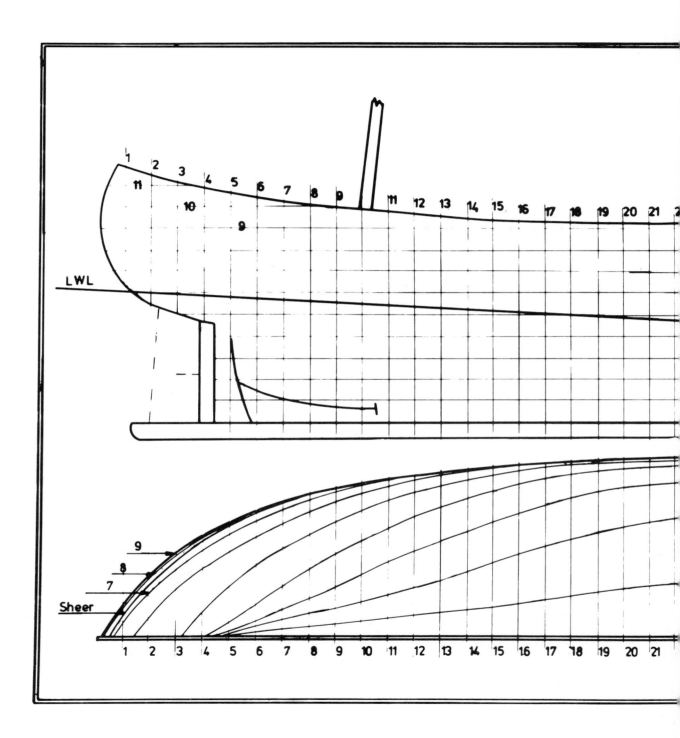

The hull of the 'Enterprise' of Keiss redrawn from the o
Alexander, Wick,

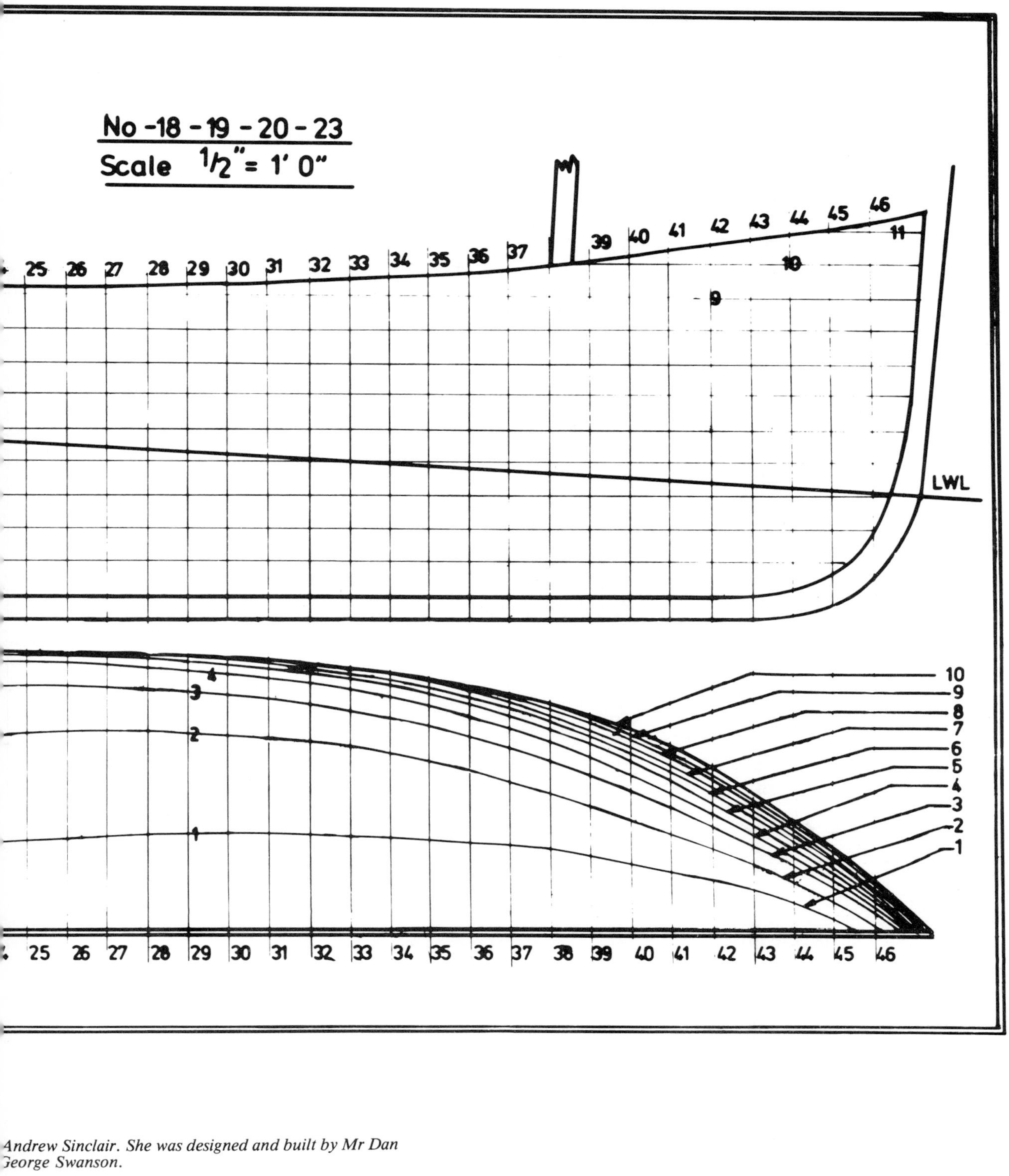

Andrew Sinclair. She was designed and built by Mr Dan
George Swanson.

A study of Wick skipper Mr Donald Wares in the 1880's. He is wearing the bowler hat which was so commonly worn ashore by skippers of the day and his dress gansey, in which most of the traditional stitching is visible. Wick fishermen wore their button arrangement on either shoulder.

Photograph by permission of Mrs J. Gatt, Fraserburgh.

A typical fishing family in the first decade of the century, where the father was a fisherman, the mother and the eldest daughters all gutters. This is Mr Benjamin Noble, of Fraserburgh surrounded by his children. The infant on Mrs Noble's knee became Mrs May Chalmers and was tragically killed with most of her family when a German bomb struck her home in Rosehearty, three miles west of Fraserburgh.

The ladies without whom the Scottish fishing industry simply could not have functioned between 1770 and 1960 should have a monument erected to them equal in height to the St Kilda cliffs. From Barra, Stornoway, Stronsay, Lerwick, Scrabster, Wick, Helmsdale, Nairn, Lossiemouth, Buckie, Fraserburgh, Peterhead, Eyemouth, Shields, Scarborough, Yarmouth, Lowestoft, Peel, Bunchrana, Killybegs and back to Barra they were to be found. Bobbing into farlans lipping with herring, lifting, dragging, hanging into barrels head first, and above all gutting the herring with the distinctive double action necessary first to open his throat and then to ensure that the appendix had been removed with the guts. In wind, rain, snow, shine, storm, mental or physical exhaustion they gutted, selected into five sizes and packed about 30 to 40 herring each a minute. A crisis was caused in Lerwick on Wednesday 19th June 1929 when there was exceptionally heavy fishings but sales came to a standstill at 11 am because two days standing in torrential rain had reduced the lassies efficiency by 40% and they simply could not handle any more. As a result the fleet did not sail and prices hit rock bottom. Lassies from the west coast of Sutherland would walk to Wick, Lybster, Latheron, Dunbeath, Helmsdale and Cromarty, for some a journey of 130 miles over trackless wastes that could take a week. They could still sing their beautiful Gaelic songs as they worked and then walk back home when the 16 week season was over. The coming of the railways in the 1870's made things easier, as did the fact that curers used to send schooners for them from 1840 onwards. Others travelled by fishing boat, steamer, train, lorry, cart or walked, but not so far. Whatever the method of travel, they were there when the first herring came in and when the last was gutted. And that could range from first light to the dark of a snowy winters night lit by a wadding torch or paraffin flare to electricity by 1939. The specially built curing yards were largely covered but those on the quays or open shores were not.

Gutting crews, made up of two gutters and a packer, often worked as families, as their menfolk manned the boats. There could be as many as three crews from the one family, of sisters, mothers, grannies and cousins, and they sustained strong family bonds. And because of the coming and going around the coasts, both by themselves and the fishermen, they knew an enormous amount of people and had relations all over the place whom they met frequently. They were accomplished conversationalists who rarely wasted time or words on nonsense, but who also had a very highly developed sense of humour and razor sharp tongues which were honed in the repartee of the yards.

When they came home from the yards, after perhaps six or more hours on their feet, with their stiff aprons and clothes splattered with guts, blood and scales, they would check on the family in which the elder looked after the younger infants. Generally they would be spotlessly clean within ten minutes of coming home with the apron and boots outside waiting for the next day. As often as not this was done in a house which, if it had a plumbing system, would have no hot water other than that in the little tank on the end of the stove. If they were going somewhere special the young ones could change from their bloodstained working clothes to the highest fashion in an unbelievably short time. The style of the Newhaven fishwives, a town that has been officially vandalised almost beyond belief, was famous. Married women with families to look to, did not usually need to change so quickly, but there was always a relative to visit; or in the 1920's and 30's a husband to be supported, comforted, encouraged or driven through the black despair caused by the loss of his savings and a debt that looked beyond control.

The arrival of the seine net fishings made as big a change in the lives of the fishermen's wives as it did for the men themselves. No longer were they required as a necessity to mend nets, or suffer the eye strain that went with trying to see the dark twine by the light of a paraffin or Tilley lamp. It was only in the 1930's that electricity became generally available, but by that time mending was on a much lesser scale, even with herring nets. There were mending contractors, but not many could afford them. The seine net, apart from the fact that the mending could usually be done by the crew, was not so easily understood by many wives in the way they had understood the straightforward herring net. This meant that they had taken another step away from the days when, not all that long before, they had to carry their husbands out on their backs to the boats when there were no harbours. This was to keep the men dry, and the ravages of rheumatism at bay, for as long as possible.

Life also became easier when mass produced underwear arrived, not long after the seine net came with its less demanding requirements. It meant the beginning of the end of the time when the wives were continuously knitting. It was not uncommon to see a small group, waiting for the drifters to come in, or even in the street blethering, all with their arms going like bees wings. Factory made ganseys also began to make their appearance but the practice of knitting and making all flannel underwear continued till well into the 1960's. The men all required at least four spare sets of long woollen drawers, and as many ganseys to see them through if they were away from home for any length of time. Ganseys are of course still knitted today but this is no longer the necessity it was. A gansey knitted on number 11 or 12 gauge double ended steel needles, round on a belt, had the appearance of woven cloth, so beautifully was it made. They were all knitted to the same general design, with a very deep rib to grip and warm the kidneys, which were also protected by the flannel belt they had made. The sleeves were short to prevent the wool from getting wet and irritating the wrist. Many ports had their own individual patterns, in which the stitching represented the Ear of Plenty, the shore, stones on the beach, waves, anchor cables and other tokens of good luck. In the last century a fisherman's home port could be instantly recognised by the arrangement of the buttons which had been let into the neck and shoulder of his gansey. They were unfastened when the gansey was taken off to prevent the neck from stretching and so retain its insulation seal, just like the rib. Wick had four evenly spaced buttons. Other ports had different arrangements of two, three, four or five buttons, in groups or pairs, on the left or right side. When the ladies were not attending to these things they could well be shelling mussels with their short bladed knives, or redding and baiting lines.

The years 1938 and 1939 were in much the same pattern as the previous three except that they were unfolding in the gathering thunderheads of war. Many fishermen were in the Royal Naval Reserve a tradition which had stretched back to the time of the Press Gang. The law permitting the operation of Press Gangs has never been repealed and they are still law but the practice fell into

Photograph from the Johnston Collection by permission of the Wick Society.

A Chief Officer of Coastguard and a Chief Petty Officer of the Navy lean against a naval gun at the coastal defence battery at Wick about 1890. They are surrounded by instructors from the gunnery school 'HMS Excellent' and coastguards whose duties included instructing fishermen reservists. The ramrods and traversing track for the muzzle loading cannon are clearly visible. There was a strong tradition of fishermen joining the RNR since the Press Gang ceased to function.

disuse in 1853 when continuous service, in peace or war, was introduced by the navy. However before the fishermen got into the shooting war with Germany, they had already been in an 18 year battle of wits with the long suffering body of men who manned the 'Norma,' 'Freya,' 'Brenda,' 'Minna,' 'Vigilant,' 'Rona,' and 'Vaila;' the British Sea Fishery Officers, as they were known, and who were informed of their responsibilities this way

4. Duties of British Sea Fishery Officers.—The duties of a British Sea Fishery Officer are:—

(1) To enforce the Sea Fisheries Act, 1883, as amended by the Fisheries Act, 1891, and subsequent Orders in Council on all fishing boats, whatever their nationality, inside the British Exclusive fishery limits. These limits are not the same for all foreign vessels (*vide* Chapter I., para. 2).

Photograph by permission of Mr D. Corse, Marine Superintendent, DAFS, Edinburgh.

The fishery cruiser 'Minna' built by Murdoch and Murray, Port Glasgow in 1900. She was 146 ft long, capable of 11 knots and was decommissioned in 1939.

(2) To enforce these provisions on all British fishing boats anywhere.

(3) To enforce the Conventions on all foreign fishing vessels to which they apply in all conventional waters (outside exclusive fishery limits). These duties can only be exercised by Sea Fishery Officers who are also Commanders of Naval Cruisers.

(In Scottish waters additional duties fall on Sea Fishery Officers; these are referred to in Chapter III).

5. Offences which may be dealt with by all British Sea Fishery Officers.—In the exercise of these duties, a British Sea Fishery Officer has authority to deal with the following offences with regard to all fishing vessels inside British Exclusive Fishery Limits and British fishing vessels anywhere:—

(1) Causing injury to any person belonging to another boat, or damaging another sea fishing boat, or damaging gear belonging to another sea fishing boat.

(2) Concealing nationality.

(3) Anchoring between sunset and sunrise among drifters.

(4) Improperly shooting nets near other vessels when drifting.

(5) Anchoring nets on a drift net fishing ground.

(6) Making fast to another boat's gear.

(7) Failure of trawlers to keep clear of drifters and long liners.

(8) Cutting entangled nets without mutual consent or necessary.

(9) Cutting entangled long lines without necessity.

(10) Neglecting to rejoin long lines cut by necessity.

(11) Lifting gear the property of others.

(12) Using an instrument for cutting or destroying nets or having such an instrument on board.

(13) Failing to hand over gear salvaged.

(14) Failing to observe the Collision Regulations. This applies to Icelandic and Faroese waters only.

(15) In English Channel only. Fishing for oysters or carrying oyster dredgers between 16th June and 31st August. This applies also to French fishing vessels.

(16) Not conforming to the international rules for lights at sea.

(17) Discharging fire arms.

(18) Throwing missiles.

(19) Using threatening language.

(20) Fighting or brawling.

And with regard to British fishing vessels only:—

(21) Being improperly marked, or gear being improperly marked.

(22) Not having Certificate of Registry on board.

And with regard to foreign vessels only:—

(23) Fishing within British exclusive fishery limits.

(24) Entering British exclusive fishery limits for a purpose not recognised by International Law.

It is also an offence in the British Isles to manufacture, sell or expose for sale, any instrument serving only or intended to damage or destroy fishing implements.

Photograph by permission of Mr D. Corse, Marine Superintendent, DAFS, Edinburgh.

The third 'Vigilant' which replaced the vessel shown overleaf. Built in 1935 by Denny of Dunbarton. She was 135 ft long with a gross registered tonnage of 209 tons.

Photograph by permission of Mr D. Corse, Marine Superintendent, DAFS, Edinburgh.

The fishery cruiser 'Vigilant', originally named 'Violex', bought in 1894 to replace the sailing cruiser of the same name. She was sold in 1936 and replaced by the third 'Vigilant'.

As the Wick skipper Rab More of the 'Alert' puts it "The haddie disna ken far the line is." This ignorance on the part of the haddie, and its relations, led to a contest of wits, skill and sheer farce that would fill an encyclopedia were it all to be told. Most complaints came in from the public and inshore fishermen and they all had to be investigated. Like other men the crews of the cruisers liked to be ashore at the weekend if possible and were often tied up on a Saturday. This of course became the favourite time for inshore fishing. Most of the cruisers at that time were steam powered and the seine net men would wait till they thought that the steam pressure had fallen below working levels when she could not sail. They would then proceed to fish right up to the main road, secure in the knowledge that even if the inevitable complaint was made, it would take the cruiser a couple of hours to get under way. On such occasions they were well advised to be far out of the way when it eventually did arrive with a fuming skipper looking for something to vent his anger on. Timing was extremely important, particularly for latecomers who may not have heard that the whistle had been blown, or that the cruiser was lurking in the shadows.

It was not all one way of course and cruiser skippers would have dirty rags and wadding smouldering in the funnel to give the impression that they still had a head of steam. Sometimes it worked and they got peace. In the hard times of the 1930's fishermen could have been caught poaching far more often than they were. It may be difficult for them to believe but cruiser skippers were largely sympathetic towards them. Often when they thought they had outwitted the cruiser it was because they had been allowed to escape.

Cruisers, except when they were on relief, were allocated certain areas and the following illustration, as indeed with all references to poaching and convictions, must be made without names or places.

A seine net boat was a stone's throw from a part of the coast, with many headlands, and had caught an enormous bag of fish. She was about 60 feet long and had taken 100 boxes aboard which put her well down by the head. An over ambitious attempt to lift more fish at one time than the net could stand had caused it to burst and they were sitting in a sea of cod when the cruiser appeared from nowhere. The skipper of the cruiser, who obviously was not familiar with what fishing boats did, asked what they were doing there. The reply was worthy of the question. "Naethin" There was a pause while the cruiser put her helm over "Ye hae twenty minutes tae gang an dae it some ither place." Whereupon she turned and left.

Skippers who were convicted several times could be imprisoned, but in fact only one skipper ever was. He was not even aboard the boat when it was detected but as it evaded the cruiser at the time, he was accused and convicted. The skipper of a vessel, which had belonged to the same men for 20 years could suddenly be changed, according to the frequency with which it had been caught poaching. Promotion could be rapid if the cruiser was coming up fast and several teenagers have found themselves skippers, when the owner, who had been at the sea for 30 years decided to resign his position.

Photograph by permission of Mr D. Corse, Marine Superintendent, DAFS, Edinburgh.

Officers of the fishery protection service photographed at the turn of the century, probably aboard the 'Minna'.

The opportunity to resign was not so available after 3rd September 1939. Out of a total of 17,000 Scottish fishermen about 10,000 served in the Royal or Merchant Navies. By 7th October 71 drifters had been requisitioned and a total of 143 trawlers, 294 steam drifters and 234 motor boats were to be on service by the end of the war. They were on minesweeping duties, where the wooden hulled vessels soon showed their worth against magnetic mines, minelaying and general fleet support at naval bases as far away as Ceylon. Twenty nine were sunk as a result of direct enemy action and some were in action very early on in the war.

On 14th October 1939 the drifter 'Daisy' was on station in Scapa Flow in the vicinity of the battleship 'Royal Oak' when she was torpedoed by a U-boat. Before the unbelieving eyes of the witnesses she slowly rolled over taking most of her sleeping crew with her. Fortunately for those who managed to scramble to the deck the 'Daisy' was already on her way and in a singularly heroic action rescued 300 men from the vicinity of the 'Royal Oak' which might have blown her up or sucked her down at any moment. It might be worth noting for posterity, since the old Scots tongue is vanishing before the triple onslaught of the media, the teaching profession and the social order, that the 'Gowanlea' of the first war meant 'Daisyfield.' It is a peculiar coincidence that both these vessels should have an association with this bright little flower. Eight hundred and ten men lost their lives on the 'Royal Oak' and there were 424 survivors most of whom were landed in Thurso without proper clothing. Scores of families, many of whose sons were already in service, threw open their homes to accommodate the men in an act of care and hospitality rarely equalled.

Photograph by permission of Mr. J. G. Addison, Cullen.

The 'Daisy' which rescued 300 men from the stricken 'Royal Oak.'

On 6th November 1940 the armed merchantship, 'Jervis Bay,' was suicidally attacking a German pocket battleship to allow the convoy which she was escorting to scatter and escape. In that convoy was the tanker 'San Demetrio' which was abandoned when her cargo of petrol caught fire. Her crew, which included fishermen from the Western Isles, later reboarded her, put the fires out and took her to the Clyde. Eighteen of the crew of the 'Jervis Bay' were from Caithness including fishermen from Wick and Keiss. Nine of them were killed in the action.

On 20th May 1941 the Germans began the only successful airborne invasion in history when they attacked the island of Crete to which the Greek government and the remnants of the retreating British army had been evacuated. There, in the middle of this cockpit where ferocious fighting raged for

Photograph by permission of Mr W. Stewart, Lossiemouth.

Skipper William Stewart, DSC in his fore and aft naval rig, but not wearing his ribbons.

Photograph by permission of Mr W. Stewart, Lossiemouth.

Skipper William Stewart, DSC, MBE, JP, skipper of the 'Rival' and 'Sireadh'. In the snowstorms of 1955 he carried barrels of high octane aviation fuel through a south east gale to Wick in order that the helicopters which were supplying isolated communities could continue.

Photograph by permission of Mrs J. Gatt, Fraserburgh.

The dramatic launch of the second 'Comfort' for Mr. Benjamin Noble, at Noble's yard in Fraserburgh. Her end was equally dramatic as she was rammed and sunk by a British destroyer during the Dunkirk evacuation.

days, was skipper William Stewart of Lossiemouth, in command of the minesweeper 'Lanner.' At Suda Bay, on the north west corner, under continuous attack from dive bombers at mast height, he landed 1000 soldiers from Greece, as well as survivors of 'HMS York' and a Norwegian tanker. The Germans gradually forced the defenders back and for a second time Skipper Stewart had to embark and try to bring the remnants of the defenders to safety. The 'Lanner' was the last vessel to leave Crete still flying the white ensign and had insufficient coal to keep steam up till they reached Egypt. She got there by burning all the wood aboard and under air attack during which she shot down at least one aircraft. Skipper Stewart was awarded the Distinguished Service Cross for protracted and sustained courage in face of enormous odds.

On 4th September 1939 the Fishery Board for Scotland was taken over by the Scottish Home Department, and the Herring Industries Boards powers were suspended from 23rd November, under the Emergency Powers Acts. Thus came to an end the career of the Fishery Board after 60 of the most eventual years that Scottish Fishing ever had, or will see. While the Board was the classic civil service department in the way it carried out its duties, it did not have much effect on the thinking of the fishermen. Their annual reports were masterpieces of detail and statistics. They probably contained too much information for politicians of the average intelligence to absorb. The size of their reports declined with the importance of the herring fishing and their last in 1938 was a pale shadow of former years. It was still a substantial volume and the Department of Agriculture and Fisheries, who assumed their function eventually, ceased to issue seperate reports on fishing in 1980. This may be a sign of the times as fishings are no longer the major national industry they were, but a component of the much wider European concept whence future decisions will come. In that context, Scottish fishing will assume a smaller importance in British governmental eyes than when it had a Board to itself.

Photograph by permission of Mrs J. Gatt, Fraserburgh.

The 'Rotche' built for Mr Benjamin Noble after the loss of the 'Comfort' at Dunkirk. She was probably the only fishing boat constructed during the war which immediately began fishing rather than being commissioned for military service. She is shown here in Balaclava harbour, Fraserburgh, just after her launch.

Wartime restrictions on fishing vessels exceeded those of the First World War, because warfare had made great progress in the meantime. The use of radio, echo-sounders, which were becoming widespread in trawlers, and direction finders were all severely restricted. It was forbidden to carry passengers except in the islands and fishing grounds were greatly restricted. With all the able bodied men at sea, and many boats with them, fishing was confined to small areas which could be worked under licence only. In the Clyde estuary only 30 boats were licenced at one time on the Ayrshire grounds, causing much dissatisfaction as there were always more applicants than licences.

Vessels which had been requisitioned by the Government were hired on the system known as Charter-Party. Under this the Government agreed to compensate owners for the loss of their vessel if it was sunk. Under the Compensation (Defence) Act of 1939 trawlers and drifters were hired at a fixed rate of compensation if they were lost. This was fairly low, especially in the case of drifters as most of them were 30 years old and had not been all that well maintained during the difficult '30's. It was a different situation with the newer motor boats and their values were open to negotiation because many were less than ten years old. At the end of the war all the drifters were returned to their owners with a lump sum in lieu of a refit. The owners were not given a choice as they had in the previous war because it was becoming policy to have steam drifters scrapped as quickly as possible. The Herring Act of 1944, the Inshore Fishing Industry Act of 1948 and the White Fish and Herring

Photograph by permission of Mr J. Lawrence, Fraserburgh.

Fraserburgh's famous Tarry Mangle in operation with its equally famous owner, John Lawrence, feeding it with his back to the camera. This device was the only attempt ever made to mechanise the backbreaking and filthy job of tarring the bush rope, or leader, which ran beneath a drift of herring nets to take the strain of the haul. In a summer Mr Lawrence and his sons, John, Alex, and occasionally Francis would tar over 200 miles of leader, a length which would have stretched across the mouth of the Moray Firth and back again. The handle is being turned by Francis Lawrence while John (jun), coils the tarred rope.

Industries Act of 1948 all made increasing amounts of money available by way of grants and loans for the replacement of obsolete drifters and the purchase of new boats. In modern terms sums of about £25,000,000 in grant and £40,000,000 in loan. By 1948, 281 men had qualified for assistance under schemes for herring fishing. Eight hundred and thirteen had been given assistance for inshore boats, including yawls. In 1950 a boat of about 60 feet cost £8200, between £180,000 and £200,000 in the values of 1985. It must be remembered that these boats had little more than a winch, coiler and a radio.

Fishermen had been allocated extra rations during the war and had been allowed to buy oilskins without the clothing coupons which were necessary for everything else. For the couple of thousand who were able to continue fishing there were other, if lesser, difficulties than enemy attacks and restricted grounds. The Japanese occupation of the Philippines cut off the supply of manilla for ropes and sisal had to be used as an unpopular substitute. Similar difficulties were experienced with the supply of cane for the quarter cran herring basket. Under the Act of 1889 the law required that the basket had to be made from cane and willow, and a special dispensation had to be passed on 20th March 1943 allowing the use of willow only. It was the same story with the cutch or bark, used to preserve both herring and seine nets. Normally it came from Burma, but as battles were raging there, Borneo cutch, creosote, cuprinol and even copper sulphate crystals had to be used instead.

The end of the war saw the fishermen returning to a world of social transformation as had never been seen. It was also the beginning of the end for the herring fishings in the traditional manner, although few would have believed that in 1945 or 46. The main fishing grounds had recovered their stocks and looked as if they were going to last for ever. During the war the Admiralty had built over 300 vessels, MFVs, Motor Ferry Vessels, designed for use as fishing boats when hostilities ceased. They came in four classes or keel sizes, 45ft, 61½ft, 75ft and 90ft and were offered to fishermen under the grant and loan scheme, known as the Grunt and Groan Scheme. One hundred and seven were allocated to Scotland and by 1948, 85 had been taken including five of the 90ft boats. Not many of the 45ft boats were taken up as they nearly all had petrol engines which were hopelessly uneconomic for fishing. There was a waiting period of nearly two years for a Gardner engine and often, to their cost, fishermen would fit any engine they could get their hands on. By 1948 when fishings were pretty well back in full swing the number of motor boats over 45ft of keel had risen from 276 in 1938 to 505, and the number of steam drifters had dropped from 402 to 228 in the same period. There had been 854 in 1920. Seine net landings at Peterhead that year was 26000 cwt, the amount being handled in a week in the 1980's. In 1950 motor boats landed 2,998,000 cwt of fish, 59% of the total Scottish landings. The fleet comprised a total of 5222, of which 3843 were motor boats and 967 were still registered as sail powered. The remainder were steam trawlers, drifters or liners.

Photograph by permission of Mr John Lawrence, Fraserburgh.

Mr John Lawrence (sen), left and his son John (jun), pause while the barrel of tar is replaced with a full one. Mr Lawrence (sen), performed this work for 35 years in Fraserburgh and at a rough calculation must have tarred about 7000 miles of rope in that time. He cleaned the tar off his hands with margarine, which he referred to as "Maggie Jean".

As in the first war scientists had been busy and the advances that had been made in the performances of such things as radar, radio, radio direction finding, asdic, or echometers as fishermen knew them, were all available. As had their fathers in the first war, they too had a great deal of first hand knowledge of the new equipment which, with the exception of trawlers, had been quite rare in 1939. The echometer had come a long way since Henry Hughes installed their first, which they do not seem to have patented, in 1928 in the 'St. Endelion.' In 1947 not many smaller vessels had an echometer, but an important event took place which persuaded observers that it was high time they got one.

The herring fishing season at Whitby had all the appearance of being a failure and many skippers were on the point of giving up, when a ringnetter, appropriately called 'Hope,' under skipper David Wood, arrived complete with a Kelvin Hughes MS 20 echometer. He immediately detected the herring at 30 fathoms, much below the usual depth, and persuaded the skippers around him to lengthen their buoy ropes to let the drift down to the necessary depth. The rest is, or should be, history. In its progress to the fantastically accurate instruments they are today, the echometer and its cousins with which all modern boats are festooned, went through four main phases. It began with an electric hammer, ear phones and a stop watch, progressed from there to a dial, then a strip of recording paper on which the bottom was outlined. From 1947 onwards they were operated on the new breed of valves developed during the war. These were replaced by transistors in 1963 and by 1970 had printed circuits which gives them the unbelievable accuracy they have today.

Photograph by permission of Mr J. G. Addison, Cullen.

Steam drifters being broken up on the foreshore between Sandhaven and Fraserburgh in the late 1940's as part of the government's modernisation scheme. While the steam drifter broke more hearts than ever they uplifted, these elegant vessels deserved a more dignified end than this.

The story with radar is similar. It made its first appearance in a fishing boat on an Icelandic trawler in 1947. Like the other instruments radar has made an enormous difference, particularly with regard to the loss of life and vessels. No longer is fog the menace that it was due to the twin eyes of radar and electronic navigators which operate to an accuracy of inches. After centuries, from 1953 onwards the knowledge of landmarks became as obsolete as the knowledge of how a dipping lug sail performed. Like radio, radar took some time to achieve widespread acceptance from its original conception. It, like radio, is the work of many men, and is an echosounder which works in the air, and picks up signals returning from nearby solid objects. A man called Lewis Fry Richardson filed a patent on an idea which used radio waves and he thought might be useful for detecting icebergs in the busy North Atlantic. That was on 20th April 1912, five days after the 'Titanic' disaster.

The fishermen returned from war to find that the price of fish had been fixed, called the control

Photograph by permission of Mr J. McDonald, Wick.

Boats were supplied with an auxiliary set of sails until after the Second World War. Here the 'Royal Burgh' and the 'Fisher Boy' dry their full set. When the 'El Alamien's' engine smashed at the Butt of Lewis, her skipper, Alistair Smith, sailed her to Scrabster.

price, to ensure that it would be available cheaply in spite of wartime shortages. Not only was the legislation going through to assist in their smooth absorbtion back into the industry, by way of grants and loans, but assistance was also available to set up co-operatives. In 1948 money was allocated to allow fishermen to acquire premises for administering their associations and several places, notably Buckie, took advantage of this. The idea was that it would be a beginning towards the creation of self help organisations for such things as box pools, net mending and purchases of stores such as oil and ice which were coming into increasing demand. Even the simple act of getting the fish from the boat to the quay had a complicated history.

Before there were harbours the women carried herring ashore in the creel baskets which they slung on their backs. However as the catch was usually only a cran or two that did not take long. The advent of the bigger boats, landing on quays meant that the herring was landed in the quarter cran basket with two men heaving on a burton purchase slung between the masts, or from a mast. Capstans mechanised the process as did the arrival of the derrick at the same time in steam drifters. The advent of seine netting was different, as all the pioneers had was the quarter cran baskets for herring. Lined fish had been landed with them, or thrown ashore, but not with the frequency that seine netting demanded. To begin with the fish was landed by basket and tiered, or left in the basket if they were of a size that fitted it. When the merchant bought them he took them away in his open mouthed barrels, called kits, or in boxes with swivelling metal handles on the ends, which normally held the lid on. These boxes were for cured white fish or salmon. Fish were also generally ungutted, because most of the buyers also had a herring work force who could easily dispose of the comparatively small quantity of seined fish. As the volume of landings grew, so did the need for something to put them in, and salesmen and curers began to supply the boats with boxes. A boat which did not have boxes had either to leave the fish on deck, put them in the herring lockers in the hold, or put them on shelves in the hold, which usually only trawlers had.

Photograph by permission of Mr G. Swanson, Keiss.

The 'Enterprise', of which there is a hull drawing at the end of this book, lying at Stromness. Orkney was a favourite fishing ground for Caithness seine net fishers during the 1940's, 50's and 60's.

Wartime shortages of wood caused the creation of boxpools which required fishermen to put all the boxes available in to a general store and to hire boxes as they needed them. The system certainly worked but it had drawbacks in as much as boxes had to be landed at the port to which they belonged or the chances of getting them back again were remote. The practice had now developed that fish were being removed to the yards in the boxes in which they were being landed. Local yards would return them, as there was usually somebody keeping track of what was going on, but if a boat was away from home, an increasing trend, then the fishbuyer was quite likely to send the boxes away to his market by train, and later lorry. This could be anywhere, and it meant the almost certain disappearance of the box. To a certain extent it was offset by the acquisition of boxes from other ports but the system was hopeless. Boats bought their own boxes to see if this would ease the situation but generally they were supplying the fishbuyers with free packaging. Million of fishboxes vanished between 1950 and 1970 when companies such as the Wood Group established box pools on sufficient scale to make the system work no matter where the boxes were landed. These boxes are hired at a fixed rate. Fish were by 1950 being landed largely in a gutted condition which attracted a higher price, because the buyers, many of whom did not process the fish, no longer had the work force to handle them otherwise. Boxed fish always attracted a better price than shelved fish, and lined fish the best price of all as the inshore boats always landed them in the best condition. The practice of landing

Photograph by permission of Mr P. McCabe, Peterhead.

The 'Strathnairn' in the idyllic setting of the Caledonian Canal.

ungutted fish returned in the 1970's when huge catches of fish, just on the borderline of the legal size, were landed by crews who either could not handle the quantity or the prices had fallen to the extent that the labour was not justified.

The dwindling female work force ashore turned more and more to the large factories of Peterhead, Fraserburgh and Aberdeen but never on the same scale as the herring needed. There they are still employed, in conditions which bear no resemblance to those of 50 years ago and no longer gut. They are filletters, smokers, dressers, cooks and occasionally kipperers.

By 1954 there were only six steam drifters left, five at Peterhead and one at Eyemouth. The number of motor boats over 45 feet of keel had risen to 628 and one vessel with a keel considerably longer than the others landed in August 1954. She too was a pioneer but one whose example has only been followed by her sister ships so far. The 'Fairtry', owned by the whaling company Salvesens of Leith, arrived home after a voyage to Newfoundland and Greenland, with 460 tons of frozen fish, of which 240 tons were filleted in 7lb catering packs. She also had 80 tons of fish meal and 4200 gallons

The 'Fairtry'.

of liver oil aboard which her crew of 84 had processed during their three month voyage. While only a company with Salvesen's resources could afford such an outlay, the skipper owners of the smaller seine net boats were also beginning to think in terms of trips, albeit on a much more modest scale.

The practice of putting in a days fishing, regardless of success and coming home at night began to go into gradual decline for a variety of reason. With it went most of the fleets from the smaller ports over the next 20 years. The increasing size of the boats, which by now were nearly three times the size of the yawls which had begun seining in 1920, gave them a much bigger range and carrying capacity. The versatility of being able to shift ground so quickly also provided the opportunity to try to catch as much fish as the boat could carry, rather than stop with what might be considered to be a good day's fishing. If good fishings were found there was little point in leaving it for tomorrow as somebody else would almost certainly have caught them before then. This was not an option that had been open to the driftermen who had to settle for what they got and came in every day if they could, unless they were a long way out with little or no herring.

The economic pressures on the skippers of the new large seiners were also greater as they had to meet proportionately higher costs because of expensive equipment and thirsty engines. There was also, probably the most important of all, intense rivalry about being the best fisherman, something that was measured by the size of the catch landed and the value of the boats gross earnings. While the smaller boats with the older or less ambitious men could still, and would till the present day, pick a living by going in and out each day, the gradual drift towards present methods proceeded as the stocks in the Moray Firth and other coastal areas began to wilt before the intensity of the fishing. Slowly, led by Buckie, Macduff and Lossiemouth boats, the fleet began to range further and further. They began fishing around the north and west coasts and on both sides of the northern isles.

The crew of the 'Enterprise' after they had salvaged the 'Juny' which is seen tied alongside. They are, from right to left: William Swanson, George Swanson, skipper, Andrew Taylor, seated front, John Elder and John Bain. The man on the left, Mr William Mackenzie, was a passenger not a crew member.

Photograph by permission of Mr A. Macintosh, Thurso.

The crew of the 'Primula' taken in the 1960's. They are from left to right: James Smith; William Mackay; Ben Sinclair, Alec Thomson; skipper Angus Macintosh, DSM, Croix de Guerre. He was awarded these decorations for distinguished heroism during the Norwegian campaign of the Second World War. The 'Primula', in addition to her main purpose in life also acted as a nuclear research vessel for the Atomic Energy Authority at Dounreay and as a ferry for Her Majesty the Queen Mother during her visit to the island of Stroma.

Kinlochbervie, Scrabster, Lochinver, Mallaig and Oban became temporary, and in some cases, permanent homes for men from the Moray Firth. Others ranged into the North Sea as far as the Norwegian and Danish coasts, blazing the trail which Peterhead would put to such advantage 20 years later. And so it proceeded with the inshore stocks declining inevitably under ceaseless, uncontrolled fishings, by now conducted with increasingly sophisticated instruments, equipment and the new immensely strong polypropylene nets. The second golden age was in full swing.

The introduction of polypropylene twine and ropes gave the nets a strength that allowed a large increase to be made in their size, which in turn required more and more power to tow them. This led to an increase in both boat size and put pressure on the carrying capacity of the hold which was becoming fairly regularly filled to a capacity. A demand was created for much more compact high speed engines of a kind which the old friends of the fishermen, Gardners, did not manufacture. The American and continental makes, which took up far less room but provided the same or more power, gradually took an increasing share of the market in new engines. The engines of course were proportionately heavier on fuel and would burn in 12 hours the amount that would have done a prewar boat for a week.

A hand operated winch which was so commonly used around the coast in many small exposed harbours for hauling the yawls. It is also very similar to the first hand winches used to hoist the sails on boats in the 1870's before the advent of steam capstans. Early winches were known first as the Iron Woman and then the Iron Man.

Photograph by permission of Mr P. McCabe, Peterhead.

The 'Kestrel' with her rope reels aft, a variation of the layout introduced by the 'Cutty Sark' 50 years earlier.

The 1960's saw not only the arrival of new and expensive technology but a breed of progressive, adventurous, daring and well informed men who had grown up on seine net fishing alone. They built boats capable of not only sailing in any kind of weather but of fishing in any kind as well. Covered foc'stles began to make their appearance in the larger vessels as a measure of protection from seas, something that had been adapted from the liners and trawlers. This later was to be supplemented by a

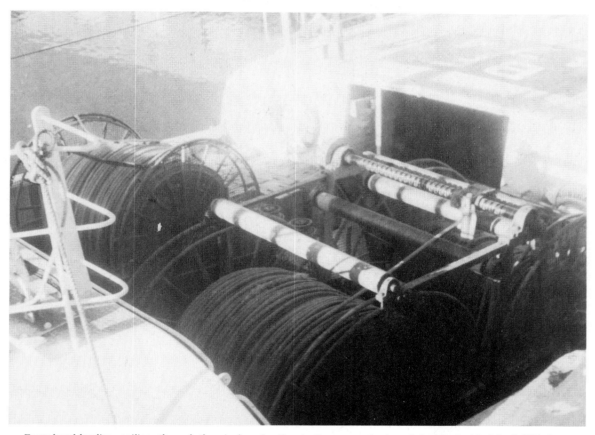

From hand hauling, coiling, through the winch and coilers to the rope reels aboard the 'Auriga' in Macduff harbour.

shelter deck and ultimately a totally enclosed working area, giving the boats the appearance of submarines. They had evolved to this profile over 25 years of discussions, consultation and co-operation between fishermen, designers and builders. The old chain and shaft drives were replaced by hydraulics, less prone to breakdown because they had fewer moving parts. Men like David Smith of Anstruther, Norman Bremner, and later his son Andrew of Wick, John Thomson of Lossiemouth, George Murray of Buckie and William Campbell of Elgin all pioneered or led the way to landings of fish with a gross value of almost unbelievable worth. And looming menacingly above them all were the Buchans and the Taits with their enormous purse seiners. The Buchans with their vessel 'Lunar Bow' were the first fishermen to introduce purse seining to Scotland, about 1966. And an earning capacity which is in excess of one million pounds a year, something the old time fishermen, who paid their hired men £6 and a pound of tobacco for the season, would find incomprehensible. The day when the Iron Man, the mechanical hand winch for hoisting the sail was the ultimate technological development, has long gone.

During the 1950's and 1960's it was a story of unchecked expansion, steadily increasing catches, with prices in support. The White Fish Authority now administered the grant and loan schemes which were available for the installation of everything from engines to the dreadful gantrys aft, which ruined

Photograph by permission of Mr P. McCabe, Peterhead.

The third of the famous line 'Argonaut 111' probably the most outstanding of them all. Her skipper Mr David Smith dominated the gross landings value in the 1970's.

Photograph by permission of Mr N. Bremner, Wick.

Skipper Norman Bremner, left, of the Wick boat 'Boy Andrew' and skipper Andrew Strachan of the 'Challenger' of Peterhead. Both very prominent as fishermen and organisers within the fishing industry during the 1970's and 1980's.

Photograph by permission of the "Glasgow Herald".

Skipper Andrew Bremner of Wick with one of the most successful vessels ever to sail in the history of Scottish fishing.

The 'Ocean Challenger', BF 130, and the 'Be Ready' on the slip at Macduff. Their powerful construction is quite visible.

Photograph by permission of Lossiemouth Museum.

Skipper John Thomson of the Lossiemouth boat 'St Kilda'. He was a prominent figure in fishermen's organisations and the blockade of 1975. He is seen here talking to Mr Pete Lewis on the wheelhouse.

Photograph by permission of Mr A. Martin, Campbeltown.

The 'Fair Morn', a dual purpose ring and seine net boat.

The 'Sagitarius' dwarfs the 'Utilise' in Macduff harbour showing how the size of seine net vessels has increased since the war.

The 'Shalimar' almost ready for launch in December 1984 at Thomson's yard, Buckie. Scenes such as this have been familiar in Low Street since the turn of the century. The 'Shalimar' has a Kelvin 500hp engine giving the company an association covering 80 years with the Scottish fishing fleet.

Photograph by permission of Mr P. McCabe, Peterhead.

The 'Joysona' punching on.

Photograph by permission of Mr P. McCabe, Peterhead.

The unusual 'Adelphi' which was built for Mr Peter Murray of Anstruther in 1976 to a design by J. Miller & Son of St. Monans. Her wheelhouse was on top of the galley for visibility but this style did not acquire any popularity.

Photograph by permission of "The Press & Journal".

A section of the blockade at Aberdeen in 1975. It has been opened to allow the P & O ship, 'St Rognvald' to sea, to maintain supplies of consumer goods to the Shetland Isles, when the islanders complained of the effect that the blockade would have.

the appearance of many a stylish boat. There was hardly a fisherman worthy of the name, who was not prosperous and as the 1960's bore to a close, there was hardly a cloud in the sky. By then the Highlands and Islands Development Board, in 1966, had assumed responsibility for the administration of finance to fishing in that area with the Department of Agriculture and Fisheries the rest of the country.

The approach of political union with the European Economic Community brought with it doubts and there was deep suspicion of how the Government would negotiate entry as the conditions of the Treaty of Rome, which created the Community, required that the fishing fleets of member states had free access to each others resources. The Scottish waters offered a particularly attractive proposition to continental fleets from which they had hitherto been excluded. In the event entry was negotiated with access to fishing grounds limited by licence but in a way which most fishermen found quite unsatisfactory. Matters deteriorated and by 1973, two years after entry, heavy fish imports were upsetting a market which had been strong for the previous 20 years. Iceland rang the death knell of Hull and Grimsby by extending her limits to 200 miles, thus putting more pressure on the home grounds. The quota system allowed foreign vessels to fish in waters from which Scottish vessels were banned, a repetition of the situation of the 1920's. Matters became worse when the Arab/Israeli war trebled the price of oil in a year, which for boats with a four or more hundred horsepower engine was serious indeed, particularly in the face of falling prices. It looked as if the old story of feast and famine, so familiar to the herringmen, was going to repeat itself.

Photograph by permission of "The Press & Journal".

The blockade at Aberdeen at its most complete in 1975.

Photograph by permission of Mr P. McCabe, Peterhead.

The 'Rotche' called after Mr Noble's wife, whose tee-name meant that neat little bird the Little Auk in the Fraserburgh dialect. In conjunction with the 'Endeavour', skippered by John McLeman, she towed airplane wrecks aside on the Heads of Ayr to clear the fishing grounds.

Photograph by permission of Mr P. McCabe, Peterhead.

A fine study of an elegant dual purpose boat, the 'Girl Olive'. The last skipper to fish for herring in the traditional way was almost certainly skipper Peter Duncan of Peterhead about 1971.

One thing that the fishermen had developed since the war was a much more aggressive attitude towards those who could influence the course of the industry. The days when some politician with a plummy accent could send them away dissatisfied but passively accepting his explanation, were almost gone. When the dockers in Aberdeen tried to dictate to the seine net fishermen how fish would be landed they transferred to Peterhead. Not all that long before, they would have done nothing about these ridiculous demands which levied a charge on the fishermen for landing their own fish. And in 1973 a concrete sign of the times was manifest with the formation of the Scottish Fishermens Federation, reminiscent of the old Driftermens and Line fishermans Association of 50 years before, but a much more robust organisation. Under the presidency of Mr A.I.B. Stewart of the Clyde Fishermans Association, the Fife, Firth of Forth, Mallaig, Pelagic Fishermen, their Salesmens section, Shetland, White Fish producers, and their Salesman Section combined with the purpose of achieving political and market influence, both in London and Brussels. It was not to be long before they were playing an active part in a quite unique and unprecedented event. Dissatisfaction rose as returns fell during 1974 and on 31st March 1975 the fishermen of Scotland, for the first time in their history acted in unison and blockaded the major industrial and fishing ports in protest at the state of the industry. They were put under great pressure to lift the blockade with threats of all kinds of legal sanctions and imprisonment for the leaders. After four days the blockade was removed, partly because of half promises from the Government and the European Commission, and partly because there was never a great deal of enthusiasm for it anyway. In retrospect they achieved little or nothing but it was the first, and so far only sign, that fishermen had found the unity and militancy so often used by other industries. Whether they will need it again, when the massive Spanish fleet is on the verge of entering the European Community's fishing operations, remains to be seen. Slowly but surely the Scottish fleet is becoming part of the European fleet and will be subject to decisions over which it will have less and less influence.

The story of how, or if, it will prevail lies in the future.

Postscript

It was not my intention to write a postscript until 13th March, 1985, when I went to Gourdon to see Miss Moira Watt about her grandfather, Mr Charles Moir. There I had the pleasant surprise of finding the firm of A. Gove and Son in full swing with the staff as busy as bees filletting and packing the codlings which the Gourdon line boats had caught that morning. It was not a sight that I had expected to see but it brought to my mind the fact that so many small places are struggling bravely on in the face of the super-port and the super-fisherman, as the small shop is with the supermarket. So I decided to do something no historian worthy of the name would do, I will voice my opinion of how I think things are. I excuse myself on the grounds that I am only a storyteller, not a historian.

One of the lessons of history is that nobody ever learns anything from them and todays fishing methods is a classic example of this. The future of the fishing fleet has been left unplanned and to its own devices. It also uses devices that are the most deadly used for harvesting anything anywhere. Unfortunately it has only been licenced to kill and assumes no responsibility for the replacement of stocks. No farmer or crop grower could survive without ensuring the source of his next harvest, by way of maintaining his breeding stock or seed supplies. Fishermen alone are afforded the privilege of not having this responsibility but even the oceans are not infinite. There is no hiding place to which fish stocks can retreat, and retreat they most certainly have as the empty harbours around the coast stand in melancholy testimony. Even the bustling, driving, energies of Fraserburgh and Peterhead are at one and the same time so strong yet so fragile, in an industry where forward planning is something somebody else does. And as fish stocks dwindle and recede into the Atlantic, the advent of the Spanish fleet carries with it a grim warning for the smaller ports such as Buckie, Macduff, Whitehills and a dozen others.

The present day fisherman is driven by a need to find up to £4000 a week, just to remain in business. No other business incurs overheads of this kind, or has to acquire a piece of equipment

The picture of the large boat, the 'Rain Goose', squeezing the small boat the 'Maureen' in Gourdon harbour, and neither of them with a future, could foretell the fortunes of the Scottish fishing industry as we know it.

costing £750,000, and is then left to wrestle the investment back any way it can or likes. The result is that the fishing fleet is put under continuous economic pressures that old time fishermen only had nightmares about, even with his trials and tribulations. Hard times, which they had aplenty, were always brought about because of history, never shortage of stocks. Poor seasons simply meant that they had failed to find herring, but they always came back. Today it is different.

The difference lies in the instrumentation and the seine net, or its variants, which are the most destructive devices ever used. The instruments tell exactly where the fish are and the net does the rest. It has never been calculated, because returns are not made, but from what I have seen myself, I would guess that for every fish landed by seine net boats, another five have been destroyed. Two or three boxes of immature fish have been shovelled over the side for every box landed and these could have grown to ten or 15. That is happening day and daily with the nearly 1500 boats which are catching white fish. Not them all, all the time, but extremely frequently. So can anything be done, do we want anything to be done, or should it be left while we hope for the best, as things are just now?

Apart from their utter professionalism, and commitment to their trade, nearly all fishermen, no matter how their vessels may bristle with electronics, are very strongly aware of their heritage, their traditions and deeply committed to them. They are also keenly aware of the need for conservation, nobody more so, but with the economic pressures they have to face, their priorities are sorted out for them by the balance sheet on which there is no allowance for wishful thinking.

There can be no retreat from technology at sea, any more than computer operators can be expected to pick up a quill pen, or haulage contractors will start carrying packs on their backs. If any defence is to be made of fish stocks, assuming the European Economic Community can be persuaded to listen and control things thereafter, then the only practical way is to limit the size of vessels and fishing methods. At the moment it is a free for all, anywhere, with no such thing as a protected breeding ground where stocks can rejuvenate. I can see no alternative to closing coastal waters off in ten mile wide zones where fishing methods and boat sizes are strictly controlled, with relaxation in methods introduced the further the grounds are from the coast.

The fishing fleet is not in business to provide picturesque scenes for landlubbers or to give the idea that everybody lives in Grannie's Heilan' Hame. What future it has will have to be carefully considered by fishermen, scientists, politicians, boatbuilders and everybody with any connection, directly or indirectly. It is disturbing to think that an industry which has over £1,000,000,000 invested in it by some of the most enterprising men anywhere has so little thought for the next 10, 20 or 50 years. A careful, controlled approach could see firms like Cowie and Banks of Wick, and Gove of Gourdon, and many others with a secure future. Because if they have a secure future so must the fishermen. I would like to think that was possible.

Acknowledgments

As I read the letters which I have been sent, my notes and listen to my tape recordings I cannot escape the conclusion that I have merely edited this book and that it was written by the following people. Obviously some have made greater contributions than others, but all have assisted me to the best of their considerable abilities. Nor can I overlook the great courtesy and hospitality extended to me by people to whom I was a complete stranger, and the trouble that many of them took to get in contact with me. The following are the real authors of this book.

Firstly the men who patiently answered my questions either on a tape recorder or wrote me at very great length:
William Stewart, D.S.C., M.B.E., J.P., of Lossiemouth, skipper of the 'Rival' and then the 'Sireach'.
William Thain of Wick, skipper of the 'Zoe'.
Jimmy Bremner of Wick, skipper of the 'Fisher Boy'.
Rab More of Wick, skipper of the 'Alert'.
John Macleod of Wick, skipper of the 'Mairi Bhan'.
Alistair Henderson of Wick, crew member of the 'Stack Rock'.
Hugh Carter, Lybster and Wick, crew member of the 'Maid of Honour'.
Angus Macintosh, D.S.M., Croix de Guerre, Thurso, skipper of the 'Primula'.
Alec Thomson of Thurso, crew member of the 'Primula'.
John Rosie, Wick and Thurso, engineer with Bruce and Duchart.
Mr George Simpson of Wick, fishcurer, shipowner and ironmonger.

Then the people who fully and freely responded to my enquiries:
Miss Pat O'Driscoll of the *Fishing News* who provided me with a very great deal of important information.
Professor M. S. Laverack, B.Sc., Ph.D., F.I. Biol., F.R.S.E., of the Gatty Marine Laboratory and Mr R. N. Smart, keeper of Manuscripts, both of the University of St. Andrews.
Dr J. R. G. Hislop of the Marine Laboratory, Aberdeen.
Mr R. Allan, Chief Executive, Scottish Fishermens Federation.
Mr R. M. Coppock, Ministry of Defence, Foreign documents section.
Mr Andrew Cordiner of Peterhead.
Mr I. H. Sproull of Kelvin Diesels.
Mr N. E. Brown of Kelvin Hughes.
Gardner Diesels.
Petters Ltd.
Mr D. Edgington of the Stationary Engine.
Mr D. L. Mayne, Petter Diesels.
Messrs A. & J. Campbell, Lossiemouth.

Then the organisations and people whom I met or corresponded with on a more casual basis:

Mr Angus Martin, author of *The Ring net Fishermen.*
Public Records Office.
Town Docks Museum, Hull.
Science Museum, London.
National Maritime Museum, London.
Post Office Archives.
Highlands and Islands Development Board
Sea Fish Authority, Edinburgh.
Victoria and George Cross Association, London.
Museum of Science and Technology, Birmingham.
Norfolk Museums Service.
The Patent Office, London.
Royal Scottish Museum.
Welholme Galleries, Grimsby.
Whitby Philosophical Society.
Aberdeen University Library.
National Portrait Gallery, Edinburgh.
Gallery of Modern Art, Edinburgh.
Glasgow District Libraries.
Ms R. Galer, Cockermouth.
Mr W. Sinclair, Wick Harbour Trust.
Miss A Henshall, Society of
    Antiquaries of Scotland.
Capt. Alec Buchan, Peterhead.
Mr J. Mackay, Halkirk.

Ordnance Survey, Southampton.
Reference Centre, United States Embassy.
Beccles and District Museum.
Glasgow Museum of Transport.
Imperial War Museum.
Admiralty Research Establishment, Dorset
Orkney Library Service.
Eyemouth Museum.
Scottish Fisheries Museum, Anstruther.
Mr Neil Short of Glasgow and Campbeltown.
Mr A. Parker, Perth.
Miss M. Watt, Gourdon.
Mr William Stewart, of the 'Transcend',
    Buckie.
Mr George Slater, of the 'Fame', Buckie.
Mr R. Hibbert, Kirkwall.
Mrs M. Morrison, Campbeltown.
Preston and Thomas, catering equipment
    manufacturers.
Dr S. V. Kerr, Mechanical Engineering
    Group, University of Strathclyde.
Mr J. Brown, Fishery Officer, Wick.
Miss J. Tudor, Institute of Marine
    Engineers.

Mr A. McLaughlan, Hon. Sec. Institute
of Marine Engineers.
Mr W. MacDonald, Fraserburgh.
Mr P. Ridgeway, Trinity House.
Mr G. Wilson, Macduff and Thurso.

Christian Salvesen & Co.
Mr D. Stewart, Falkirk.
Mr J. Lawrence Fraserburgh.
Mrs N. Ritchie, Macduff.
Mechanical Engineering Group,
University of Strathclyde.

The boatbuilders and designers whose own handiwork is the highest testimony they could ever receive:
Millers of St. Monans.
Jones of Buckie.
Macduff Boatbuilding and
Engineering Co.

Forbes of Sandhaven.
Mr S. McAllister, Campbeltown.

The editors, past and present of the following newspapers whose assistance was considerable:
The Press and Journal.
The Fish Trader.
The Fishing News.
The John O'Groat Journal.
The Caithness Courier.
The Northern Ensign.
The Northern Times.
The Kincardineshire Advertiser.
The Fife Herald News.

The Banffshire Journal.
The Northern Scot.
The Fraserburgh Herald.
The Buchan Observer.
The Grimsby Evening Telegraph.
The Hull Times.
The East Anglian Daily Times.
The Fish Friers Review.
The Campbeltown Courier.

Finally the people of my acquaintance, other than those mentioned already, who assisted with illustrations or information, without which this book would have been less informative: Mrs Jean Vandecasteele, Mr Andrew Sinclair. Both Mr Jim Buchans of Thurso.

The members of the Wick Society; Mr Donald Robertson and Mr John Robertson of Aukengill; skipper George Swanson of Keiss; Mr Ian McDonald, photographer, Wick; Skipper Norman Bremner of the 'Boy Andrew'; five men whose abiding interest in the history of fishing and fishing boats have created an enormously important reserve of information. There no doubt are others but these men are my personal friends; Skipper James George Addison, Cullen; Mr Phil McCabe, Peterhead; Mr Peter Bruce; Mr John Barnetson and Mr Joe Reid.

The members of the Lossiemouth Museum committee and Museum employees: Mr & Mrs Jim Gault of Lossiemouth and their son Iain; Mr and Mrs John Gatt, Fraserburgh; Mrs Ann Leel, Rosehearty; Mr John Buchan, Peterhead; Mr Jimmy Campbell, Halkirk; Mr Donald Sinclair, Wick.

And Mr Jim Matheson, friend and mentor for quarter of a century.

Finally the books:
The Herring by John Mitchell.
The Harvest of the Sea by James Bertram.
Encyclopaedia Britannica.
Electroaccoustics, The Analysis of Transducion and its historical background
by Frederick Hunt.
Sea Fisheries, Their Investigation in the United Kingdom, 1956,
edited by Michae! Graham.
Annual Reports of British Fisheries Society.
Annual Reports of Fishery Board for Scotland.
William Carmichael McIntosh by A. E. Gunther.
The Ring-net Fishermen by A. Martin.

None of the above have any responsibility whatsoever for any of the views expressed in this book. These, along with any conclusions drawn, or any errors, are mine alone and I alone am answerable.